Scrum for Hardware

To my dearest friend
JOE

Paolo Sammicheli

Scrum for Hardware

Paolo Sammicheli

ISBN 9781983373312

This is a Leanpub book. Leanpub empowers authors and publishers with the Lean Publishing process. Lean Publishing is the act of publishing an in-progress ebook using lightweight tools and many iterations to get reader feedback, pivot until you have the right book and build traction once you do.

Contents

Acknowledgements

This book would not have been possible without the many people who support and encourage me every day. My biggest challenge is not to forget anyone now.

First, I would like to thank the people who helped me write this book: Francesca Martinuzzi for the Italian edition and Anna Spertini for the English edition.

A decisive factor has been the contribution of my most passionate readers, who reported any inaccuracies and provided suggestions (in alphabetical order): Allen Jones, Davide Roitero, Lapo Cioni, Luca Bertoldo, Marcello Semboli, Silvia Bindelli, Tiziana Cascino.

Thanks to my friends and fellow coaches, whom I deeply respect; each of them in his or her own way, consciously or not, has created in me the urgency to start writing this book (in alphabetical order): Alberto Brandolini, Andrea Provaglio, Andrea Tomasini, Claudio Perrone, Fabio Armani, Gaetano Mazzanti, Jacopo Romei, Lapo Baglini, Raffaello Torraco, Samuele Guidi, Stefania Ciani.

Huge thanks goes to Avanscoperta[1]. Again Alberto Brandolini and the great Alessandra Granaudo. When this book was just a bunch of notes and post-its they believed in me and started organizing the first workshop[2] of Scrum for Hardware.

I also would like to thank my family, which always supports and encourages me even without actually understanding what my job is.

And of course, my infinite gratitude goes to Joe Justice. He is the myth that inspired me to write this book, at the same time he is the

[1]http://www.avanscoperta.it/

[2]http://www.avanscoperta.it/it/training/scrum-for-hardware-course/

humblest, most modest, and kindest person I know. A modern hero who – I am sure – will be in schoolbooks one day.

Dedication

I would like to dedicate this book to the people who contributed to make me who I am and who are no longer with us.

Germano, Patrizia, Renato.

You are always with me.

Foreword

What would happen if we all could deploy a superior product or service every one week or even faster? That changes long lead procurement, separate test organizations with queues, project status meetings, and the sources of risk from "can we do it ?" to "will they use it ?" The idea of a "Development Phase" and a "Production Engineering Phase" lose meaning or utility for project planning and funding in a system that moves this quickly.

This book takes the stance that markets are rewarding faster development and time to market.

Shorter development times mean less risk and less cash outlay. This book comes during the turning point of all product development. Software development embraced agility at scale, and now no customer will even entertain a 10 year software development life cycle. Hardware companies, like financial services groups and governments, are driving Agile manufacturing and specifically Scrum for Hardware are in every time zone globally. We are seeing this acceleration around the world from luxury niche to mass production to military grade. The quest for half price, half time projects has forced the question, investigation, and adoption of daily standup meetings, empowered Product Owners, and highly trained Scrum Masters sprinting across teams of teams doing new product development on the factory floor.

Paolo Sammicheli's work is the result of collaboration with my own work, my clients, his own clients, and the rich professional peer group of expert practitioners and the earliest adopters such as Peter Stevens, Hubert Smits, Peter Borsella, and many more. What we are learning is that all of the technical patterns that revolutionized software for twice the work in half the time, such as the XP practices, the Scrum PLoP, UATDD, and software design patterns for performance and reusability, have direct translations across domains with similar speed increases. In the words of Jeff Sutherland, co-creator of Scrum, "Scrum did not start in software and it will not stay there."

So what does Scrum for Hardware look like? Imagine a manufacturing shop floor, with concrete floors and suspended heating ducts. Then imagine groups of 4 to 5 people, each group clustered around a piece of flexible manufacturing equipment, test fixtures, and computers. Tens of teams, hundreds of teams, in some cases tens of thousands of teams. Each team has a big board to organize the flow of work inside their small group, and a labeled "input" and "output" for parts or sub-assemblies, with quality indicators called the Definition of Ready and Definition of Done. Parts and sub-assemblies are shuttled non-linearly between teams by autonomous carts or excited interns. Integration happens inside each team, with no part being allowed to be called "done" unless integration tests successfully pass. Each team is responsible for not only producing their piece of the parallel puzzle, but also for improving it, testing it, and validating it in production, every sprint. And the shorter the sprint, the faster the product is reinvented.

This book is the first significant publication on the topic, the most complete and authoritative. If the Agile transformation of the Software industry has any parallels outside software, and if the current client adoption rate is any indication, this book will be the reference for executives, shop floor managers, and team members globally. And it is clear this book and books like it will grow with case studies from readers just like yourself. Every aspect of Scrum for Hardware is observed from teams delivering and retrospecting to improve, to Kaizen. That would mean the source of ammunition for this book is the clear production and process notes of the readers. So let's keep up the awesome.

Joe Justice
Creator of Scrum for Hardware and eXtreme Manufacturing.

Introduction

This book is being published through the Agile Publishing[3] method. This means that it has been published online in several times, well before being completed, in order to allow me to receive rapid and frequent feedback from my most passionate readers. It also means that the content and form of the final draft will be affected by the feedback from my readers. From yours as well.

THANKS IN ADVANCE!

Your tips will allow me to adjust the text and to create the best possible book on **Scrum for Hardware**.

Did you like what you read? Do you have any questions I did not answer? Do you feel that something is missing? Is there any unclear phrase?

Write me at **feedback@scrum-hardware.it**

Copyright

[3] https://leanpub.com/manifesto

[4] https://creativecommons.org/licenses/by-sa/3.0/

- **ShareAlike** — If you remix, transform, or build upon the material, you must distribute your contributions under the same license as the original.
- **No additional restrictions** — You may not apply legal terms or technological measures that legally restrict others from doing anything the license permits.

Sharing my work with a permissive license so others can freely use it is the best way I know to create a better world and to thank the giants who came before us.

Book Structure

This book is divided into two parts: the Stories and the Method. The stories go with the reader along the same path of understanding I have experienced with **Scrum for Hardware**. I have chosen this approach to allow everyone to become familiar with the topic in a lighter and smoother way, using a narrative style. The second part of the book, however, summarizes the methodology and it can also be used as a reference for quick access.

SHU - HA - RI

The progression of the ideas expressed in the stories follows the *SHU-HA-RI* scheme, used to describe the stages of learning to mastery in Japanese martial arts.

The **SHU** stage can be described as *"Follow the rule"*. In this beginning stage, the student follows the teachings of one master precisely and he concentrates on just practicing thoroughly in order to acquire the basic knowledge of the main moves. The teacher, according to his experience and style, decides what the student must learn at this stage.

In the **HA** stage, described as *"Use the rule"*, the student begins practicing the art, learning the underlying principles and variations of already-learned moves. He enriches his language and departs from the orthodoxy of the previous phase.

The **RI** stage is described as *"Be the rule"* or *"Transcend"*. At this stage, the student begins to build his own style: he knows the rules and can deliberately decide to break some to create his own style.

Of the five stories in the first part, the first two chapters introduce the characters, the third chapter sets the basic concepts (SHU), the fourth illustrates some motivations and alternatives (HA) and the fifth shows advanced concepts and personal interpretations of methodology (RI).

Now, it is time to dive into the stories. Enjoy your read!

The Stories

Joe

In 2008, Joe Justice was a software consultant living in Denver, Colorado. He worked for Avanade, a large software company, joint venture of Microsoft and Accenture, developing interesting software projects for large businesses.

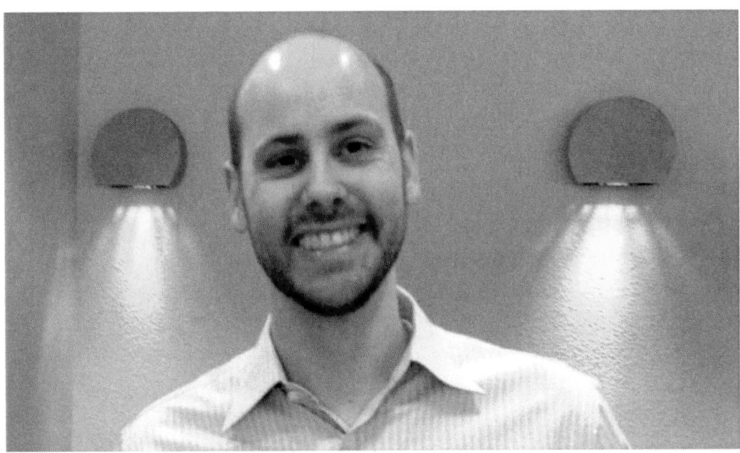

At the beginning of the year, he received a phone call: an Accenture employee was forming the team for a new project for the Bill & Melinda Gates Foundation, the organization founded by the American magnate and patron of Microsoft and considered the richest man in the world. Joe's curriculum seemed extremely suitable for that project: besides learning about the .NET development environment and Microsoft Sharepoint, the two main technologies of the project, Joe also had experience with Scrum[5], the Agile development[6] method that the Gates Foundation had decided to

[5]In the second part of the book you will find the description of Scrum and all the technical terms used hereafter.

[6]https://en.wikipedia.org/wiki/Agile_software_development

adopt for all new projects. Scrum's experienced staff was extremely rare in Accenture, so they offered Joe to fly to Seattle every Sunday and go back home every Thursday night for the following months. The idea of working with the Bill & Melinda Gates Foundation was very exciting and Joe did not hesitate to accept; he would be the Scrum Master of the Avanade team at the Foundation and would teach Scrum to the entire organization. Joe knew Scrum well, he had used it since his first job in Denver as a developer; he considered it the only serious way to develop software in a business context.

Joe had started to become interested in computer science since he was a kid. Being the youngest of five children Joe was very intrigued by the games of his three sisters and his older brother John. In particular, that strange object – a computer called Commodore Vic 20 allowing to watch new worlds and live exciting adventures on his TV thanks to some tapes – really fascinated him. When he was about to go to university, Joe chose the faculty of computer science, emulating his older brother who had already graduated and was enjoying the economic boom[7] in the late 90s, earning good money. Joe had received a scholarship offer from a very prestigious university and he was enthusiastic about starting this journey. However, something went wrong: shortly before starting the courses, he received a letter from the university stating that the scholarship was allocated to the Hispanic minority and there had been a mistake. He was not qualified to access it. Joe, an adolescent and inexperienced person at that time, did not think to seek advice from a lawyer; he consulted with his school secretary and, thanks to the knowledge of the student placement officer, he obtained a scholarship from the University of Wyoming. It was an alternative far below his expectations, but Joe was just OK with it and decided to accept.

AI, a young Japanese student, was attending classes on the same campus, where she also held a language and culture course about her country, as required by the international scholarship that had

[7]https://en.wikipedia.org/wiki/Dot-com_bubble

brought her to the US.

Joe made no secret with his friends of his passion for the Japanese culture: he had received it from his mother who had spent her childhood in Japan to follow her father, a prominent US Army General, on a mission to the island. Joe's roommate, who knew about this, met AI in class and told him immediately: "You must absolutely know my Japanese teacher; she is definitely your type. I'm sure you'll like her". "I don't like older women," Joe replied. "She is our age! Trust me, you must know her".

For Joe it was love at first sight, and as soon as he left university, he asked her to marry him. They were young, newly graduates and with little money. They decided to get married and to celebrate their wedding in Hawaii, so that friends and families could join them more easily from Japan and the United States to celebrate all together. They would then spend their honeymoon exploring Hawaii renting several cars along the road.

One morning, great sports car enthusiast Joe was driving a small convertible on the road to Hana. He just felt in heaven, with his young wife sitting by his side and a gentle breeze coming from the forest and refreshing his face. Suddenly, despite feeling so well with a smile spread from ear to ear, he saw that paradise slowly blur in front of him. "If every single individual of the 7 billion populating the planet would like to enjoy this same pleasure – he thought – the forest could no longer exist. It would be replaced by a bare clearing devastated by acid rain and the air would smell of exhaust gas."

Ever since he was a child, Joe had naturally developed a strong ecological sensitivity. He still remembers that when he was 4 or 5, he prevented his older sister from killing a grasshopper with ether, which she needed for a science school research. Little Joe, in an attempt to save the insect, cried and threw such a tantrum that he lost his senses by hyperventilation, alarming the whole family.

And now, the only thought of a devastated forest made him feel almost physically distressed. Such stomach burning feeling wiped that smile off his face for the rest of the trip and that disturbing image began to haunt him even at night. He felt guilty, as if he was doing something wrong or unfair. It was exactly during this trip that Joe all of a sudden fully understood the ecological meaning of the word "unsustainable". This thought was very disturbing to him and he felt he had to react and to do something. But what exactly?

The Challenge

The XPrize Foundation is a nonprofit organization based in St. Louis, Missouri, which organizes public competitions to encourage technological innovation. It is a moral institution aiming at identifying solutions to complex problems with its initiatives, and facilitating the financing of projects that can benefit humanity in different fields (medical, aerospace, environmental, etc.). In 2008, with sponsorship from Progressive Insurance, the Foundation announced an Automotive XPrize competition with a 10 million-dollar prize. Participants were challenged to build a four-seater eco-friendly vehicle that could be legally registered in the United States, producing less than 200 grams/mile CO2 equivalent emissions, able to achieve 100 MPGe (100 miles per gallon equivalent of petrol, that is 100 km per 2.8 liters) and that could be manufactured for the mass market. Over one hundred competitors took part into the competition including individuals, companies and universities from all over the world.

Wikispeed's Birth

It was immediately clear to Joe: he had to participate in the XPrize. Contending with the construction of an ecological car would have been the best way to overcome the discomfort he had felt during his honeymoon. Unfortunately, while being a car enthusiast, Joe was totally new to any mechanical expertise. Before that moment, he had not even ever changed the oil in his car and he was well aware of the need to learn many things. However, he did not let himself be scared by these initial obstacles and decided to focus on his goal: he placed a large board in his garage and he hung there a sticky note saying, "Win the XPrize".

How to proceed? Where to start? Joe knew only one method to develop something serious: **Scrum**. He started to apply the "user story splitting" method to his car, that is, targets were broken down into sub-objectives, thus becoming smaller and more reachable in acceptable times. The first two objectives written by Joe on two different sticky notes: "build a car that can be registered" and "build a 100MPG car". Joe recurrently split them into subtasks, so that his board got full of sticky notes within one afternoon only. He knew that he could not do it alone; so he began to share this idea on his blog, telling the world about his experiments, his mistakes and any new learnings. He asked specialized communities for help and advice; and people from around the world began to answer, offering suggestions and opinions. Joe replied to anyone who could provide a little help, he updated his followers and asked for further information. Many mechanics, electric technicians and simple hobbyists began to be interested in the project. Someone even wanted to meet in person "that guy on the internet" who wanted to build the most ecological car ever designed, and strangers started arriving to spend the weekend with Joe after flying at their own expenses over the US. Wikispeed[8] was born: a community of enthusiasts who, like Wikipedia, was developing collaboratively and openly a 100 MPG car to participate in the XPrize competition.

Toward XPrize

In 2010, Joe and his wife had moved to Seattle, Washington for some time. The Bill and Melinda Gates Foundation project had been going on for two years and some weekends, instead of going back to Denver, Joe had asked AI to join him in Seattle. Like any good Japanese, AI has a very wide food culture and the excellent cuisine of the typical restaurants in Seattle, along with the variety of choice of international restaurants, had convinced her that it was worth moving there. In addition, Seattle was the headquarters of very important companies including Amazon, Microsoft and Starbucks; it seemed a very interesting city from different points of view.

The Wikispeed project was going on quickly: it counted a group of 44 people coming from 4 countries and actively helping Joe, it had a Facebook group[9] with a thousand fans already and a Youtube channel[10] with many followers. After the evaluation phase of the documentation for admission to the competition, Joe and his team started the operation phase and they had built in three months only their first prototype called SGT01, Super Grand Touring 01.

The SuperGT[11] class is a car racing championship that takes place in Japan with road cars. They are probably the fastest vehicles that still resemble normal cars; better performance is obtained only from cars similar to Formula 1. Joe had always been fascinated by those competitions and, in his imagination, the car he was planning would have to look as much as possible to a racecar, beautiful and

[8]http://wikispeed.org
[9]https://www.facebook.com/WIKISPEED/
[10]https://www.youtube.com/user/WIKISPEED
[11]https://en.wikipedia.org/wiki/Super_GT

charming, and at the same time, it had to consume so little to be the most ecological car ever built.

The first simulated tests showed[12] that the car could reach 104MPG on urban cycle and 114MPG on extra-urban cycle: already perfect to win the contest! In addition, weighing only 1300 Lbs. (about 589 Kg), it could go from 0 to 60 miles per hour (nearly 100 Kph) in less than 5 seconds and reach a top speed of 149mph (about 240 Kph). The prototype went like greased lightning! On April 6, during a trial run, Joe ended up colliding with a wall. Luckily, the crash tests carried out on the simulator confirmed very realistic: Joe did not hurt too badly and, with a one-day work and not too much expense for the materials, Wikispeed was as good as new. On April 12, the team obtained the official confirmation[13] so longed-for by everyone: Wikispeed had been admitted to the final selection, called Shakedown, which was to be held from May 2 to 8, 2010 at the international circuit of Michigan, 100 km west of Detroit and location of the famous NASCAR racing. It was great news.

The development team at the Bill and Melinda Gates Foundation was also very excited by the idea and everyone went out of their way to allow Joe to take the necessary vacation to get the business done.

However, it became necessary to find a specialist mechanic quickly, as Wikispeed had the engine of the Honda Civic and, if necessary during the final selection, the team had to be able to intervene without hesitation. Moreover, the race was only less than three weeks away! Joe and his friends published an ad on Craigslist humorously titled “Mechanic/MacGyver (Michigan International Speedway)”:

> Team WIKISPEED is competing in the final rounds of the Progressive Automotive X Prize, and we need a

[12]http://wonderfulworldofwikispeed.blogspot.fr/2010/04/faq.html

[13]http://wonderfulworldofwikispeed.blogspot.it/2010/04/we-did-it-detroit-here-wikispeed-comes.html

> fantastic Honda mechanic to support our team at the Michigan International Speedway the week of May 2-8. We are building a prototype car that will go 100 mpg and will retail for under $20k. The challenges we will hit will probably be pretty novel– no repairs are routine on a prototype car. Ideally, the candidate would be willing to work at a reduced rate or gratis, since we are a small team of volunteers. An attitude similar to the TV show MacGyver's help.

With that single ad, they got an answer by Bryan, a certified technician with experience on Honda engines. In addition to working for free, as long as taking part in the Wikispeed project, Bryan refused some job offers, which were not so profuse in that crisis period in the Detroit area.

Moreover, a certain Todd, owner of a company producing Plexiglas material, offered his help to build and install for free the transparent canopy that would protect the pilot, in return for the only flight to Seattle.

Finally, Mike, a robotics enthusiast who was attending a Yahoo-themed forum, showed up unannounced at Joe's garage where volunteers were working at Wikispeed. No one had ever seen him before, but he spent the whole afternoon working hard, and solved some wiring problems that Joe, despite his efforts, had not been able to come to grips with for weeks.

The Big Day

May 5: eventually, the big day! The entire Wikispeed team is along the Michigan International Speedway – palpable excitement is in the air. The team members have not slept for 3 nights to finish the car according to the competition's rules.

Everybody invested time and expertise into the project and everybody also feels it as his own. It's Wikispeed's turn. The jury examines the prototype and some problems arise. The team does not let this get it down and keeps working: in a few minutes, Wikispeed is disassembled into its main modules (chassis, engine, front dashboard, etc.) and all the participants work in pairs and in parallel on the components.

The jury and rival teams are impressed by the speed and readiness with which the Wikispeed team solves the highlighted problems one by one and congratulate several times. After finishing the work, the team rolls the car in the designated area for the final inspection. All together towards glory!

Just before the inspection, Joe asks his brother John to help him move the seat belt straps. It was an optional recommendation in the list of change requests but it seemed like a simple thing to do in a few minutes. Lack of sleep and lucidity played its part. Drilling the frame with the drill, Joe accidentally shears an electric cable inside it. Turning to Mary Wilkes, the expert electrician of the team, he begged her: "Can you fix it?" Unfortunately, it was not possible in the few minutes left before the final inspection and when the judges arrived, the car could not start. The team appealed to the judges asking a little more time to solve the electrical problem by showing that it had just occurred, but the extension was not granted.

That was a moment of great disappointment for everyone, however compensated by the satisfaction of being positioned tenth on the final ranking, surpassing prestigious and well-funded competitors as TESLA, TATA Motor and the Team from Boston MIT.

Wikispeed SGT01

More importantly, Wikispeed obtained a wide media coverage: the story of Joe and his volunteers appeared on numerous blogs and online magazines, the number of fans continued to grow steadily after the end of the competition and, despite having no victory in the XPrize, the Wikispeed project began to be considered a triumph.

The Ingredients for Success

Sometime later, an article on Fortune[14] listed some elements that had led to the success of Wikispeed, suggesting that firms should consider the following four principles that helped them:

1. Reach out passionate people

"No matter how many smart people you have at your firm – said the article on Fortune – there are a lot more on the outside. Competitive success hinges upon the ability to connect with others and take advantage of the knowledge that they can bring to the table. So, the benefits of connecting with and bringing together passionate people can be significant." Since the very beginning, Wikispeed uses social networks and specialized forums, getting help and suggestions from passionate people around the world.

2. Keep timelines short

Traditional corporate projects require the creation of two- to five-year strategic plans and detailed blueprints. On the other end of the spectrum, Team Wikispeed works in 7-day cycles – they're constantly reflecting on different results and what they can do better in the next cycle and the learning and adaptation cycle is so fast that it also allows non-skilled people to quickly achieve very ambitious results.

3. Make the project modular

If you have a monolithic product, it will be very difficult to evolve and improve quickly, because the impact of any change will be such as to compel you to review important parts of the entire

[14] http://fortune.com/2012/06/18/how-companies-ought-to-train-their-staffers/

work. On the opposite, Wikispeed consists of independent modules, connected to each other through clear and predefined interfaces. This way, Team Wikispeed manages to improve a single module with no recourse to the entire work, with the possibility to see the results of the changes within the same iteration week[15].

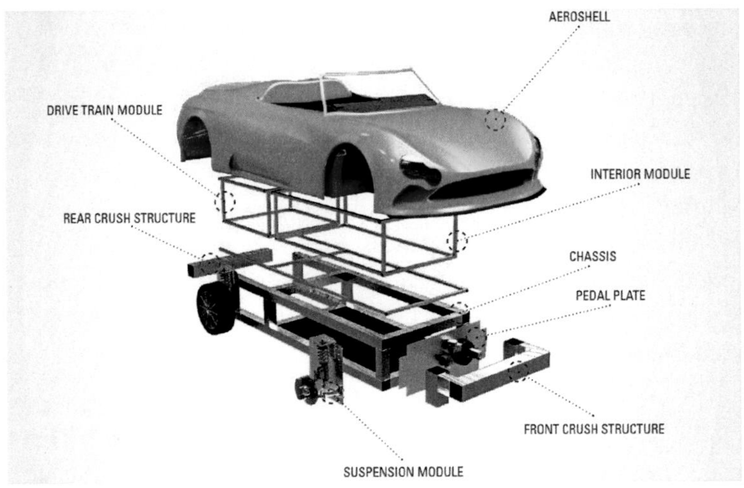

Wikispeed's Modular Architecture

4. Create opportunities for hands-on learning

At Wikispeed, continuous learning is encouraged and planned. Volunteers work in **pairings** of inexperienced and experienced individuals who take on small projects and skills are quickly and mutually transmitted between team members. Volunteers work as much as possible on different modules, so they acquire **skills**[16] on the entire car.

[15]Further details in the Agile Architecture section.

[16]See the T-Shaped Skills section.

Detroit Auto Show

In January 2011, Team Wikispeed received one of those offers one cannot refuse: they were invited to participate free of charge at the largest car show in the world, the Detroit Auto Show. All of the most important car brands on the planet would be present. The team members were extremely excited, but also literally terrified by the opportunity they were offered. Wikispeed's body used for the competition, and nicknamed the "orange shoe box", was absolutely not up to the task. For an international auto show, it was necessary to design something more attractive. The team contacted some distributors of composite materials, but estimates and conditions were desolating – they would need 36,000 usd and three months to get the desired results, but there was no such time nor money. What to do?

Once again, the connection was decisive. A design-specialized, Wikispeed-enthusiast, technician spent various sleepless nights to create the design and sent his CAD project for a new bodywork from Germany, which was later called the "Le Mans Version". Also in this case, nobody had ever met the author of a contribution that proved to be decisive.

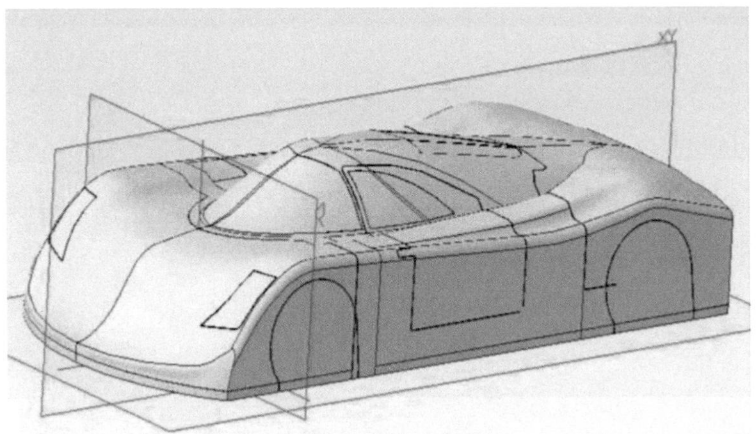

CAD of Le Mans version

In Joe's garage, volunteers began modeling the bodywork with pressurized foam, first on a reduced scale, and then, with the aid of a CNC machine, they generated a real-size 3D model.

Bodywork Model

Joe took a vacation to attend a course on composite materials, and after a few days, he had already acquired the basic knowledge to attempt an experiment. The team used carbon fiber sheets softened with a special solvent, so that they could perfectly adhere to the model. They then painted the bodywork of a nice "race black" and, with a strenuous smoothing work and some stickers, the most beautiful Wikispeed that had ever been seen came into existence. It was an incredible achievement, especially considering that the car body cost only 800 usd and three days of work.

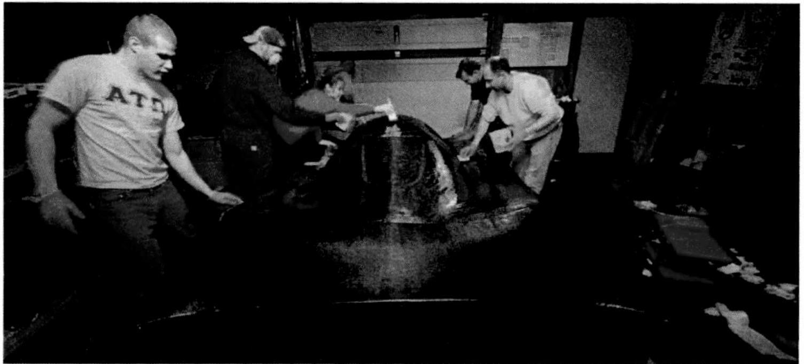

Painting Stage

Transport of New Body

The fact that Wikispeed, in addition to offering great performance, was also beautiful was in turn a decisive factor because, with great team surprise, the car was placed on the main floor of the show, right in the middle of Ford and Chevrolet.

Detroit Auto Show

Joe was still frightened by that environment – he expected to be snubbed by the white collars of the other booths. Instead, one by one, the managers of each automobile company shook hands, complimented him, and many wished him to start a real automobile company of his own. Joe was astonished: why did his competitors encourage him? Subsequently, Joe stated in an interview that, in his view, the managers of the big companies were frustrated by the slowness with which things change in larger companies and hoped that a new, small, aggressive and ecologic competitor would put the right pressure needed to generate a real change in their organizations. This explained, according to Joe, the warm welcome he was given that day. Again, media coverage was huge. Wikispeed was mentioned by big newspapers such as Wired, National Geographic, New York Times Online, Forbes and many specialized blogs including Autoblog[17].

---

[17]http://www.autoblog.com/2011/01/12/detroit-2011-wikispeed-sgt01-low-cost-super-mpg-car/

TEDx Rainier

The peak exposure stage for Joe and the Wikispeed team arrived in December 2011, when Joe was invited to speak to Rainier's TEDx[18]. TED is the most prestigious conference format in the world, so that the main event, which takes place in California annually, can only be attended by invitation; the videos of the TED talks, on the other hand, remain available free of charge online and have a great follow-up. TEDxs are events independently organized according to TED format and rules, and in short have reached such a level of interest that many of the highlights in the TED site[19] are just shot at TEDxs. Joe's video on Wikispeed, which at the time of writing of this book has reached 90,000 views, was the turning point for the project.

Joe Justice at TEDx Rainier

From a costume phenomenon, Wikispeed was starting to become an example to follow. Even important companies, who knew the Agile software development methodologies and were looking for a way to innovate their product creation process, saw in Wikispeed

[18]https://www.youtube.com/watch?v=x8jdx-lf2Dw
[19]https://www.ted.com/

the proof that improvement was possible and began contacting Joe and Team Wikispeed.

John Deere

John Deere is one of the world's largest agricultural machinery manufacturers. John Deere, a blacksmith, founded the company in 1837 at Grand Detour, Illinois. He was also a great innovator, who, like the others, produced pitchforks, rakes, horseshoes but one day created a steel plow that for pioneering peasants became the conquest tool of Midwest grassland. On that innovation alone, the company grew for almost two centuries billing about $24 billion in 2007. John Deere executives learned about the story of Wikispeed in 2012 from this TEDx video and some articles in magazines. Curious, though they knew more, they sent three managers to Joe's garage in Seattle, over 3,000 miles away. Shortly after their return, Joe received an invitation to the headquarters of the company in Milan, Illinois, to illustrate the story of Wikispeed during the initiative "Frugal Engineering and Innovation". At the meeting, they talked about modular tractors and a startup that was creating open-source agricultural modules, called Open Source Ecology. At that time, John Deere was building the 8030 model, a large modular tractor platform, and Joe projected a statement during his talk that had been given five years earlier by the chief engineer of the company:

> The development process of the 8030 model is completely predictable: we know how much we will spend, how many resources we need and when we deliver the product to the market.

Just after that, however, Joe exposed interesting information contained in a document that the company had sent to him before the meeting:

> The 8030 project had been delayed by 6 months, the staff involved worked 12 to 14 hours a day, and some key features had to be omitted.

The tractor that was launched on the market had great commercial success and was very profitable. But in spite of this, Joe showed to the executives that the development of new products was becoming more and more complex, as the world around them was changing very quickly and it would be wise to review the way budget estimates and schedules were processed. Jonh Deere had been producing tractors for 175 years, the company was very self-confident and, in showing the quotation and data that denied it, Joe feared being sent away, or at least criticized. It was not so: on the contrary, the managers invited Joe to repeat that intervention on a cruise ship during the company's annual meeting, and on that occasion Joe said clearly that in his view the annual budget planning should not be done annually anymore. In an interview, Joe later stated:

> I cannot tell you the details because I signed a confidentiality agreement, but the other day I received a phone call from a John Deere manager asking me what a Wiki-Deere might look like.

Boeing

Not long after, Boeing also contacted Team Wikispeed. It was easier this time, as their headquarters are about a 20-minute drive from Joe's garage; but it was not less exciting. Joe and other volunteers were invited to see the 787, 777 and 767 production lines in the world's largest enclosure. Boeing's production facility is so large that clouds form inside and sometimes even rain falls from them! People in the distance look tiny, yet they are only at one quarter of the building. Entering, Joe felt being on the set of "Indiana Jones and the Raiders of the Lost Ark". After a guided tour of the production line, Joe met some Boeing executives. They were interested in learning more about Wikispeed and finding out if there was "a Wiki project" in their field. At the meeting Joe mentioned Maker Plane[20], an Agile company that declares to use the "Wikispeed method". Joe knew the founders and had exchanged mails with them. "They are building two models, a 4- and a 6-seat. It will be exciting to see what they can do", Joe said in a subsequent interview. In the same interview, Joe explained the reason why more and more companies began to be interested in Wikispeed. The widespread fear of the eventuality that more and more sectors would see the birth of another "Google", or "a group of guys, who in their garage, invent a way to make a better product, spending less, faster, and that with this idea create a competitor that cannot be bought".

Agile Alliance 2012

In 2012, the Wikispeed Team was well known on the international Agile scene and Joe was invited as a keynote speaker to one of the most prestigious Agile conferences in the world: Agile 2012 of Agile Alliance[21] in Dallas, Texas.

[20]https://makerplane.org

[21]https://www.agilealliance.org/resources/videos/keynote-joe-justice/

AGILE2012
DALLAS, TEXAS
AUG 13-17
MANAGING A COLLABORATIVE MULTI-NATIONAL TEAM IN REAL TIME
Keynote Speaker: Joe Justice

At the end of his speech, a participant asked a question to Joe:

> Joe, do you see the Wikispeed manufacturing becoming a large scale manufacturer?

His answer explains why, at the same time, he changed his profession and, from a software developer, he became Agile Coach:

> About 76 million new cars were built and sold last year. Current analysts predict that about that same number will be made again this year. We think at least 60 million of those should get 100 miles per gallon. That said, I don't want to have to figure out how to do the economies of scale on 60 million cars manufactured in a year. Even worse than that, I don't want to see news that some manufacturing plant was shut down and 4,000 people in a neighborhood were laid off at once because they've just been put out of business by Wikispeed. I want Wikispeed to succeed and I want it to succeed in hundreds of thousands of cars a year, because that's the number that will make an appreciable difference in the amount of fuel consumed and the

> amount of emissions emitted. We could sell ten of these at 100,000 usd each and my pocket book would be pretty happy, or we could sell 100,000 of these at almost cost and make a difference for the environment. That's much more what I'm interested in.

Joe was only interested in creating a positive impact on the planet. And he began to understand that teaching others to do likewise, according to the Wikispeed model, was the best way to boost its impact in less time.

Scrum Inc

Scrum Inc is the consulting firm founded by Jeff Sutherland, inventor and co-author of Scrum. Joe had known Jeff as he had attended a training session, and Jeff had visited the Wikispeed garage curious about the project. On September 9, 2013, Joe's entry into the team was announced[22] on the ScrumInc website. Joe started to hold his own workshop: in Boston's garage, he taught people how to apply Scrum to the construction of a Wikispeed vehicle. Not long after, ScrumInc published a webinar[23] where Joe and Jeff showed the secrets of the success of Wikispeed and what Scrum for Hardware was. In May 2015, Joe became Certified Scrum Trainer[24] for Scrum Alliance[25], the nonprofit association founded by Scrum's pioneers around the mid-2000s. From Joe's entry on, ScrumInc began to include in Scrum Master Courses examples from various areas, releasing the methodology from software alone. In the second Webinar[26] regarding Scrum outside Software, which ScrumInc published at the end of October 2015, Joe has the title of President Scrum@Hardware. He had gained a stake in ScrumInc

[22]https://www.scruminc.com/joe-justice-joins-scrum-inc-team/
[23]https://www.scruminc.com/scrum-in-hardware/
[24]https://www.scruminc.com/the-awesome-joe-justice-is-now-a-cst/
[25]https://www.scrumalliance.org
[26]https://www.scruminc.com/scrum-for-maximum-awesome/

and was now the leader of this new movement. The international community of Scrum for Hardware was already growing, but Joe wanted to see it grow even more. And he was wondering what to do.

Paolo

My name is Paolo Sammicheli, Sammy to my friends, and I was born in Siena, a charming town in Southern Tuscany, famous for its Palio[27], a ancient horse race held twice a year. I am a software developer: that has always been my passion. I was eleven when I first saw a computer. It was my Commodore 64, a real novelty for those times, and a luxury. It had just arrived from faraway America and it cost nearly one million Italian liras, a real asset for a kid like me. The "64" in its name was a reference to its 64kb RAM, which was twice bigger than any available in personal computers, by the way, not so widespread at that time. It was the early eighties: we programmed in BASIC and software was loaded using 5¼-inch floppy disks or cassette tapes – we were pioneers. I soon realized that this was what I wanted to do in my life and, at twenty years old, Information Technology had become my profession. At the dawn of 2008, turning point in Joe's life, I was a computer scientist with an interesting, innovative and envied job. At that time, I was working as a Technical Director of the Central Italy branch for an Italian software house, which had offices in Siena and Perugia, with part of the staff also based in Florence and Pisa. As a Software Architect, I personally supervised Banca Monte dei Paschi di Siena[28], one of the oldest customers of the company and one of the top three in terms of turnover. Yet, although my job was consistent with my early plans, it was not what I actually loved the most. As a teenager, I volunteered for many years on ambulances for the Siena's Confraternity of Mercy[29], a welfare office with 750 years of history, also taking part into humanitarian missions in Italy and abroad with the Civil Protection Group. So when, in the late

[27] https://en.wikipedia.org/wiki/Palio_di_Siena

[28] https://en.wikipedia.org/wiki/Banca_Monte_dei_Paschi_di_Siena

[29] http://www.misericordiadisiena.it

1990s, I discovered the Free Software[30], it was love at first sight. All those programs developed by volunteers, which you could legally copy, study and modify, represented a technology plus volunteering combination that I sensed particularly close to my understanding of the world. I was one of the most active members in the Siena Linux User Group[31]. My friends were there too, and we organized conferences and events aimed at raising awareness on free software in schools, universities and sometimes even in town squares.

I am what I am because of who we all are

The free operating system that was spreading most rapidly in 2008 was Ubuntu[32]. In the Bantu language, spoken in Central Africa, Ubuntu means "humanity towards others" or "I am what I am because of who we all are". Building a better computer system, accessible and free for everybody: this was the vision of the founder of the project, the South African entrepreneur Mark Shuttleworth[33]. I joined the project in 2006 and thanks to my volunteering I quickly earned the esteem and friendship of the Italian community. Towards the end of 2007, I mainly dealt with translation and marketing, I had founded the **Italian Ubuntu Marketing Team**, and I had set the goal of organizing in-person gatherings for the community members, who usually had online contacts only. I then started working at what would become the semi-annual meeting of the Italian community: the Ubuntu-it Meeting[34]. I suggested organizing the first meeting in Siena, in the Conference Hall of *Via delle Sperandie*, in the heart of my Contrada[35]. They liked the idea

[30]https://en.wikipedia.org/wiki/Free_software
[31]http://siena.linux.it
[32]https://www.ubuntu.com
[33]https://en.wikipedia.org/wiki/Mark_Shuttleworth
[34]https://wiki.ubuntu-it.org/UbuntuItMeeting
[35]https://en.wikipedia.org/wiki/Contrade_of_Siena#Chiocciola_.28Snail.29

and, on January 26th 2008, the first Ubuntu-it Meeting[36] took place.

Ubuntu-it Meeting, January 2008

The meeting allowed us to hold very prolific discussions and strengthened our mutual bonds of friendship. In particular, I finally met and bonded with Milo, another cornerstone of the Italian community as well as a prime contact at Canonical Ltd, the company founded by Mark Shuttleworth sponsoring and supporting the Ubuntu project. It is worth noting that the idea of creating a regular meeting was not originally coming from the Italian community. The international community of the project had already organized semiannual meetings called Ubuntu Developer Summits, also commonly known as UDSs. These events took place shortly after the release of a new version of the operating system, that is twice a year[37], and it was the occasion in which we discussed how went the last release and what to include in the following one. Each release[38] of Ubuntu had a nickname that was assigned to it before its development, and had the "adjective – animal" scheme with the same initial, which changed in progressive order (e.g.: Gutsy Gibbon, Hardy Heron, Intrepid Ibix, etc.). The code name announcement for a release was a special moment; Mark Shuttleworth declared it via his blog, also revealing other details as the release's objectives and the date and location of the following UDS. A few months after the

[36]https://wiki.ubuntu-it.org/UbuntuItMeeting/20080126

[37]https://wiki.ubuntu.com/Releases

[38]https://wiki.ubuntu.com/Releases

first Ubuntu-it Meeting, during the announcement, Milo and I were chatting on IRC[39]. The code name for the new release of Ubuntu was Jaunty Jackalope and the UDS would be held early December in a place that appeared to us simply as wonderland: Mountain View, California, Google Campus. Within seconds, we decided we could not miss this opportunity. I put off my holidays in December and we started looking for a cheap flight.

California Dreaming

That trip to the USA was the turning point for my professional and personal life. Milo had already been there four times but it was my first. We decided to get there some time prior to the UDS, so we had a week and plenty of time to visit Los Angeles and Las Vegas. The flight was long and tiring, but once there, everything seemed to be paying off. Our sense of awe and wonder grew at every corner: Hollywood, the Studios, Beverly Hills, Santa Monica Pier. I felt like I was in "Grand Theft Auto - San Andreas[40]". It was an extremely violent videogame on fashion at that time, which had also become famous for introducing the opportunity to explore freely the world in which action was set. Therefore, you could virtually visit cities strongly inspired and very similar to Los Angeles, San Francisco and Las Vegas between a gaming mission and the next. But the things that struck me most were not actually the iconic locations in California, but something that from that point on would radically change the way I was learning new things: the discovery of American bookstores. In the United States, bookstores are huge, they are provided with a café with tables, chairs and couches, where all the people spend hours reading quietly. I was flabbergasted. Being able to enter a bookstore, take a book, sit down in front of a cup of coffee, read it, and eventually put the book back on the shelf and go away seemed impossible to

[39]https://en.wikipedia.org/wiki/Internet_Relay_Chat
[40]https://en.wikipedia.org/wiki/Grand_Theft_Auto:_San_Andreas

me, coming from Europe! I thought that was only allowed in public libraries – In Italy, given the continued cuts in the culture budget, possibly not even there. Milo, however, knew these places very well, like Barnes and Noble or Borders, and took me there since the first night. Furthermore, *what* you could find on those shelves! "If these books are new here, let alone in Italy. This is the easiest way to become a guru with little effort!" I thought. I realized this was an once-in-a-lifetime opportunity to me, so I bought several books, almost exceeding the weight limit of my luggage. In particular, I brought home two beautiful photographic books on how to design and deliver successful presentations, just published in the US and still unknown and unavailable in Italy: "Presentation Zen[41]" and "Slide:ology[42]". Milo and I envied our Californian peers for many more things though. Amazon, for example: in 2008, the online sale of books and electronics was not available in Italy yet. At that time, eBook readers, such as Kindle and Nook, which had recently become popular in the USA, not only were unavailable in Italy, but also they were denied to those with a foreign credit card. Even more, what about Android? The first release was in June of that year, and the stores had just received the G1, the first Android phone, with a physical sliding keyboard. One day, Milo and I lingered to try one of these phones on display at a big T-Mobile store, and we got a hefty fine for leaving our car in a no-parking zone. All these technology and knowledge gems would have been useless in Europe, even if we had bought them. "Damned DRMs[43]! They leave us behind! - I complained angrily – Not only we do not have these wonderful tools, we are also forbidden to bring them home! It is not fair!" Milo supported me, feeling broken. He had already experienced that frustration on other occasions, so much that he had almost resigned to that.

[41]http://www.presentationzen.com
[42]http://www.duarte.com/book/slideology/
[43]https://en.wikipedia.org/wiki/Digital_rights_management

Fosscamp

After the long tour in Los Angeles and Las Vegas, the trip continued to San Francisco. For the two days prior to the UDS, Canonical Ltd. organized an Unconference[44] called "Fosscamp". Unconferences are gatherings where there is not a clear distinction between audience and speakers and whose agenda is created by attendees. Fosscamp aimed at gathering the members of Ubuntu with participants and enthusiasts in other Open Source projects. It was held in the same location of the UDS, and this allowed us to savor in advance the climate of the UDS. At the Google campus, after taking some routine photos in front of the entrance, we ventured inside.

Mountain View, December 2008

A guard hurried to ask where we were heading and pointed us to where we could park. The strange canopies over the parking lots turned out to be solar panels and we noticed some electric mini-cars nearby. In 2008, all this seemed like science fiction to us! At the entrance to the Google Campus, there was a billboard saying: "Low-Fi Wiki" and containing the agenda[45].

A session on the future of human-computer interaction caught our attention, especially since we saw Mark Shuttleworth among the

[44]https://en.wikipedia.org/wiki/Unconference

[45]For details on this type of conferences, see the Openspace section.

names of the promoters. We decided to attend it. Among the dozen of participants sitting around an oval table, a young girl (which I later found to be only 16 years old) with a very knowledgeable look piqued my curiosity. She was chatting from her PC on several IRC chats by pressing the keyboard keys at an awesome speed and, not satisfied with that, she often used a large pda[46] which she held on her side. Googling the name I had glimpsed on her badge, I saw that she was a famous developer for KDE[47]. One of the speakers, discussing multiple-screen devices, suggested: "Look at that girl: it's obvious that a single screen is not enough for her!" Milo and I realized that the talent of the participants was well above our expectations.

Ubuntu Developer Summit

Prior to 2008, I thought I was an expert conference organizer. Since the beginning of 2000, I had coordinated the Linux Day in Siena every year, with more than 200 attendees; in 2004, I had been involved in the planning and management of an international conference, always in Siena, hosting the Free Software Inventor Richard Stallman and representatives of governments and universities from Brazil and Argentina. Yet, all I knew was nothing compared to the UDS. Beyond the impressive numbers, given the 600 attendees, the conference lasted for a whole week and the organizational structure was completely new and unusual to me. It was an open conference format, which I later found out called Open Space Technology. The conference did not have a definitive program; each participant could suggest an hour-long session and put it into agenda, available online at the summit's website[48]. This meant that the agenda of the following day changed every day, adapting with new emerging ideas and integrating with the most

[46]https://en.wikipedia.org/wiki/Palm_(PDA)
[47]https://en.wikipedia.org/wiki/KDE
[48]http://summit.ubuntu.com

interesting topics. The sessions were divided into Tracks: Desktop, Server, Foundation, Community, UX, etc. For each Track, there was an easily recognizable Track LEader with a special T-shirt, making sure that the sessions were planned harmoniously.

One of the tracks Milo and I were most interested in was the one about the Community. To encourage the flow of discussion, the track was divided into special sessions, called Community Roundtables, where the agenda emerged from the discussion itself. They where similar to those I later found out to be called Lean Coffees[49]. The substantial difference was that, while in a Lean Coffee each topic has an exact time slot, usually 10 minutes, in a Community Roundtable the topic was thoroughly explored using a popular Popcorn Discussion model. As with popcorn, which is to be removed from the fire when it stops popping, when talks started decreasing and interest falling, the session leader closed the topic and introduced the following. Another interesting aspect was the so-called "Law of two feet", namely: "If at any time during the session you find yourself in any situation where you are neither learning nor contributing, use your feet and go someplace else". What most impressed me was the fact that all these organizational rules, models and formulas were not explained nor documented: simply, the leaders and the majority of participants did so, and

[49]http://leancoffee.org

everyone behaved accordingly. All this created a special – unusual – atmosphere. Where I had worked, especially in banking, I experienced just the opposite. If there was not a rule, if we did not explain something, nobody did anything and the meeting ended up slipping into chaos and resulting in a huge waste of time. Yet, this organization was a company! Beyond a few dozen volunteers, the rest of the 600 attendees were employees of Canonical Ltd. or other companies who were there for work but acted as if they were having fun, so excited about the things they did, and they really worked hard! I had never seen so cooperative and productive meetings, not even in my volunteering activities. In addition, this system worked non-stop for 8 hours a day, 5 days in a row. What a wonderful thing! On that trip, I decided that the UDS was something I could not miss.

Ubuntu Developer Summit - December 2008

Crowdsourcing of the most boring job

In a software company, the tester's job is the most boring one: it was not my opinion nor an absolute truth; it simply was what I had always heard in my work experience. Until the spring of 2010.

The winter UDS[50] in 2009 was held in Dallas, Texas, November 16th to 20th. Milo and I, having also participated in the May edition in Barcelona[51], at that point, were two veterans of the event and everybody knew us. As you know, coffee breaks are the most interesting part of summits. Informal conversations in front of a coffee or having a beer after dinner often lead to great ideas and successful initiatives, where everything reflects exactly the definition of the English word serendipity[52]. During one of these moments, I was introduced to Ubuntu's new Quality Assurance Director Marjo Mercado, who suggested, while we were having a beer, that volunteers should be more involved in the testing activities. Some years before, I had founded and managed the Italian Marketing Team[53] obtaining great results in terms of participation. So at that moment, I felt that having a big group of volunteers who massively experienced the current version under development would increase gossip and rumors on the new features, creating a lot of expectations in the blogosphere. It was a fantastic way to use guerrilla marketing, contributing to improve the software at the same time. I knew what I was supposed to do and assured Marjo that, back to Italy, I would work on that idea. There was another wonderful aspect of Ubuntu, both in the national and international community: if you wanted to do anything, all the doors were wide open. Long story short, I gathered a small group of national community cornerstones willing to help, prepared the wiki presentation pages of the new workgroup, created the mailing list and announced the new project. We experimented with a new leadership model: instead of appointing an administrator, we started with a group of "experienced members" willing to mentor the newbies. The group had no hierarchical structure and activities were carried out through "adoption": there was a table with the list of versions to be tested (there were two platforms at that time,

[50]https://wiki.ubuntu.com/UDS-L
[51]https://wiki.ubuntu.com/UDSKarmic
[52]https://en.wikipedia.org/wiki/Serendipity
[53]http://wiki.ubuntu-it.org/GruppoPromozione

i386 and amd64, and various flavors: ubuntu, kubuntu, xubuntu, netbook edition and mythubuntu) and the volunteers declared in advance what version they wanted to test. At this point, a special server, called ISO Tracker, sent out e-mails for every new release, with form where the volunteer could report the test results and the list of all detected bugs. Towards mid-January 2010, the first tests of the founding members began and, thanks to their example, other community outsiders began to join little by little. At the same time, the most committed members and mentors started to opt gradually out, until when only Sergio Zanchetta and I were left. In less than four months, the group grew from 4 to 13 people, seven of whom had never contributed to Ubuntu before. In the first tested Ubuntu release, 10.04 Lucid Lynx, consisting of 7 Alpha and Beta releases, the group performed the impressive number of 227 complete interactive tests on the operating system. These required booting, checking operations through a list of basic steps such as application, document and file opening, and finally surfing the web visiting the ubuntu.com website. Sergio and I presented these data in a special session of the Ubuntu Developer Summit held in Brussels from 10th to 14th of November 2010. The managers at Canonical Ltd. were enthusiastic: they had never seen a group with such a turnout and productivity in such a short a time, without even taking into account the fact that in Italy the free Software was not so widespread. Other groups immediately followed the Italian example, including France, Israel and China. It seemed impossible, yet, testing received a resounding interest among the enthusiasts. Had we managed to transform the most boring job into something fun?

The Italian Version

Towards the end of July 2011, Milo suggested a preview to the Community Council[54], the coordinating body of the Italian com-

[54]https://www.ubuntu-it.org/comunita/struttura/

munity where I was in charge. The creation of automatic procedures to generate the CD with a language other than English in the international list of translations was under consideration. They just started with some technical trials and the final decision would be taken in the following UDS[55], held in Orlando, Florida, from October 31st to November 4th. As usual, Milo and I participated and several volunteers from Italy also joined us, including Silvia, who is now his wife. I took part in the session devoted to CD localization and there was not much to talk: everyone agreed on the opportunity to start the project, so much of the time was used for technical clarifications and organizational arrangements. Producing Ubuntu CDs outside the original infrastructure required to recreate elsewhere all the automated *build* and *continuous integration* mechanisms that had refined in Canonical over seven years of work: a hard task, but considering that we could count on a large group of testers, I suggested Italy as the pilot nation. My proposal was accepted and, when I returned home, I started the (by this time very well known) activities that were necessary to start a new working group. Dario Cavedon, a great friend of mine and historic member of the community, offered to help and I was very pleased to accept. I knew I would have to spend several nights at work staying up late and an expert contribution was more than welcome. All localized CD customizations had to be collected in a single package[56], called ubuntu-defaults-nn, where nn represented the country code – ours was called ubuntu-defaults-it. The planned customizations were:

- Localization settings (language, currency, decimal point, etc.).
- Browser bookmarks.
- Default radio stations in the media player.
- Additional desktop icons.
- Additional programs (e.g. dictionaries and spell checkers).

Once we created the package, we would upload it to the official

[55]https://wiki.ubuntu.com/UDS-P/

[56]https://help.ubuntu.com/community/InstallingSoftware#What_is_a_package.3F

Ubuntu servers. The procedure was to download the File System[57] directory onto our computer including all Ubuntu main packages, including the Italian default one. From that edited File System, an .iso image[58] was generated to create the CD or the USB stick, which users would use to install the operating system. The whole procedure was performed automatically by a very long *BASH script* I had created on purpose, and many tests and corrections were needed to obtain a stable and reliable procedure. Each run of the whole process took almost an hour and, as we expected, Dario and I spent several nights working on the project until late. Once ready, the .iso image was uploaded to a web space and indexed by a dedicated ISO Tracker Server, which rallied volunteers for tests: each upload required another hour, given the limited nature of our ADSL connections. Luckily, after a few months, when the script started to work smoothly and did not need any more checks, we migrated all the instances on the cloud where, for the cost of a coffee, we could run the whole procedure in about twenty minutes. Beyond the technical aspect, the Italian CD was also the first occasion where so many Ubuntu-it groups were involved in the same aggregating project. While the Translation Group was responsible for the linguistic part and the Test Group played a huge role in quality control, the Promotion Group took advantage of the novelty for an intense marketing campaign. The Development Group was also of great help as I was a "newbie" I did not have all the skills to develop the .deb packages required by my Maintainer role of the default package. The initiative was a huge success. The first version of the Italian CD containing Ubuntu 12.04 Precise Pangolin was massively downloaded. At that time, Flavia and Luca, two other very active members of the community, were updating their book on Ubuntu, published by Hoepli[59], and they had the idea of including the Italian CD in the book. They asked me to write the preface and I was very pleased to accept; it was my first timid foray

[57]https://help.ubuntu.com/community/LinuxFilesystemTreeOverview

[58]https://en.wikipedia.org/wiki/ISO_image

[59]http://www.hoepli.it/libro/ubuntu-linux-1204/9788820351779.html

in the publishing world.

Discovery of Agile

Just when I was busy with the Ubuntu Italian CD, in the spring of 2012, I realized that it was time to leave my job. I did not share some of the strategic choices of my company, which was expanding abroad by reducing staff in Italy, and the management style was too different from what I was used to in Ubuntu, so much that the feeling of not being in the right place just grew more and more every day. It was a hard choice: changing job would mean leaving Siena and an extremely comfortable life. After 12 years, I knew everyone at the customer's facility and my technical knowledge was enough to work without stress. Moreover, having ordered and devoured English books from Amazon since 2008, coming first from the US (taking forever!) and then from Italy, allowed me to become a guru in my environment with little effort. Competition was low and mediocrity widespread. People were just struggling along. A friend of mine who had moved to London a couple of years earlier and that I had met during my visit to Canonical offices in 2010, knew that I was "looking around" in search for a new job and told me about a free position in the company where he worked. It was an application for Dev Manager, but as the company was in full Agile transition, Scrum Master's competences was also required. I knew Scrum and Kanban from the long discussions that came about when someone in Ubuntu from a different team using one of the two methodologies wrote a blog post claiming that one was better than another. The financial offer was well above my expectations, and the perspective of moving to London for work, to breathe an atmosphere much more similar to the one I had known during the UDSs really appealed to me. I changed my Skype status into "You were not made to live as brutes[60]" and I sent my resume. The

[60]https://www.goodreads.com/quotes/266943-consider-your-origin-you-were-not-formed-to-live-like

interview did not go as I hoped. For some reason, the fact that I was not graduate took its toll and the only weapon I could use to fight in this fierce competition were the beautiful experiences in Ubuntu; which unfortunately, in a highly competitive labor market, were not enough. I came back home and, in an effort to strengthen my curriculum, I began to take some certifications: after qualifying in traditional Project and Service Management, I enrolled in the Certified Scrum Master[61] course from Scrum Alliance. The two day course held in Bologna by the energetic Andrea Tomasini, an Italian Agile Coach living in Berlin, came as a revelation to me. I knew the rules of Scrum but I did not understand its true essence, its underlying principles and values. The more I explored this approach, the more I felt it familiar. I understood that working Agile meant working with that sense of participation, involvement and motivation that had pervaded my experience in Ubuntu. I realized that just the lack of all this made my daily work unattractive. Working Agile meant bringing in your job that productive fun I had experienced in Ubuntu. "Wonderful – I thought – from now on I just want to do this". As soon as I was back to work, I started experimenting what I had learned with my colleagues.

The Agile Community

From that moment on, I had just discovered the same passion I had in Ubuntu. I began attending conferences and meetings with other Agilists. Meeting to exchange ideas and learn from each other was, after all, what I was most used to. I started to devour books on Agile. In the community of Italian Agilists, I found a similar climate to Open Source. After just one year from the first Scrum Master course, I attended another course for Product Owner and I founded the Tuscan Agile Community[62] on Meetup. I made friends with two Scrum Masters working in the Florence area, Raffaello Torraco and

---

[61]https://www.scrumalliance.org/certifications/practitioners/certified-scrummaster-csm
[62]https://www.meetup.com/it-IT/ALT-AGILE-LEAN-TUSCANY/

Manuele Piastra, whom I occasionally saw to have a pizza and beer together. Meanwhile, I was losing interest in Ubuntu. In 2012, Mark announced that the focus of the project was "convergence" that is creating a single system running on computers, phones, tablets, and TVs. The greatest efforts, therefore, were revolving to the mobile world, which I did not feel particularly attracted to. In addition, the decision in the beginning of 2013 to stop the Ubuntu Developer Summits in favor of online quarterly meetings, coupled with some (in my opinion unfair) layoffs, broke down the bond of the latest 5 years. Ubuntu was changing and I began to outgrow it. One of my recent works in Ubuntu was a talk at the November 2014 meeting, where we suggested a parallel between Ubuntu & Agile[63]. The change had begun: Ubuntu had stopped fascinating me, and Agile was attracting me more and more.

The First Training

In Empoli, spring 2014, speaking in front of a pizza while organizing an Agile Lean Coffee cycle, Manuele told Raffaello and me that he was waiting for a response after an interview in London. I still cultivated the idea of going to the UK, but I could not find a satisfactory job. Starting from a very comfortable situation, with a good paycheck and a permanent contract, I had set some minimum standards for the job offers that drastically reduced the number of what I considered acceptable, and the few interesting ones turned out above my profile. I also had talks with dream companies, such as Amazon and Google, but failed them. On the other hand, I was an expert about London. I knew which agency I should call to find a home, what the best living areas and phone companies were where I should go in order to network with other Agilists etc. We finished the evening talking mainly about London and the next day I sent to Manuele a plethora of links I had saved in a special folder on my computer. A few weeks later, Manuele contacted me on Skype:

[63]https://www.slideshare.net/xdatap1/ubuntu-agile

"Paolo, I have two news for you. The first is that I got the job, I'm going to London! The second is that I had a teaching job for a Scrum course in Perugia in September but I cannot go. Would you like to teach there?" I nearly fell off my chair: "Wow Manuele, congratulations! Sure of course! Teaching Scrum: that's cool!" I then found out that the course was funded by the Italian Fondo Imprese and lasting seven days, for bureaucratic reasons. "Why seven? The Scrum Master course is two days plus other two for Product Owner. I did a one-day DevOps course. What else shall I tell them?" I asked the training agency guy, who was quite categorical: "Come on, we are in July and the course is in September, you have plenty of time to prepare it. Maybe add some practice exercise." I spent the whole summer preparing slides. It was a devil of a job: preparing the material for 56 hours of lesson from scratch was a mammoth task. Many friends of mine helped me sending me links and material and by the end of August I had done it! I had prepared my first Agile course. Of course, to fill all that time I did not only cover Scrum but also Kanban, Lean Startup, Scaling and Team Coaching. The course was excellent and while I was in the classroom, I realized that teaching was what I've made for. It made me feel good. Even the students were willing to attend and had fun. That course was my luck. It had forced me to prepare a massive amount of Agile training material, which I now had in my PC, and provided me with a first expendable experience.

New Year, New You

Towards the end of 2014, the work relationship with my employer, with whom I had spent the last 12 years, had irreparably deteriorated. In mid-October, we reached an agreement that both satisfied us and signed the resignation; at the beginning of November, I was a free man. I spent the end of that year following the Design Thinking and Interaction Design courses offered online by the Interaction

Design Foundation[64], reading books and attending conferences, among which the Italian Agile Day[65], held in Ancona that year. On that occasion, I met Fabio Armani, a very skilled Agile Coach whom I had known two years before at an event in Florence. Chatting with him, it emerged that he was working as a coach for Monte dei Paschi Bank. I told him, almost jokingly, "Since the new year I'm freelance, if you need a hand, feel free to call!" He called me on January 4: he had to train two groups on the same day in Siena, and he was looking for a colleague to help him. We would work together in the morning and separate in the afternoon. On January 8th, 2015, I was working with my new title: Agile Coach. I added the new job position on LinkedIn and the participants in the Perugia course that I had held the year before left very flattering recommendations on my profile. I felt incredibly lucky: I had not even had time to wish it, and this great new job had already begun!

---

[64]https://www.interaction-design.org
[65]http://www.agileday.it/

Summer 2016

Here we are at 2016, when I am the managing directory of Klimsoft, an IT services company I founded with my friend and former colleague Alessandro Pettorali. I spend most of my time traveling around Italy as an Agile Coach, I have clients spread all over Central and Northern Italy and I work with various companies and colleagues, including Fabio Armani, my first mentor, and Raffaello Torraco, the other cornerstone of the Tuscan Agile Meetup[66]. At the end of 2015, I had followed a Scrum Inc.'s Webinar[67] about the application of this methodology outside of software: "Scrum for Maximum Awesome. Hardware, Software and Innovation". I got interested in this topic and I had recently started collaborating with the Industrial School of FESTO, a German industrial giant, which encouraged me to deepen my knowledge. I devoted a lot of time to this, I read a lot and found out that some **Joe Justice** would hold the first Scrum for Hardware "Train the Trainer" course in January. It was expensive and I had not planned it; moreover, I had already scheduled to attend a coaching course in Neuro-Linguistic Programming exactly those days, so I reluctantly discarded the idea to enroll.

You can't judge the day from the morning

At the approach of the summer and for the first time since I had started my life as a coach, something went wrong. In Rome, during a Lean Startup event for a customer, I felt an intense itching and

---

[66]http://www.meetup.com/it/ALT-AGILE-LEAN-TUSCANY/

[67]https://www.scruminc.com/scrum-for-maximum-awesome/

burning on my chest and back. I noticed a reddish skin rash with small bubbles spreading from beneath my sternum and stretching across the side to the center of my back. During a break, I went to the nearest pharmacy but the pharmacist refused to sell me anything without an accurate medical check up and sent me to the nearest medical guard, at a 15-minute drive. The doctor immediately recognized what it was: Herpes Zoster, commonly known as shingles or "Fuoco di Sant'Antonio" (literally Saint Anthony's fire) in Italian. "Its Italian name originates from the fact that in the past it was such a painful and long-term condition, that sick pilgrims used to go to Padua to plead for mercy from the Saint Patron of the city. But you don't need to: just go to a pharmacy and buy these – he said with a strong Roman accent – and you should definitely take a rest." he added. After being back in Siena, the pain had not disappeared yet, so I went to my family doctor's for medical advice. I found out that those drugs would not be enough to heal me properly: after two weeks, I showed no significant signs of improvement and I often woke up in terrible pain at night. He prescribed a more effective antiviral therapy and firmly prohibited me to sunbath. My summer was ruined! In addition to having to endure that pain, I could not even go to the beach!

Alternative Holidays

One early morning, while reading my mail, I noticed the Scrum for Hardware banner in the regular Scrum Alliance newsletter. I found out that a second "Train the Trainer" three-day course would be held in Denver, Colorado, just a month later, shortly after August. In addition, for the following two days, the same area would host the first International Conference on the subject: Scrum for Hardware Gathering. A Wikispeed Build Party — a workshop where an eco-friendly sports car would be built with Scrum methodology – was also planned the day just after the gathering. A really interesting program! Since I was looking for alternative holidays, I thought the

Colorado Mountains could be the perfect destination. The cost was pretty high but Alessandro, my business partner, encouraged me to go. I would spend a few days relaxing in the mountains, what I needed, and I would deepen a topic that I loved very much. Four years after my first time, I was going back to the USA, this time alone: Milo and Ubuntu's friends would not be there to keep me company.

Back in the USA

I landed in Denver around 6:00 p.m. local time, while in Italy it was already 3:00 a.m. of the morning after. To welcome me, an annoying storm. After getting my suitcase and finding my shuttle to the hotel among dozens of lined-up buses, I headed towards my accommodation, in the middle of heavy traffic. Once checked-in, I could eventually sit on the bed in my room, and it was already 8:00 p.m. I felt exhausted, I had left home twenty hours before, but I wanted to grab a bite before collapsing in that giant king-size bed – I had never seen such great beds in Europe. In front of the hotel, there was a 1950s-style American Diner restaurant – very nice; the cashier looked like Al from Happy Days[68], the chubby owner of the drive-in where Richie, Fonzie and friends regularly met. I ordered the first of many burgers to come for that summer. The morning after, I rented the car that would take me on my solo journey: a large amaranth red Jeep. After a couple days exploring Denver, I headed south towards Colorado Springs: the red rocks of the Garden of the Gods[69] and the National Museum of WWII Aviation[70] are among my most vivid memories. After spending other two nights in Colorado Springs, I went into the mountains, at Aspen, at an altitude of about 2500 meters. The town of Aspen is known for being the original home of the Aspen Institute[71],

[68]https://en.wikipedia.org/wiki/Happy_Days

[69]https://en.wikipedia.org/wiki/Garden_of_the_Gods

[70]http://www.worldwariiaviation.org

[71]https://www.aspeninstitute.org/

an international forum, independent and nonprofit organization born in the 1950s to revive dialogue, knowledge and humanistic values in a complex and evolving international geopolitical reality. Today, the Aspen Institute is headquartered in Washington and focuses on the most current political, economic, cultural and social innovation challenges. In the mountains of Colorado, the original auditorium is still surrounded by majestic nature that inspired Walter Paepcke, a Denver businessman, to make it the perfect place where thinkers, politicians and artists from all over the world could forget for some time their daily routine and pause to meditate on the core values of Western society and culture. Driving towards Aspen all the landscapes I met along the way literally took my breath away. Exploring the area, I discovered that the town took its name from the trees, Populus Tremuloides, commonly called Aspen, growing abundantly there. That plant fascinated me. In Aspen's woods, all trees are nourished through the same roots, they are all connected and have the same DNA, just like all the hairs on my arm are part of me, though a midge may perceive them as many distinct elements. Individual trees are parts of a single organism and whatever happens on the surface – a fire, an avalanche, a landslide – the underground net of roots continue to expand and quickly produces new plants replacing those destroyed. In the neighboring state of Utah, there is an Aspen forest called Pando[72], which is the largest and longest living organism in the world. Its estimated weight is about 6,615 tons and it is about 80,000 years old. It is the living being that best interprets the concept of resilience[73].

[72]https://en.wikipedia.org/wiki/Pando_(tree)
[73]https://en.wikipedia.org/wiki/Resilience

Aspen woods

Speaking of Agile and organizations, we often mention **resilience** as an important feature to be nurtured, given the market's shifts and the incredible acceleration of technological progress. What a wonderful metaphor thinking of a resilient organization like an Aspen forest! It resists adversity thanks to its invisible **network** of relationships.

Train the Trainer

From my Colorado Mountain tour, I went back to Denver on Sunday afternoon and I headed north of the city to the town of Westminster. I had booked my hotel a few minutes ride from the course site, which would take place at the Scrum Alliance headquarters and the following morning I showed up very early. The classroom was already full. I introduced myself to a thirty-five-year-old man sitting next to me: "Nice to meet you, Paolo" and he went "Nice to meet you, Nicola". A very familiar accent. "Italian?" I asked. "Yes, we're all Italians at this table." Eight other participants were employees of an Ivrea company, founded several years earlier by former Olivetti[74] staff. Unbelievable! During my travel, I kept

[74]https://en.wikipedia.org/wiki/Olivetti

thinking, "I'll be the only Italian... maybe I'll be the only European!" On the opposite, Italian was the mother tongue of the majority of the attendees! The course was held, of course, in English, by Hubert Smits, Peter Borsella and Lonnie Weaver-Johnson, three American Certified Scrum Trainers who, the previous January, had participated in the first Train the Trainer course.

The course also provided a CSM Certification[75]: the CSM that I had already obtained in 2012 and that saw me so keen to begin the transformation into a coach. Needless to say, the first part of the course, in which we traced the basics of Scrum, was a bit boring for me: I had already clear those concepts in my mind and I was already used to teaching them. Fortunately, typical hardware engineering practices were mentioned[76], and I was much more interested in those. On the second day, we saw the video of Joe Justice's TEDx[77]. When we were asked about what hit us most, many agreed on Joe's statement, "Morale is a multiplier for velocity across the team".

Agile Architecture

One of the reasons behind Wikispeed's success is its modular architecture; we discussed about it in depth with Hubert, who had assembled several. Modularity proved crucial to apply Scrum in the field of hardware: with extremely complicated monolithic products, it was impossible, in fact, to improve one part of the system during a maximum of a four-week sprint. Moreover, such an approach made it difficult to work on the same product at the same time to multiple teams. The Wikispeed example looked stimulating because the team worked with one-week-only sprints: excellent performance, considering that many software teams are struggling already with two-week sprints.

[75] CSM, Certified Scrum Master.

[76] See second part – Extreme Manufacturing section.

[77] https://www.youtube.com/watch?v=x8jdx-lf2Dw

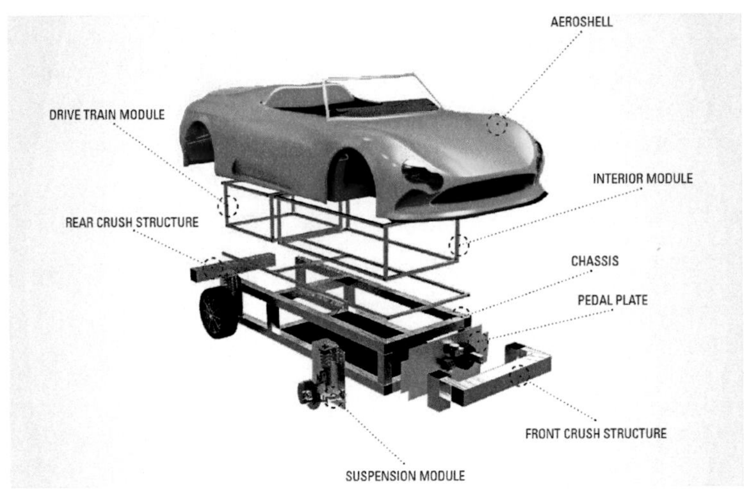

Wikispeed's Modular Architecture

Finally, we saw some examples of Design Pattern Software[78] applied to Hardware, taken from Wikispeed, which proved very useful to obtain an Agile Architecture.

The Game

The third day continued on hardware-oriented issues culminated in a game where we were divided into three Scrum teams, each with their own Scrum Master, aiming at building a modular toy car. The available material consisted of mixed constructions made up of Lego bricks for the bodywork and elements of other weird constructions for chassis, wheels and engine. One of the problems was that the two construction brands were not compatible, which made it necessary to design some integration points as well. The exercise took place in a very noisy atmosphere, mainly because of the high percentage of Italians who, at the earliest opportunity, started speaking their native language; but also in a productive way, so that in four sprints we managed to make a car that our Product

[78]See second part – Design Pattern section.

Owner considered "good enough". During the review of the car, we welcomed an exceptional guest: Joe Justice in person, who would talk later and attend the final part of the course. Joe talked to us about some new developments in the Scrum for Hardware application, particularly about some parallel manufacturing practices he was experimenting with in Boeing.

Train the Trainer, August 2016

The Conference

On the next two days, August 25th and 26th, 2016, the first **Scrum for Hardware Gathering** was held. The location was in a town called Boulder, 20 miles northwest of Westminster, in Hotel Boulderado. The hotel is a historic red brick building of the early twentieth century, which back in 2004 hosted the second Scrum Gathering, the first in the United States. This was the place where the idea of creating the Scrum Alliance took shape (as we can still read in the historical blogpost[79] by Rachel Davies). Initially, I had

[79]http://agilecoach.typepad.com/agile-coaching/2004/10/scrum-gathering-ii.html

planned to sleep in the conference hotel site, but among the reviews I noticed a few comments from Italian tourists talking about it being haunted[80]: it seemed that some guests had been disturbed several times during their sleep by unexplained noises and strange events. Though I am usually a heavy sleeper, I preferred to sleep somewhere else, in a hotel just a 10-minute drive from there. It cost half and was at the edge of a beautiful natural park at the bottom of Mountain Meadows.

The conference counted about 30 attendees. For two full days, we kept our focus on the differences between Scrum in Software and in Hardware as well as on existing experiences and success cases around the world. This was the agenda.

[80]https://www.tripadvisor.it/ShowUserReviews-g33324-d82795-r237281902-Hotel_Boulderado-Boulder_Colorado.html

---

Thursday August 25, 2016

- 9:00 Opening (Hubert Smits)
- 9:15 Disrupting the Automotive Industry (Joe Justice)
- 10:45 Combat Scrum (Mike Few, ARCA)
- 12:00 Lunch
- 13:00 Agile for Hardware – Learning from the Trenches (Jeanne Bradford)
- 14:00 Point estimating with multi-disciplinary teams (Jeanne Bradford)
- 15:15 Scrum for Life: A tale of 2 journeys (Mark Bruckner)
- 17:00 Conclusion

Friday August 26, 2016

- 9:00 Opening (Hubert Smits)
- 9:15 Agile Hardware Development with Scrum (Kevin Thompson)
- 10:45 Applying modeling to real world objects (Mac Felsing)
- 12:00 Lunch
- 13:00 Workshop: Modeling with Mac Felsing
- 15:15 Our Manifesto: Wording the Scrum4HW Manifesto and Principles
- 16:30 Retrospective
- 17:00 Conclusion

Mostly, I was struck by Joe Justice's keynote speech: with his clear and direct communication style, he gave us a real energy boost, which stayed with all the attendees for the entire conference. His speech began with a somewhat cryptic slide: 353.

Keynote by Joe Justice

With this first slide, Joe wanted to point out that Scrum for Hardware standards were the same of traditional Scrum: the 3 Roles, 5 Ceremonies and 3 Key Artifacts of the Scrum Guide[81] remain. Joe wanted to insist on the fact that working with hardware was not an excuse to dismantle or change Scrum, which unfortunately many people tend to do even in software. After the theoretical part, Joe told about the experience of some customers, including Boeing, already known by some attendees, and underlined how the supplier chain is crucial to a true agility. Finally, talking about Extreme Manufacturing, he launched an innovative idea to organize teams around product engineering: organizing team building similarly to the model by which modern microprocessor operations are processed. The results showed how this could drastically accelerate performance by simply moving from a linear to a parallel workflow. In computer processors, this is achieved thanks to very fast cache memory that acts as a buffer; In manufacturing, however, a similar result is achieved through the concept of "contract first design"[82]

[81]http://scrumguides.org
[82]See second part – Extreme Manufacturing section.

and flexible production lines. (Joe's slides can be downloaded from the Scrum for Hardware[83] website). The conference group photo was taken on the same stairway used for the photo of Scrum Gathering II in 2004, hoping it would be a good omen for the initiative.

Scrum for Hardware Gathering, August 2016

Our Manifesto

In the concluding part of the conference, we talked about how the Agile Manifesto[84] was written with a too specific lexicon for software only, even if its principles were a source of inspiration, and could not be used as it was for the development of physical products. Moreover, for someone, the word "manifesto" had in English a too strong connotation, associated with extreme political movements and revolutionaries. We started brainstorming on which principles the new statement should contain. We divided into four groups and began to generate ideas with sticky notes; after a break, each group shared what emerged, so we set for convergence and synthesis. The operations continued beyond the expected time for the conclusion, and gradually the working group became less

[83]http://scrum-hardware.com/events/i-scrum-for-hardware-gathering/
[84]http://agilemanifesto.org/iso/it/manifesto.html

numerous as the attendees left. However, we managed to make a first draft that satisfied the majority, and after taking a routine picture, we left agreeing to finish the text remotely via email.

Agile Product Charter, August 2016

The definitive version, called Agile Product Charter[85], was published on September 28th, 2016.

Agile Product Charter

We embrace Agile methods as the engine driving innovative solutions and collaboration to amplify economic, ecologic and social benefits across our planet. Through this work, we have come to value:

> Cross functional team collaboration over specialization, process and tools
>
> Modularity over tightly-coupled solutions
>
> Continuous customer collaboration over inflexible contracts
>
> Useful continuous delivery over a single comprehensive delivery

[85]http://agileproductcharter.org

> Extending development through manufacturing over fixing problems in the field
>
> Useful continuous documentation over comprehensive documentation

That is, while there is value in the items on the right, we value the items on the left more.

Wikispeed Build Party

The next morning, I left the hotel under a clear blue sky and no clouds. Such a radiant day put me in the right mood: it was about time to put into practice what we had learned. I headed to Erie, a small town east of Boulder, where Hubert Smits was building a Wikispeed car. The garage was in the open countryside and the view was beautiful. A plethora of Wikispeed pieces was scattered around the floor; there was very little of it mounted, only a suspension of the four needed and little more. We thought we had to mount pre-assembled pieces, but our Wikispeed had to be built almost from scratch, with drill and saw!

During the Security Briefing, Joe provided us with the rules on working safely and told us the schedule for the day. We organized[86] with a one day Sprint length and a daily meeting at lunchtime. Divided into three Scrum teams, each with a Scrum Master and a Product Owner, we listened to the homeowner, acting as a Chief Product Owner, describing the backlog with the Sprint Planning activities. Joe would help the Scrum Masters solve any problems and would act as a mentor when the teams needed technical suggestions. We agreed to work on three modules: interiors, body shell and suspensions/wheels. The car's internal module was to be built from scratch. There was just an aluminum parallelepiped of the right size ready to be placed inside the chassis. The suspensions

[86]See second part – Scrum section.

also had to be mounted; you could use the almost-ready one as an example for the others. For the rest, we had to watch videos on Wikispeed's YouTube channel, from Hubert's computer. The carbon fiber body shell was done, but it had been damaged during transport and had to be repaired. Considering that a member of my team had some knowledge of composite materials, having repaired by himself a tank in his own house in the country, we decided to deal with the body shell.

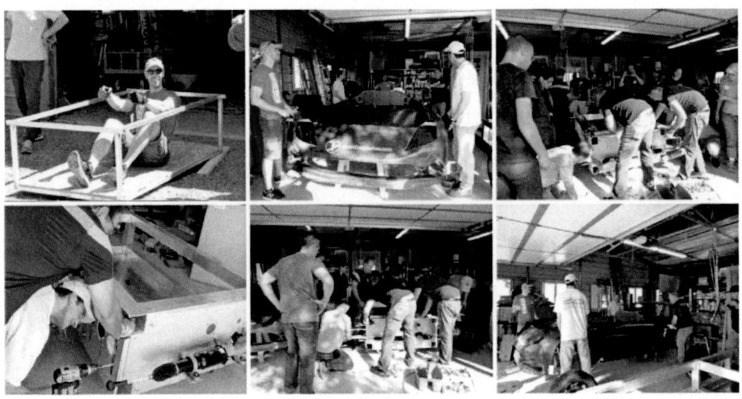

Wikispeed Build Party Phases, August 2016

We finished working at lunchtime and placed the body shell inside the shed, so that the resin used for repairs could dry out. The daily meeting was held at 12 o'clock and there we discovered that the other team taking care of the interiors had already completed the task. So we decided to take care of the chassis module helping the suspension team. We would devote to the rear ones, while the other team took care of the front module, where the steering arm and the brake needed to be mounted. However, all this would happen after lunch: we literally launched into the sandwiches we had just been offered. We all came from computer electronics and the lifestyle of most of us was very sedentary: in that moment, hunger was so much, a sign that open air and physical activity had had quite an effect on us. The work continued fast all afternoon and at about the set time we were ready for the Sprint Review: we mounted the four suspensions on the chassis and we completed it with brake disks and tires; in the front module, the steering arm and the brake pedal were working. We completed the work by placing the body over the chassis to be sure that each part was perfectly connected.

WIKISPEED Build Party, August 2016

According to Joe, we had done the equivalent of two and a half days of a regular team, and if we stayed in America for another four days, at that rate we could have started that Wikispeed car. We were very pleased, and with our frozen beer bottles in hand, we carried out our retrospective, standing in a large circle outside the garage. Many ideas on how to improve that build party emerged and Hubert took diligently note of everything.

Final Retrospective

The day was over, we all went back to our hotel: tired, but happy. What a beautiful experience! Unfortunately it was over. The next day I had to travel about 20 hours to come back home.

Back to Italy

The worst part of having a holiday in the United States is going back home. I do not know the logical explanation, but the jet lag of the return is definitely more annoying than the one on the way there: for several days, you experience a continuous drunkenness feeling with the difference that, unlike when you drink with friends, you have no fun at all. In the evening you are sleepy and in the morning as well, and all your senses are slow. Fortunately, I came back to Italy before the end of August, with no upcoming work commitments. I was thinking of a way to capitalize on the beautiful experience I had just lived; I also had promised Joe during a coffee break in the conference that I would study how to create a Scrum for Hardware community in Italy as well. Given my experience in Ubuntu, I knew where to start. The first step was creating an Italian website, translating documentation and articles and get as many pictures as possible. With that material, then, I would share the Scrum for Hardware stories on social media. So I would start to suggest the topic to conferences, to generate interest. Thus the Italian website of Scrum for Hardware[87] was born. Hubert sent me, through his assistant Katrina, the material he had published on his website in English. Therefore, I took advantage of the hot late summer 2016 to create a core group of web pages. On publication, Joe congratulated me on Wikispeed's Twitter account. Full of enthusiasm, I was preparing to face the new challenge I already knew was waiting for me.

---

[87]http://www.scrum-hardware.it

A New Industrial Revolution

A few days before leaving for Colorado I had received a phone call from Marcello Semboli, one of the historical cornerstones of the Siena Linux User Group: “A friend of mine is in the committee organizing the first TEDx in Siena and he asked me if I know any brilliant guy to suggest as a speaker”. My heart went up my throat: Marcello, with whom I had organized several conferences on Linux and free Software, had thought of me. “It would be one of my dreams coming true! What shall I do?” I said trembling with excitement. “Let me get you in touch with Massimiliano Angelini, he’ll explain everything to you”. I arranged an aperitif with Massimiliano at 6:00 p.m. in Gramsci Square, the Siena bus station, just steps away from the city center. He was with his fiancée enjoying the afternoon in a good mood: the next day he would leave for his holidays. In order to be admitted as a speaker, he explained, it was important to have a story. It cannot be a theoretical-only speech, a TED talk needs narration and it must be credible and inspiring people. “This event’s theme is **Open Doors**, we want to talk about how sharing, openness and the free movement of knowledge are synonyms of progress and growth”. “A very familiar theme to me,” I assured him, “as Marcello already told you, I’ve been up to Open Source for years. Anyway, I am about to leave too; I’m going to Colorado to meet the founder of the Wikispeed project, an eco-friendly car built by volunteers. I am sure that when I’m back I will have the right story for you”.

TEDxSiena

Upon returning from the United States, immediately after publishing the Scrum for Hardware[88] website in Italian, I devoted to my application for TEDx Siena. In a break from the Conference, I had mentioned to Joe that there was this possibility and he immediately offered to give me some material. I called Massimiliano to tell him that I was back to Italy and to ask him for some details about the organization and deadline for submitting my application. We talked for some time on the phone and, among other things, I mentioned a project he was following at that time on 3D modeling of the Bottini of Siena. The Bottini of Siena[89] are the underground tunnels built from the 13th to the 15th century for the city's water supply. They are a little engineering miracle as they are the only watercourse in the world that does not take water from a spring, but rather collects rainwater. I knew their story already at elementary school, when I visited the biggest "bottino", called "Bottino Maestro di Fonte Gaia". In that school trip, we entered one by one in a manhole at Piazza del Campo and after over an hour of underground passages, we emerged near the Antiporto[90], a fortification placed immediately outside Porta Camollia[91], the main northern door in the walls of Siena. We had walked underground for almost two kilometers! "I even found the Bottini's story in Silicon Valley, can you imagine?" I said amused to Massimiliano. "Wait, what? Tell me more, please!" he replied, curious. "In 2008 I was in Mountain View, California, for a conference, and at the San Jose Science and Technology Museum there was an exhibition on Leonardo da Vinci. Just at the entrance, there was a section dedicated to the Sienese engineers of 1500 and their Bottini". "You must mention this at TEDx! What a coincidence!" Massimiliano exclaimed. "I'll think about it. I need to find a point of conjunction with the other stories, and maybe I have

[88] http://www.scrum-hardware.it

[89] http://www.enjoysiena.it/en/attrattore/The-Bottini/

[90] https://it.wikipedia.org/wiki/Antiporto_di_Camollia

[91] https://en.wikipedia.org/wiki/Porta_Camollia,_Siena

an idea," I said.

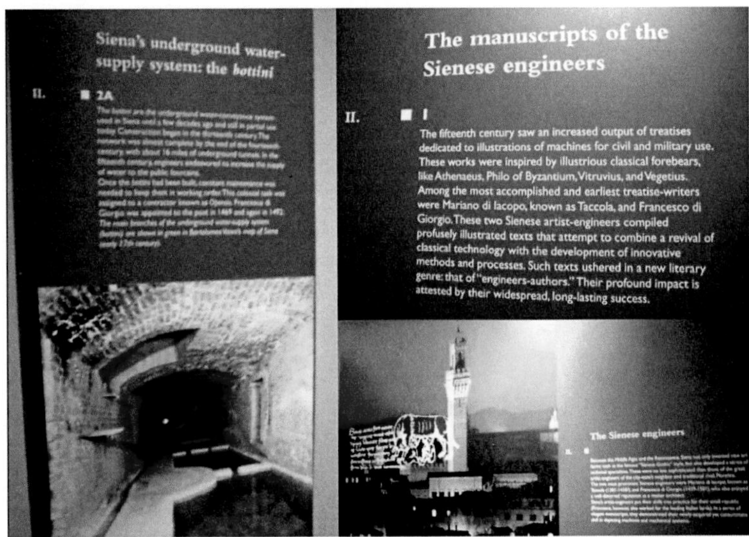

Bottini Senesi at the San Jose Science and Technology Museum, CA

I started covering the wall in front of my desk with sticky notes of my ideas for the talk. I had something, but I still was not satisfied. I wanted a *link* between the fragments and a final catchphrase. I continued my search. I spent the following weekend, the only one that year, in a seaside town. In the Gulf of Baratti, near Livorno, there was a PO Camp[92], an Agile un-conference dedicated to Product Ownership. Two pleasant days, full of interesting conversations, yet I was a little distracted: I had only one thing in my mind, my talk at TEDx. Back to Siena and to work, I had the opportunity to find the time to read and study, since my coaching appointments weren't demanding yet. One morning, scrolling through social media, I accidentally saw a video[93] by Marco Montemagno on the Fourth Industrial Revolution, which advertised an upcoming event the month after at the Milano Forum. The description of what the Fourth Industrial Revolution was resonated in my head: 3D

[92]http://www.pocamp.it
[93]https://www.youtube.com/watch?v=9_Iu6ogEAbg

printers, Internet of things, mass customization. During Gathering I had discussed with Joe about something we joked about calling it the "Hardware Compiler". We said: "If there was a sophisticated machine that could allow a single person to sit in front of a computer, draw a complex object and, pressing a button, cause a number of machines to print its parts and robots to self-organize to mount them together in a short time... well, the process would not be very different from writing software! At any moment, that person could *fill out* the object and get feedback, just as we do with software. We could use Agile methods as well as they are, even with any physical product! What's missing is technology", I said to Joe, and he replied, "That's never a problem; it goes faster than you think". Now, hearing Montemagno's words and reading articles on the subject I realized that those technologies, which according to us would have allowed making Scrum with physical products, were called Industry 4.0 in Europe. "Just a moment", I thought, "if industrial production starts to resemble software, is not that the phenomena that I have seen in the software will extend to all sectors?" That is just happening now. Each day something more becomes collaborative: Uber, Airbnb, TripAdvisor are not coincidences! Everyone will be affected. I was fascinated; I had to find out more. I had to go to the origins. I found out that the most authoritative source on the Fourth Industrial Revolution was the World Economic Forum. On the website, I found a first article[94] of the previous January, which provided interesting ideas. "Of course I didn't know this subject; they haven't been talking about it much!" I was struck by the quotation by Klaus Schwab, Founder and Executive Chairman of the World Economic Forum: "In the new world, it is not the big fish which eats the small fish, it's the fast fish which eats the slow fish".

[94]https://www.weforum.org/agenda/2016/01/the-fourth-industrial-revolution-what-it-means-and-how-to-respond/

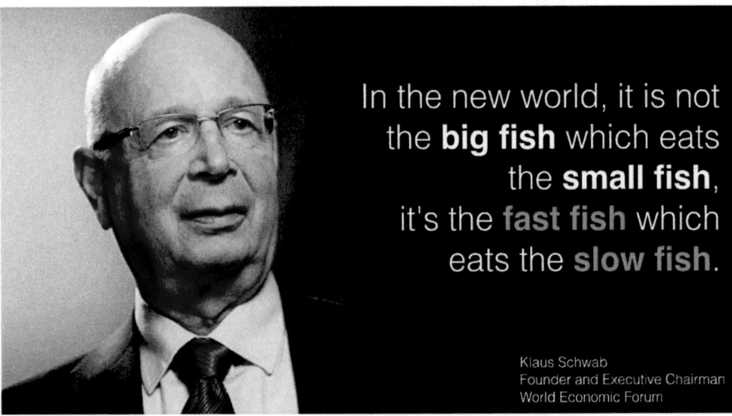
In the new world, it is not
the big fish which eats
the small fish,
it's the fast fish which
eats the slow fish.
Klaus Schwab
Founder and Executive Chairman
World Economic Forum

That is exactly what happened in Hi Tech industry since the mid-90s! I had an intuition: "Agile and Open Source are not expanding in the traditional industry because someone is asking them: it is the industry that is experiencing those phenomena because the surrounding conditions are becoming the same as HiTech!" I had found the closure for my TEDx talk.

The Big Day

The TEDx day was approaching quickly. Maurizio Napolitano, aka Napo, unexpectedly contacted me on Facebook. I met him in 2002 at the Webbit in Padua, a sort of technological Woodstock halfway between a conference and a campsite, gathering all the open source and geek souls of the moment. Napo has been for some years an Ambassador of Open Street Map[95], the project aiming at building an open and shared map of the world. He had come to see me in Siena once and we had kept in touch through social media, but I had not heard him for nearly five years. He told me "I'm back to Siena, I'll be a speaker at TEDx." "Awesome! - I replied – I'm a speaker there too!". I wanted him to be my guest: that was a perfect opportunity to meet an old friend and to better overcome

[95]https://www.openstreetmap.org

the strain of waiting. Napo landed in Pisa an hour later the expected time, almost at midnight. He was coming from Brussels, where he had attended a hearing of the European Commission on the issue of digital freedom. "How ya doing, dude?" he asked, "Nervous", I said, "I got so angry at the TEDx rehearsal. The remote control for the slides was a cheap knockoff that didn't work well, but tomorrow I'll bring my Logitech. Then there is no teleprompter, I was assured that we would have it". "It happens", he said, "I'm used to it". I shrugged my shoulders with a hopeless feeling. "Well, in Brussels I got a bad cough; let's hope my voice is still there tomorrow". The morning after, Napo was almost voiceless and coughing continually. Walking to the city center, we stopped at the pharmacy, in Piazza del Campo. "I have a bad cough, I'm voiceless, and in two hours I have an important talk at a conference", he said entering the pharmacy. "These are powerful, take one now and another one hour before your speech", said the pharmacist, "and until then, don't talk". At the entrance of the Santa Chiara Auditorium, where TEDx was held, some young college girls in business suit and high heels handed out badges. "Are you a speaker? What's your name?" said the prettiest one, with red hair and green eyes that I had started to stare since I entered. "If you stop being so formal to me, I'll tell you", I said, smiling. She went red in the face and handed me my badge. "Come on, dude! She's probably 20 years younger than you!" Napo sniggered, "Didn't the pharmacist tell you to shut up?" We cracked up laughing. I asked him to take a photo of me with my cell phone in front of a poster near the entrance, so that I could announce the start of the event on Twitter. In a few seconds, my phone began to ring. Several friends shared my Tweet and Joe from Wikispeed's account sent me his wishes. In the United States, it was early morning, who knows where he was in that moment? Napo held his talk before me, and it went great; he only coughed once, and no one even noticed. At lunch, everyone was very talkative networking to the attendees. I just thought of my talk, which was waiting for me in the early afternoon. Finally, my moment came, I went behind the scenes, they put the microphone over my ear and I took a deep sigh: I was going to become a TEDx Speaker[96]!

I shared one of the photos Napo had taken of me on Twitter, a few minutes after my speech, and Hubert Smits and Peter Borsella joined the chorus of congratulations from across the ocean. I was on top of the world!

The Fourth Industrial Revolution

To better understand the Fourth Industrial Revolution, Klaus Schwab's book The Fourth Industrial Revolution[97] was of great help.

[96]https://www.youtube.com/watch?v=Ws828wk_NDA
[97]https://www.weforum.org/about/the-fourth-industrial-revolution-by-klaus-schwab

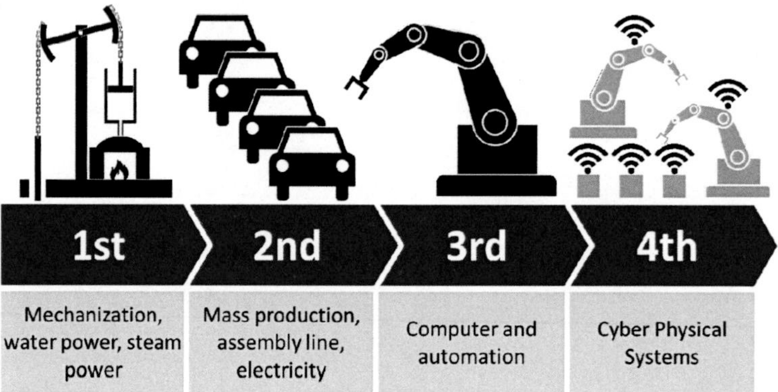

According to historian Thomas Ashton, the **First Industrial Revolution** originated in England around 1760 and involved a series of sector-oriented renovations that concerned agriculture, transport, technical and financial innovations. The change was mainly concerned with the textile and metallurgical sectors, where the flying shuttle and steam engines were introduced, but also with the agricultural sector. England was the first country where, thanks to technological innovation, a market-based agriculture was developed (not for self-consumption but for profit); many laborers, whose work was no longer needed in the countryside, moved to the city where they found employment in the emerging industry.

The **Second Industrial Revolution**, whose start is conventionally traced back to 1870 with the introduction of electricity, chemicals and petroleum, reached its full development in the last decade of 1800, when we could assist to an unprecedented technological acceleration in Europe and in the United States, which secured technical supremacy to Western countries over the rest of the world. Characteristic of the Second Industrial Revolution is the fact that technological innovations are no longer the result of occasional and individual discoveries, but of specialized research in scientific laboratories and universities financed by employers and national governments. Steel introduced new solutions in the field of mechanics and allowed the construction of more robust and resistant machines and tools than those built in iron, a weak material for its tendency to oxidize and wear out quickly. Thanks to steel, concrete could be produced, which allowed unprecedented innovations in the construction industry. A further boost to progress was the invention of Nikola Tesla (1882), alternating current, which allowed the transport of electricity over long distances and its dissemination in civil use and on workplaces.

The **Third Industrial Revolution** saw the effects of the massive introduction of electronics, telecommunications and information technology industry, since 1970. The first result of these innovations was a strong push towards progress and further technological innovation in many industries. In addition, the beginning of the process of globalization of markets fostered a more rapid dissemination of products, with fast economic, labor market and demographic changes and finally on the Western population's lifestyle. High technology capitalization, concentrated in the areas of information technology and telematics, introduced a new production system, which resulted in the sharp decline of all features based on large concentrations of manpower; the centrality of human work began to weaken both in production and in the provision of services. Slowly, albeit in a less pervasive way, such effects also propagated in the second and third worlds.

The elements that experts say will determine the current as the **Fourth Industrial Revolution**, and not a continuation of the third, are mainly three:

- Speed. Unlike the previous industrial revolutions, the current one is evolving at an exponential rate rather than at a linear one. This is due to the interconnection of the world through a dense communication satellite network, the spread of Internet and cost reduction of land and air transport.
- Width and depth. Current technologies bring new paradigms and deep changes in economy, society and individuals. The transformation is not just about products or their production

process: even key concepts like identity and property are experiencing a crisis.

- Systemic impact. The transformations affect a system that extends beyond the boundaries of companies, industries and countries, involving the entire planet.

The Fourth Industrial Revolution creates a world in which physical and virtual manufacturing systems work globally together on a flexible basis. Already in 2014, two Massachusetts Institute of Technology professors, Erik Brynjolfsson and Andrew McAfee, referred to this period as "the Second Machine Age", arguing that the world was at a point where the effects of this extensive digitization manifest themselves with great force, anticipating the automation and construction of "new and unprecedented things"[98].

The Fourth Industrial Revolution, on the other hand, does not only involve the presence of even more intelligent and interconnected machines: the spectrum is much broader. At the same time, we are seeing shocking discoveries like the sequencing of the human genome, nanotechnology, renewable energies and quantum computers; but it is the combination of these technologies and the interaction between physical, digital and biological domains that make the Fourth Industrial Revolution completely new and different from the previous.

Impact on the Market

The Fourth Industrial Revolution will allow us to witness many changes. Among these, an evolution of the traditional industry market is emerging today, making it more similar to HiTech; for this reason, it is also the opportunity to introduce Agile methodologies also outside the software industry.

[98]Erik Brynjolfsson and Andrew McAfee, The Second Machine Age: Work, Progress, and Prosperity in a Time of Brilliant Technologies. https://en.wikipedia.org/wiki/The_Second_Machine_Age

Time to Market. The first obvious deduction of Klaus Schwab's quotation on the fastest fish eating the slower one is that the speed with which the companies reach the market is a decisive competitive advantage for success. Today, industrial companies, such as the automobile industry, have five-year (if not ten-year) cycles: those who are able to reduce drastically these times will achieve a significant breakthrough. An example is Tesla[99] which, while producing very few cars compared to US giants, is gaining so much value in the stock market, to be at the time of my writing, the first car builder in the USA. The disconcerting aspect is, as Reuters reports in an April 10th, 2017 article[100], that General Motors ranked second in the stock market with a value of $5,000 multiplied by the number of cars sold in 2016, while for Tesla, the factor is equal to 667,000. This means that Tesla, with only 80,000 cars sold in 2016, is worth about a million dollars more than GM, which has sold 10 million.

Mass Customization. Additive technologies, complete automation of the production chain, and advanced assembly chains reduce the production costs of limited edition and single-piece production. This makes the market open to mass customization, which will in turn increase the demand for customization itself. Just as for software, the demand for additional and customized pay-per-action features will soon be a major business segment. Today, for example, some shoe manufacturers are offering tailor-made personalization services; such as Nike[101] and Adidas[102]. An article at the end of March 2017[103] reports that General Electric has secretly printed the engine of a helicopter, reducing parts from 900 to 16. It is evident that the limits of technology are already beyond our imagination.

Shared Economy. HiTech is a phenomenon observed since the

---

[99] https://www.tesla.com

[100] http://www.reuters.com/article/us-usa-stocks-tesla-idUSKBN17C1XF.

[101] https://www.nike.com/us/en_us/c/nikeid

[102] http://www.adidas.com/us/customize

[103] http://www.additivemanufacturing.media/blog/post/ge-team-secretly-printed-a-helicopter-engine-replacing-900-parts-with-16.

early 2000s in the world, for example with Napster[104]: the progressive democratization of value content exchanged directly between individual users. Another HiTech example: at the moment, the biggest online content owner is Facebook, which does not directly produce any of it. This same phenomenon is spreading in other areas: Uber is the world's largest taxi company and does not even own a car; Airbnb is the world's largest provider of accommodation and does not own any room. The same is happening in the most diverse fields; and this is why, as we have seen in Chapter 1, Boeing and John Deere companies have been interested in the *WIKI* phenomena in their fields for some years.

Customer Expectations. The private customer, or consumer, is getting used to a world where it is possible to have everything, immediately and at the best price. Amazon shows a countdown on many articles and warns that anyone who buys within a few hours can receive the order the morning after. In addition, it keeps the promise. Consumers become accustomed and begin to be more demanding even in working environments. I recall, in this regard, the case of a gas canister manufacturer where I held a design-thinking workshop. It was a very unusual customer for this type of business; yet, they were interested in rebuilding their *customer's journey* to understand how and why some small competitors could better satisfy their customers, making them difficult to be beaten.

Data Enhanced Products. New technologies are transforming the way organizations perceive and manage their resources, as products and services are enriched with digital features increasing their value. Tesla, for example, shows how software updates and connectivity can be used to enhance a product even after its purchase, so as to avoid its depreciation over time. On the one hand, new materials make activities more resistant and resilient; on the other, data and analysis are transforming the role of maintenance. In addition, the ability to predict the performance of an asset allows to establish new business models by extending the *consumption*

[104]https://en.wikipedia.org/wiki/Napster

service model to areas where traditionally the purchase of an asset was foreseen.

Collaborative Innovation. The importance of customer experience and analysis of resource performance data requires new forms of collaboration, mainly because of the speed at which innovations and disturbances are occurring. This applies to large companies, which often lack of expertise and of a proper mindset; but also to younger and dynamic startups, which lack the resources and the amount of data coming from a mature customer base. Clearly, they both have the opportunity to collaborate with mutual benefit. A telling example is the recent partnership between the industrial giant Siemens[105], investing about $4 billion a year in Research and Development, and Ayasdi[106], an innovative Artificial Intelligence company, founded at Stanford University in 2008. Their collaboration allows Siemens to face complex challenges for information extraction from vast databases, while Ayasdi can validate its real-world analysis approaches by increasing its credibility on the market.

The Winner Takes it All. The complexity of the factors that determine wins and losses on the markets is growing exponentially. Time becomes crucial: who first manages to delight customers in a particular niche, quickly becomes a *de facto* monopolist. The phenomenon of an industry leader with more than three quarters of market share is common in the High Tech sector. Search engines (Google), purchase between individuals (EBay), social networks (Facebook), payment systems (Paypal) are the best-known examples. It is now easily foreseeable that a similar effect may be manifested in other sectors, which traditionally saw the market competed by a plurality of operators.

---

[105]https://en.wikipedia.org/wiki/Siemens
[106]https://en.wikipedia.org/wiki/Ayasdi

A Leadership Problem

Are we living in a new perfect world? Not exactly. Half the world's population, approximately 4 billion people, not having access to the Internet are still excluded from the **Third Industrial Revolution**; and about 17% of the world population, 1.3 billion people living in poorer areas and having no access to electricity, still have not even started the **Second Industrial Revolution**. On the other hand, we are witnessing a very strong acceleration in the innovation process: while the spindle of the spinning frame, one of the key inventions of the First Industrial Revolution, took about 120 years to spread across Europe, the Internet has expanded on a planetary scale in less than 10 years. In any case, the lessons learned in the First Industrial Revolution are still usable: the extent to which a company embraces technological innovation is an important determinant of its progress and wellbeing.

A real problem, according to Klaus Schwab, is that the level of understanding of current changes, necessary for leadership training in all areas, is still too low. Current change collides with the need to rethink our economic, social and political systems. As a result, both nationally and globally, the institutional framework to govern the dissemination of innovation and to mitigate any disturbances is inadequate, when not completely absent. In a paper at the Dortmund University of Technology[107], we can read:

> "The fascination for Industrie 4.0 is twofold. First, for the first time an industrial revolution is predicted a-priori, not observed *ex-post*. This provides various opportunities for companies and research institutes to actively shape the future. Second, the economic impact of this industrial revolution is supposed to be huge."

[107]Hermann, Pentek, Otto, 2015, p.2 - Design Principles for Industrie 4.0 Scenarios: A Literature Review. https://www.researchgate.net/publication/307864150_Design_Principles_for_Industrie_40_Scenarios_A_Literature_Review

This is definitely an unprecedented opportunity. We realized, for the first time in history, that an industrial revolution is under way, during its development. This can be an advantage that allows us to adapt for our benefit and for the benefit of all, provided by embracing change and finding the best answers to this *crisis.*

In Japanese the term *crisis* is represented by two ideograms, which individually are translated into English as **danger** and **opportunity**; While the English word "crisis" comes from the Greek verb *krinein,* which means "separate, distinguish, choose, decide". In this moment of great danger and great opportunities, we will be required to distinguish and separate threats from opportunities, to choose to best way to meet each of them.

Industry 4.0 and Agile

The term **Industry 4.0** is for the first time in a speech at the Hanover Fair of 2011. It was later used by the German Government as the name of the project for the modernization of the domestic industry. This project gave rise to a series of operational recommendations, presented for the first time in 2012. The idea of "smart factories" tells about a world where global production virtual and physical systems cooperate in a flexible manner so as to allow the absolute customization of products and the creation of new operating models. The results obtained since then from Germany in production meant that the European Commission[108] gave prominence to this policy and that several EU countries, including Italy with an initiative of the Ministry of Economic Development[109], began to pursue it. Numerous studies have already been conducted on this subject so far: among the best known, those of McKinsey and Boston Consulting.

[108]Implementation of an Industry 4.0 Strategy - The German Plattform Industrie 4.0 https://ec.europa.eu/digital-single-market/en/blog/implementation-industry-40-strategy-german-plattform-industrie-40.

[109]Ministry of Economic Development, Piano nazionale Industria 4.0 http://www.mise.gov.it/index.php/it/industria40.

Enabling Technologies

The study by **Boston Consulting**[110] shows that there are a number of enabling technologies creating the assumptions of the Fourth Industrial Revolution:

- **Advanced Manufacturing Systems** – interconnected and modular systems allowing flexibility and performance, such as collaborative robots (cobots).
- **Additive Manufacturing** – 3D printing and similar technologies.
- **Augmented Reality** and enriched reality.
- **Simulations** that can anticipate feedback and experience costly operations quickly and continuously.
- **Vertical and Horizontal Integrations**, functional integrations to circulate information between all those involved in the production process.
- The **Cloud** – the ability to draw from higher computing powers only when necessary.
- **Cyber Security**, crucial aspect born from extreme systems interconnection, which opens up new scenarios in terms of safety, privacy and property.
- **Big Data** and **Machine Learning**, to provide more and more useful data to develop complex strategies and actions.

The McKinsey[111] study shows what the many "levers" are to operate according to the sought values: asset utilization, processing, warehouse, quality, procurement, time to market, after-sales services, resources and processes.

[110]Boston Consulting Group, Industry 4.0: The Future of Productivity and Growth in Manufacturing Industries. https://www.bcg.com/publications/2015/engineered_products_project_business_industry_4_future_productivity_growth_manufacturing_industries.aspx.

[111]http://www.mckinsey.com/business-functions/operations/our-insights/manufacturings-next-act

However, many analyst studies highlighted the technological aspect and disregarded the organizational aspect of companies. I felt that something was missing.

Industrial Agility

The book by Klaus Schwab, instead, fully captures what I perceived to be the biggest challenge for companies, and introduces the concept that underlies the Industrial Agility explicitly[112]:

> All these different impacts[113] require companies to rethink their operating models. Accordingly, strategic planning is being challenged by the need for companies to operate faster and with greater agility.

How can we combine the need to *follow a plan* with *responding to change*? The answer seemed obvious to me, considering that it was a step of the Agile Manifesto[114], but for a manager who only spent

[112]Klaus Schwab, 2016, p.57 - The Fourth Industrial Revolution. http://www.weforum.org/about/the-fourth-industrial-revolution-by-klaus-schwab.

[113]Reference to those described in the Impact on the Market section of the Fourth Industrial Revolution chapter.

[114]http://agilemanifesto.org/iso/en/manifesto.html

his career in the traditional industry, also considering cultural and lexical differences with the HiTech world, this could not be taken for granted.

To help understand that the changes required to implement the Industry 4.0 project had to be not only technological but also cultural, I published in a first article on January 3rd 2017[115], the concept of **Industrial Agility** with an iceberg model that I had started to use in presentations and training. This model shows the Practices, Methods, Agile Principles and Values which, borrowed from the HiTech context, could be used with great benefit even in the traditional industry.

Practices

Practices are solutions to individual problems; they are the most visible part of an organization and are easy to imitate.

[115]Paolo Sammicheli, 2017 - Industrial Agility - How to respond to the 4th Industrial Revolution. https://www.linkedin.com/pulse/industrial-agility-how-respond-4th-revolution-paolo-sammicheli.

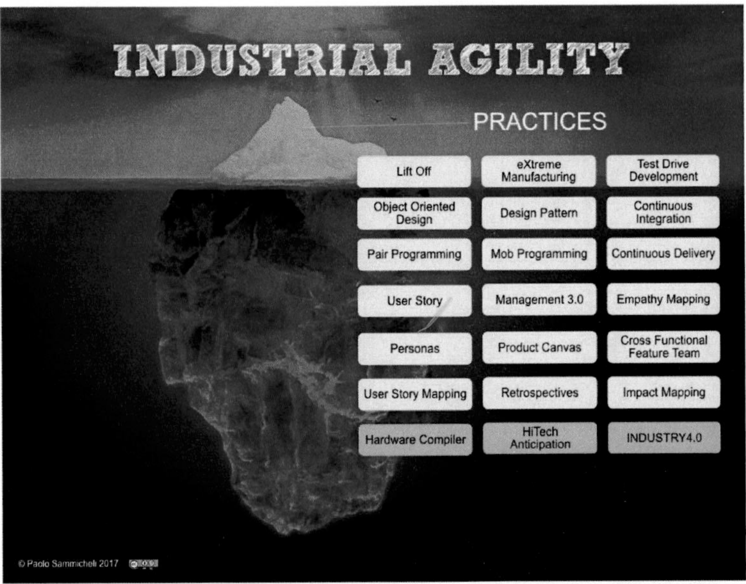

Being strongly related to the context, it is quite common that they do not represent the best choice for every occasion; there are many, and some are alternatives to other choices. Since there is not the so-called "silver bullet" that works everywhere, and that practices are only the most superficial part of a business, they are commonly published and shared by Hi-Tech companies and are disseminated in conferences and blogs. There is a widespread tendency to share, that generates real practice communities. Practices reported in dark orange in the diagram are those that come from Industry 4.0 and that will be detailed in the second part of this volume, in the Feedback Loop chapter.

Methods

Methodologies are the framework in which the processes and the flow of communication are drawn.

Various are shown in the diagram. The first two are used to represent the workflow: Scrum and Kanban. Both work well in HiTech and have already been used in industrial applications. The following two refer to the understanding and discovery of customer needs in order to create new business or improve the performance of existing ones: Lean Startup[116] and Design Thinking[117]. The idea of combining Lean Startup with Design Thinking and Scrum is not new in the software world. I personally learned it from Jeff Patton at his Product Owner course and in his book User Story Mapping[118]. The last two are related to change management and continuous improvement: Lean Change[119] and Popcorn Flow[120].

[116] https://en.wikipedia.org/wiki/Lean_startup
[117] https://en.wikipedia.org/wiki/Design_thinking
[118] http://jpattonassociates.com/user-story-mapping/
[119] http://leanchange.org/
[120] https://popcornflow.com/

Principles

Principles are what drives us in areas where there are no explicit methodologies or practices.

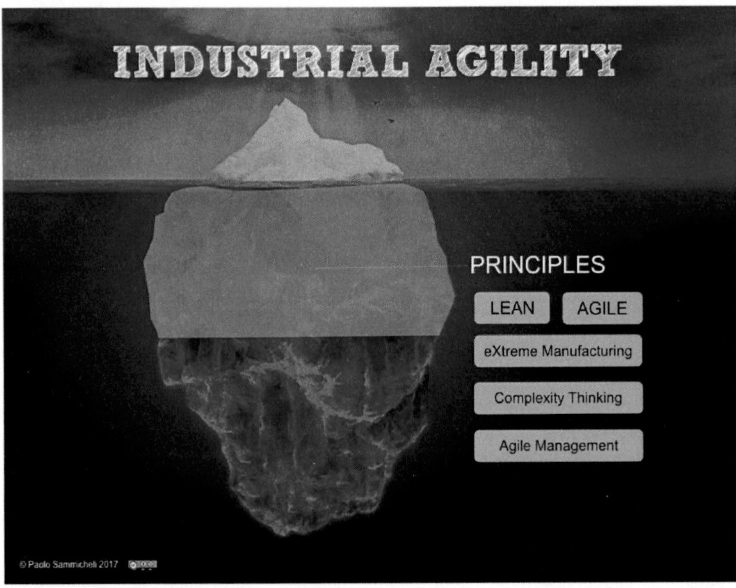

Speaking of Industrial Agility we take the principles from Lean Manufacturing[121] and the principles behind the Agile manifesto[122]. In addition, we are assisted by eXtreme Manufacturing[123], Complexity[124] and Agile Management[125].

Values

Values are the foundations of each organization; they are what defines the organization's behavior in unexpected situations.

[121] https://en.wikipedia.org/wiki/Lean_manufacturing
[122] http://agilemanifesto.org/iso/en/principles.html
[123] See In Practice section, Extreme Manufacturing chapter.
[124] See Appendix, Cynefin chapter.
[125] See In Practice section, Agile Management chapter.

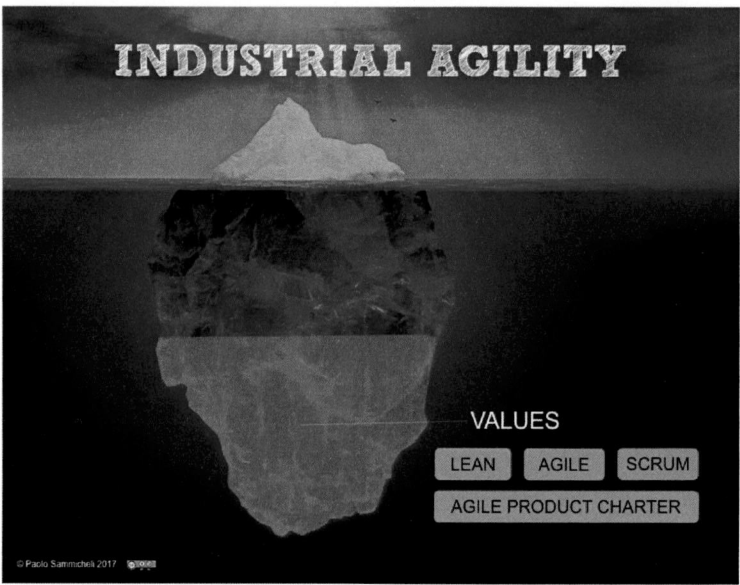

In addition to the values of Lean Manufacturing[126], those of the Agile Manifesto[127] and **Scrum**[128], we find the **Agile Product Development Chart**[129], created during the first *Scrum for Hardware Gathering* specifically for industry.

Conclusions

What is the reason why I wanted to associate an iceberg with **Industrial Agility** components, suggesting a kind of hierarchy? The reason is that if the subtle components, principles and values were omitted in practices and method adoption, the obtained agility would sink just like an iceberg without its hidden part. This is known in HiTech companies and there are no reasons for not thinking that similarly must be done in traditional industries; indeed, for the reasons we will see in the practical section, the outcome

[126]https://en.wikipedia.org/wiki/Lean_manufacturing
[127]http://agilemanifesto.org/iso/en/manifesto.html
[128]See In Practice section, Scrum chapter.
[129]See Summer 2016 chapter, Agile Product Charter section

could be even worse. Companies, rather than trying to imitate pre-packaged organizational models, typical of large consulting firms, would do well to go along a path that takes into account the principles and values, in other words, the culture of the company. A type of route of this type is described more in detail in the second part of the book.

First Feedbacks

During the first months of 2017, I turned these ideas into a talk, which I proposed to the Mini Iad of Vimercate[130]. I was faced with a crowd of about fifty people, some of whom were the Italians I had met in Colorado the year before, now great friends of mine. After my speech, the many tweets and compliments of the audience strengthened in me the idea that this theme deserves to be deepened and further disclosed. The week after, I presented to the **Agile London** the same intervention in English; the video[131] is available on YouTube. Even in this case, the topic aroused interest; but I wanted Joe's opinion, so I sent him a message.

[130]http://www.agileday.it/mini/2017/vimercate/#sammicheli
[131]https://www.youtube.com/watch?v=Nwirg6DVgGI

Three Meters above the Sky

The trip to Munich in March 2017 was the first of the most intense and exciting months I remember. Again, I had the opportunity to meet with Joe Justice, and this time I would help him in the classroom as a co-trainer. I was so excited at the idea! A few days before leaving, while I was at an industrial client for some coaching sessions, I received an email from Joe with a link where I could download the course slides. He asked me to pick a couple of sets, study them and be ready to explain them to students by myself. I had already taken several English lessons before, but having to use materials that I had not prepared myself and with such a little time to organize, made the situation much more difficult and challenging to me. I downloaded the file, which exceeded one Giga byte, with the typical slowness of Wi-Fi in hotels, and I was flabbergasted. I realized that the file contained the original documents used by Jeff Sutherland to teach Scrum, enriched with Joe's experience in Wikispeed, Boeing, John Deere and many other customers. The *Holy Grail* of Scrum for Hardware! Every single slide had several notes with references to books, scientific papers and articles on the internet and it was the synthesis of profound and very complex concepts. As Joe himself later confirmed, "Every single slide is the quintessence of hours of study. In this presentation, there are over 20 years of Jeff's research, work and refining". Long nights locked in my hotel room were waiting for me, to get ready in time.

I landed in Munich shortly after lunchtime and headed to the hotel where I was staying, which was also hosting the course. Joe had arrived a few days before to present a keynote speech at a conference and had brought Senna, his 3-year-old daughter, with him. I had seen on Facebook their photos while they were visiting Munich and I could not wait to meet him again.

Munich

The appointment with Joe was set for five o'clock. I explored the surroundings to pass the time. The hall accessed directly via a staircase to an underground mall that I discovered was extended all the way to the subway stop. To get to the hotel I had walked for about 10 minutes outside, which was very pleasant as it was a nice day. However, knowing that in case of rain I could get to the subway, and then to the airport, without having to go outdoors, seemed to me a great comfort. These Germans, so efficient!

When I returned to the hall I met Joe and Senna accompanied by Nina, the young baby sitter. Joe's wife had stayed in the United States with little Bruce, just five months old. Senna hugged me affectionately, even though she had never seen me before. Nina and Senna would spend the rest of the afternoon at the playground and in a toyshop while we would get ready for the day after. I told Joe that I would go into my room to get my computer. "I'll wait for you here in the hall while I check my mail on the phone", he said. "I'll be right back". I took the elevator to the second floor. "What a great opportunity, finally in class with Joe!" My thoughts were suddenly interrupted by a strange noise and an abrupt break. It took me just a few long seconds to realize that the elevator had blocked and I was trapped! I tried to push the buttons for the ground floor and other floors, but it was useless. I then pushed the emergency button and after a few moments, a voice started talking to me from the built-in intercom in the push-button. In German. I tried to make myself understood but the voice was disturbed. What a bad luck! It took thirty endless minutes before the clerk could manually action the elevator to take me on the floor. When I reemerged, he asked me if I was okay: "All right", I said, without paying too much attention; I did not want Joe to wait any further. I ran into my room, got my computer and rushed down the stairs. Joe was waiting for me in the lobby, on the couch where I had left him. I told him what had happened. “Incredible, I’m sorry! Let’s go now; my daughter will be back soon”. We had lost almost an hour and we still had to start.

The course we were holding in Munich was explicitly dedicated to Hardware. I found out that Joe held three different types of course: CSM standard, with examples from every field, CSM in Hardware, with specific examples and details, and Scrum in Hardware course outside the CSM certification that was designed for a more experienced audience. The material was divided into slide sets no more than an hour long, having a title on the cover in User Story[132] format. The course was offered using Scrum itself: the participants were divided into Scrum Teams with a Product Owner and a Scrum Master and the two days were divided into 4 half-day Sprints. Each slide set had a story point score that took into account the number of slides, the presence of videos, and any interactive games or activities. For each Sprint, we showed the Sprint Backlog and the list of sets to be presented on that half day on a blackboard, which was well visible by all the participants. A Burn Down Chart was updated with the progress of the work done during the day. Joe asked me to play the role of Scrum Master of the course by showing progress and removing any obstacles that would arise.

[132]https://en.wikipedia.org/wiki/User_story

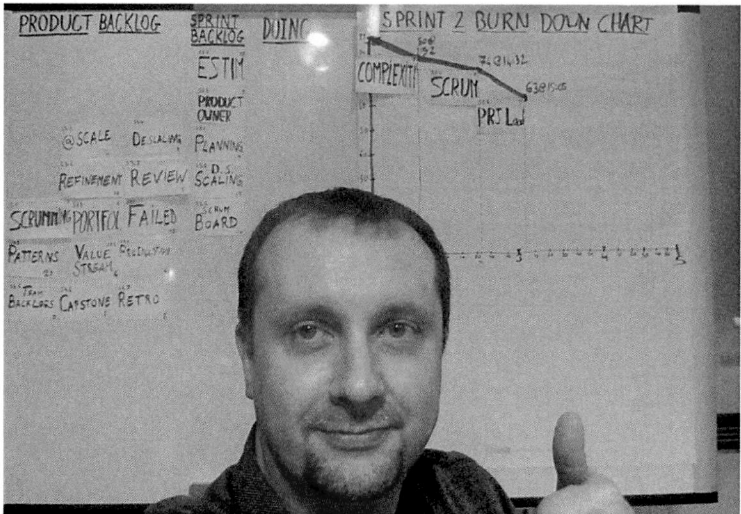

This way of teaching Scrum fascinated me. The use of the same method to conduct the course provided content concreteness and participants could enjoy a practical experience, much easier to understand and remember. The lessons were fascinating: Joe often quoted Jeff Sutherland's anecdotes and explanations, thus providing a particularly orthodox idea of Scrum close to his inventor's vision. I was struck by Joe's explanation of what Jeff called the "true essence of Scrum": *The OODA Loop*[133]. The OODA acronym, which stands for *Observe, Orient, Decide* and *Act*, was developed by the military strategist John Boyd[134], US Air Force fighter pilot and officer, and later also applied outside the military field, for the understanding of business strategies and learning processes. This innovative approach favored agility and adaptation as opposed to brute force in conflict scenarios, showing that it was not always the strongest to have the best. According to Jeff Sutherland, Scrum is the best way to have an OODA loop as fast as possible in manufacturing companies and, according to the motto that he had learned in his military career, "The pilot who goes through the

[133]https://en.wikipedia.org/wiki/OODA_loop
[134]https://en.wikipedia.org/wiki/John_Boyd_(military_strategist)

OODA Loop faster than the other guy, not the one who's flying the slightly superior plane, is the guy who wins".

The two course days literally flew, and without even knowing it, it was time to say goodbye. We would meet the week after in San Diego, California, for the Global Scrum Gathering[135].

San Diego

My flight to San Diego had a long stop in Chicago and when I arrived there it was already night. Luckily, I could dine in a late pub, in front of the hotel. I ordered a fish burger, suggested by the local waiter, delicious and, unlike many typical American dishes, light. Back to my room, I found a mail from Joe in the mail, confirming that I could attend also the two trainings scheduled the week after in Sweden and then in Switzerland. "Awesome! The adventure goes on", I thought.

The next morning I arrived at the hotel's conference venue. I had provided volunteer availability in the event and had to prepare the bags to be distributed to the participants, over a thousand! I could thus have a look behind the scenes of Gathering: the most impressive conference I ever took part in. I got a mixed feeling of excitement and challenge that I had not felt since the times of volunteering in the UDS crew[136].

The gathering opened with Jeff Sutherland's keynote speech. Eventually I would meet Scrum's author! Jeff tackled the topic of Scaling that is how to move from a few teams to an entire company using Scrum.

---

[135]https://www.scrumalliance.org/courses-events/events/global-scrum-gathering

[136]The Ubuntu Development Summit (UDS) is described extensively in the second chapter.

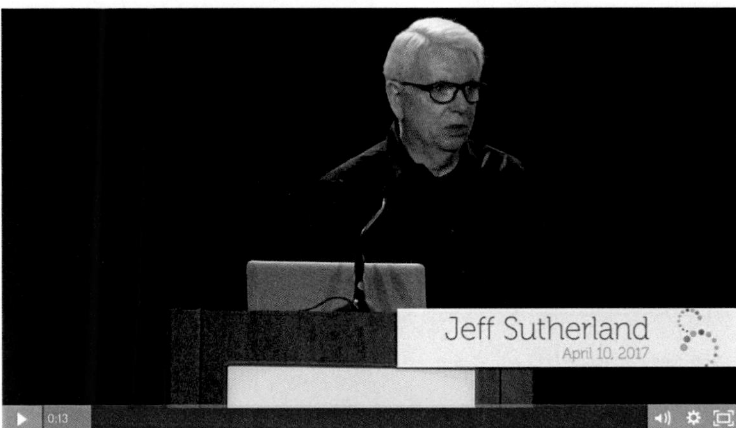

This is a debated subject, as many different frameworks use Scrum as a founding component, some of which are highly criticized. Jeff talked about companies trying to scale Scrum before even having it run fully into a single team, citing real examples; he also cited Jim Johnson's study, which analyzed 50,000 projects developed around the world, some with traditional Waterfall methodology, and others with Agile. The good news was that successful Agile projects were 4 times more than Waterfall; the bad news was that 61% of Scrum's projects were not delivered in time, within the limits of budget or customer satisfaction. This was Jeff's biggest problem; its mission: teaching the Teams how to do Scrum properly. According to Jeff Sutherland, you need to teach Scrum without using a specific implementation and therefore limited to a particular context. It is not just about talking of Scrum for Hardware, but about Scrum in every office of a company, up to senior management where managers apply teamwork, using Scrum to eradicate waste and impediments from the whole organization. He mentioned the recent case of 3M, the world famous Post-It sticker giant, where Scrum was extending to every branch of the company. However, to extend Scrum, it is first and foremost to have a single team working excellently and only then to replicate the experience in the rest of the company. Given that teams that work best, globally, have an average of 4.6

components, Jeff defined the ideal number of members in a team at five. The best way to scale Scrum seemed to be to create 5-member Teams, to make them work well and then extend the method to other Teams. Each Scrum Master will meet on a daily basis with other four Scrum Masters and will form a "Scrum of Scrum" of five members. They will use Scrum to handle the backlog of any impediments coming from each team. Every obstacle that cannot be solved in their field will be brought to a top team called "Scrum of Scrum of Scrum" and so on to the apex team called EAT: Enterprise Action Team, where top management receives and deals with non-solvable impediments using the same methodology. In the same way, the Product Owners will be organized so that there is a Chief Product Owner every 4/5 Teams and that prioritization needs are managed at various levels up to top management.

The structure with which Scrum extends in companies is of *fractal* type, and according to Jeff, in order to create it, it is enough to apply rigorously what is already prescribed by the Scrum Guide. The difficulty lies in the mindset of people anchored to their command and control *status quo* on which they have built power and prestige.

I spent the last night before leaving for Italy having dinner with Luca Bergero, one of the Italians known the year before at Boulder's Scrum for Hardware Gathering. On the piers of San Diego harbor, in a restaurant that cooked with simplicity excellent fresh fish of the day, tasting tuna on the plate, octopus with potatoes and fish tortillas, I found out that Luca was also experimenting with Scrum in his hardware teams. By exchanging experiences and anecdotes, we ended up being very late, despite the fact that the following morning I had an early awakening, flying to Chicago and Rome.

Stockholm

My flight landed in Stockholm at around 11 pm. To purchase bus tickets for the center, I realized that the Ryanair flight had landed in a secondary airport, as it often happens with low-cost flights. I had not thought of that. With too many trips in a short time, I missed an important detail: I arrived at the hotel not before ~~than~~ 1 am.

The morning after I showed up earlier anyway in the offices of Crisp[137], the company that hosted the course. Joe had already arrived and was preparing the classroom. I started to help him prepare the day backlog and the burn-down chart. Unlike the course in Munich, this did not give Scrum Master Certification by Scrum Alliance but it was more concerned with hardware and engineering practices. My excitement also stemmed from being in the company of Henrik Kniberg[138], a Swedish coach, author of successful books, very famous in this sector. Among his creations, most of all I had admired the animated video PO in a Nutshell[139]. I was stunned as he could enclose within minutes much wisdom on a topic as complex as the Product Ownership, using light and humorous style. Not surprisingly, the video, at the time of my writing, has over one million views. Unfortunately, that morning Henrik was not in his office. To do the honors, there was Reza Farhang[140], a very nice Certified Scrum Trainer, Henrik's business partner. The course comprised 16 people from various leading companies of mechanical and electronic products. The most interesting part was what for Joe was the secret to making *twice the work in half the time* about the patterns extracted from the best performing teams and documented on the Scrumplop[141] site. That day, the pattern of yesterday's weather[142] struck my attention. I knew it already but the explanation by Joe emphasized a feature that I had never really noticed. Accepting in the Sprint a number of story points at most equal to the average of the last Sprint was a prudent choice, that in practice many teams do not follow to the letter. But this

[137]https://www.crisp.se

[138]https://crisp.se/konsulter/henrik-kniberg

[139]https://www.youtube.com/watch?v=502ILHjX9EE

[140]https://www.crisp.se/konsulter/reza-farhang

[141]http://www.scrumplop.org

[142]https://sites.google.com/a/scrumplop.org/published-patterns/value-stream/estimation-points/yesterday-s-weather

practice allows, once the team takes confidence, to slightly increase the velocity. This phenomenon was represented in the burn-down chart as a line crossing the x-axis to end up with a negative number, which had happened to us in the sprints of the course.

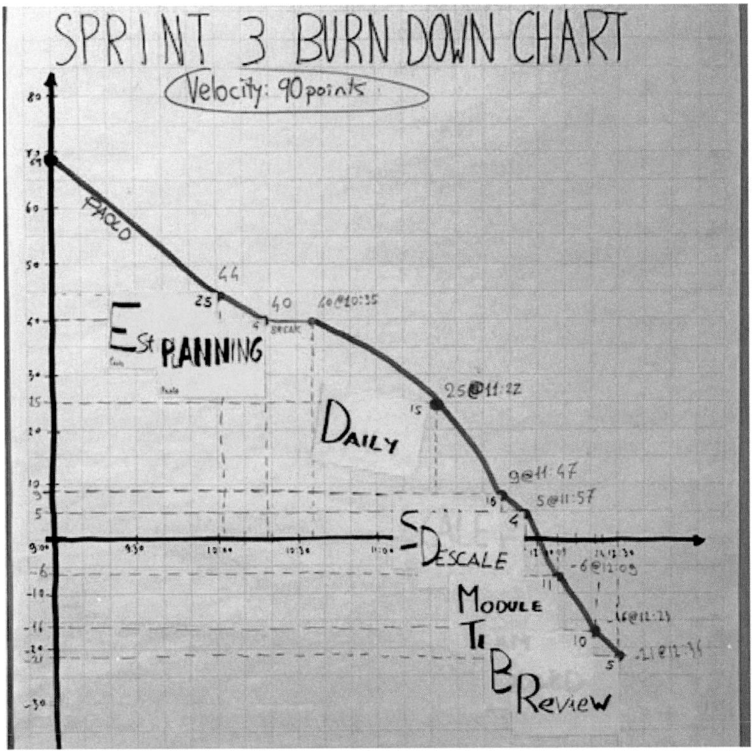

Seeing acceleration improves team morale, which according to Joe, is the true productivity multiplier. A Scrum Master, therefore, must ensure that the team never goes in **over committing**, accepting more story points of the average of the last three sprints, and that the Product Owner has any story ready to be processed, in case the team finishes first. This was the secret of "Teams that Finish Early Accelerate Faster[143]". For some time, I have tried to give a

[143]https://sites.google.com/a/scrumplop.org/published-patterns/retrospective-pattern-language/teams-that-finish-early-accelerate-faster

rational explanation for this phenomenon, which is anti-intuitive and is rarely understood by managers, who instead tend to insist on increasing the amount of work for the team. The mistake is to compare cognitive performance with physical one, such as with muscles. To improve in the gym, what we do is increasing the weight from time to time; this way our muscles respond by creating additional mass and strength to handle increasing weight gradually. But the brain is not a muscle and has the worst performance in the presence of stress. Therefore, the workload does not allow producing more; instead, it reduces performance. Reducing the load and letting the team get used to the rhythm makes the performance increase of course, and at this point you can also increase the workload; but only for the improvement margin already produced, in order not to generate stress. At the end of the course, we took the ritual group photo.

The course was over, but not my journey into Wonderland. Henrik, busy elsewhere during the day, invited us to his house for dinner. Joe, Reza, Riccardo (one of the participants in the course) and I took a taxi to Kniberg's house, in the countryside on a lake. It was a very nice evening! Henrik showed us how he created his films, making a short video[144] where he joked about having a bath in the lake, which he along with his wife, Joe and Riccardo had had a little before, while I was watching them from the pier taking pictures of them

[144]https://www.youtube.com/watch?v=IwAes7_6DV0

from their phones. At dinner, we tasted a deer stew, very flavorful, seasoned with the Chianti Riserva, which I had brought from Italy. After dinner we continued enjoying a great rum, accompanied by a bar of chocolate, and we ended up being late again talking about Scrum, the Agile scene and various anecdotes that Joe and Henrik shared with us.

Linköping

The appointment with Joe was at 9.45 am at Stockholm Central Station; from there we would take the train to Linköping, a small town with just under 100,000 inhabitants in southern Sweden, headquarters of Saab Aeronautics, the military industry that produces, using Scrum, the *Saab JAS 39 Gripen* fighter aircraft. On our arrival, the weather was variable, rainy with pungent and annoying sleet. We ventured to discover the historical center and soon Jörgen, the manager of the Saab that would guide the next day joined us. We visited the center, with some old mansions and impressive churches. "Churches are mainly used by immigrants", Jörgen told us "luckily! Otherwise, they would be abandoned. Only a very small percentage of Swedes are religious". The whole town was very clean and tidy aspect, a little jewel of precision. With a walk about half an hour, we reached the channel that divides the center from the industrial district and climbing up a short tree-lined road we arrived to his home. Jörgen lived in a beautiful three-story wooden villa, with the garden around where his three children were playing with other children. As we began to prepare dinner, we talked about Sweden, about its well-organized social system and about its culture. Jörgen described himself as a normal middle class person, while in my view he had a standard of living well above the European average. He lived in an independent house of at least three hundred square meters with garden. His children went to school on a bicycle in a clean and orderly town with a low crime rate. His most interesting work was from home about a kilometer, which he rode every day in just a few minutes by bicycle, or on foot in case of snow. The airport was two hundred meters from his office and had a simple connection with Amsterdam, from which you can fly around the world, three times a day. Even Joe remarked that compared to American standards that kind of life was well above average. "If it were not for the cold and for the little light it would be perfect", Jörgen said jokingly. "In fact, climate is a factor to be considered, especially if you have grown up in Tuscany", I said laughingly. It was April, I had left Siena with over 20 degrees while in Linköping it was still snowing.

We talked about Saab and the Gripen, the military aircraft built at the local factory. The first model came into service in 1996 and since then a progressive letter distinguished the models progressively, alternating one-seater and two-seater versions: the first single-seater edition is called **a** while the two-seater **b**; the second edition single-seater **c**, two-seater **d** and so on. The latest version, **JAS 39e**, had captured the attention of the specialized press as it was a multi-role hunter[145] of the fifth-generation competing of the infamous **F-35** but with a purchase cost five times lower and an operating

[145]That is, the same aircraft can effectively carry out air-air, air-ground and reconnaissance missions.

cost of 18%. Thus, while the F-35 project was renamed *Fiasco-35* on the Internet due to the continuous delays on delivery dates and the costs that grew annually, **Gripen e** attracted the interest and sympathy of the specialized press.

Copyright Saab AB

Let's take a Selfie

Early morning Joe and I walked to Saab, a kilometer and a half from our hotel. Upon arriving at the plant, we noticed the sign above the building. We knew we would not be allowed to take pictures inside and we decided to take a selfie on the road in front of the building. At the entrance, a very big lady asked us if we had by chance took pictures outside; we candidly confirmed, showing our pictures in our phones. She replied that it was forbidden and that she was supposed to warn her boss. We apologized for the inconvenience by suggesting that we could just delete them but she answered that only her boss may decide about it. The security officer, a thug in uniform with gun, handcuffs and baton arrived at the entrance to meet us. He repeated the questions that the lady had asked us before: "Why did you take a selfie?", "As a souvenir", "Did you know it is forbidden?", "We knew it was forbidden here, not from the road". With a glance, I begged him to finish that pantomime, in the picture, you could only recognize the sign, and we had not photographed any sensitive information: "Can't we just delete these photos please?" He looked at me with a solemn air,

"These pictures are against the law, and I cannot replace the law. We are obliged to call the police. Wait for us in that room in the meantime". Joe and I entered a comfortable waiting room. Jörgen reached us, who seemed amused by the situation. We apologized for the incident and he assured us that there were no problems. "However, at this time you cannot leave the room, so I'll bring my computer here so we start working while we wait for the police". It was a surreal situation: we were formally arrested for spying on military equipment, but a Saab manager was showing us secret information from his computer. No later than 10 minutes after, the police had already arrived at the entrance gate. The two agents replied to the questions we had already answered twice, and saying that the photos did not contain any details, they spoke via radio over the headquarters asking for the permission to cancel them. "We will now erase these photos from your phones. The crime will not be transcribed". Joe replied with an enthusiastic *Yeah*, as his favorite team had just scored, and we had "high five" as he loves to make him in important situations. Our records were still clean and we could start our much-desired visit.

A few days after the accident, Jörgen sent us a screenshot of an online newspaper in which they talked about us.

Corren.se NYHETER 24CORREN AFFÄRSLIV SPORT KULTUR & NÖJE ÅSIKTER HITTA MER TIPSA!

SENASTE NYTT 21:00 De ordnar kvalet i helgens 3D-skytte 20:30 Inget terrorhot bakom betonglejon 20:00 LISTA: Här kör de miljövänligast

Tog en selfie vid industri

LINKÖPING Polisen fick ingripa mot två personer som tagit bilder vid Saab i Linköping.

Danijela Komad 09:45 | 2017-04-24

Klockan 8.36 fick polisen ett samtal från ett vaktbolag som agerat mot två personer som brutit mot fotoförbudet vid Saab på Åkerbogatan.

Personerna, två män som är utländska medborgare och som varit besökare på industrin, ska ha tagit en selfie med mobilen utanför området där det råder fotoförbud.

– Det var inga känsliga detaljer i bilden, utan det var de två som poserade framför en skylt med förtagsnamnet på, säger Fredrik Kliman, polisens presstalesperson.

– Men man får ju inte fota på det området så selfien fick raderas.

Förutom att bilden raderades fick männen också en tillsägelse av polisen.

Ingen brottsanmälan har upprättas i ärendet.

> For a selfie in front of an industry
>
> LINKÖPING. The police arrested two people who took a photo in front of the Saab at Linköping.
>
> At 8:36 am, the police received a call from the security staff of a company that was acting against two people for having violated the ban on making photos at the Saab of Åkerbogatan. The people involved, two men of foreign nationality who were visiting the industry, should not have made selfie with the phones in front of the area where it is forbidden.
>
> "There was no sensitive information in the photos, only the two posing in front of the company name", said Fredrik Kliman, the police spokesperson. "But the photos should not be made, so they were deleted".
>
> Beyond the cancellation of the photos, the two were under police custody.
>
> The case, being not a crime, has not been transcribed.

I was very surprised by the timing of the incident. According to the article, the police were called at 8.36, and it is likely that Joe and I were at the entrance at 8.30. The police interrogation and the cancellation of the photos will have taken about 15 minutes, more or less. The amazing thing is that the time of the article is 9.45. We ended up in the online newspaper in less than an hour. When it comes to Swedish efficiency!

The Gripens

> **Note**: The material in this chapter has been declassified by military secrecy and published by Saab itself in the White Paper[146] and in the webinar[147] available on

[146]Owning the Sky with Agile: Building a Fighter Jet Faster, Cheaper, Better with Scrum - J. Furuhjelm, J. Justice, J. Segertoft, JJ Sutherland. https://www.scruminc.com/scrum-papers/

[147]https://www.scruminc.com/scrum-military-aviation/

Scruminc.com

Finally, we entered Saab's building and, in a meeting room, we met with Jörgen and Björn, one of Saab's internal Agile Coaches.

We discovered that the development of **Gripen E** had about 1,000 engineers organized in more than 100 teams. The agile framework used by Saab included Lean, Scrum, Kanban, Extreme Programming and other unspecified engineering practices. No methodologies and practices were mandatory and standardized but each team had full autonomy to experiment and change practices in their context. This meant that the teams had a different Agile maturity. Each team, however, followed the same three-week pace as for everyone starting and ending the same day. "That way anyone can tell you what day of iteration we're in Saab", said Jörgen. "Each team can use any Agile method, the only constraint it is to show how much it produces every three weeks. Scrum is simply the thing that works best for most of the Teams".

In Saab, most of the decisions are delegated to the team level as much as possible. Each Team is responsible for both technical and process decisions. They self-organize and improve the way in which they operate. The hierarchical organization is minimized and all efforts aim to maintain a broad sense of transparency.

Developments are synchronized, in addition to a three-week, 12-week release, or four sprints, featuring short-term goals. The aircraft is built according to the principle of a very high modularity "we thought of our aircraft as a giant LEGO® model" Jörgen told us at a meeting. Replacing the engine, for example, is a one-hour operation and makes the operating cost of the aircraft very low. This also makes it possible to develop and evolve the individual parts of Gripen quickly, as the module dependence is minimal. Considering the difficulties and the cost of the tests, Saab has internally developed a sophisticated simulator with which any engineer is able to modify anything, such as a bolt in the diagram of the device, from his workstation and see the metrics confirming or denying the goodness of a technical choice.

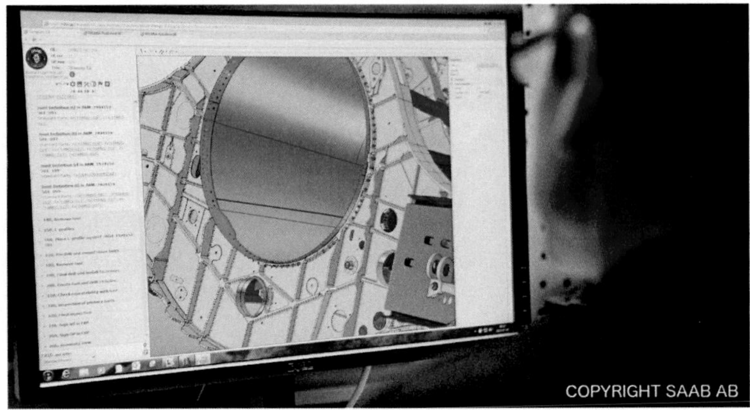

In addition, Saab has eight full-time employee pilots at Linköping's site, available to provide team advice, and the military airport infrastructure needed to carry out all real testing locally.

During the lunch break, Jörgen took us to the parking lot at the back of the plant, which had a Saab totem, so we could get a photo of him without risking being arrested again, as we were taking it at the opposite direction from the building.

The details of the visit to Saab Aeronautics were presented for the first time in Italy during the **Agile Business Day** in Venice, in September 2017, of which a video[148] (in Italian) and the slides[149] are available.

Zurich

The morning after, we went to the Linköping Civil Airport to take our flight that via Amsterdam would take us to Zurich, where we would hold the last scheduled training in Europe for that period. The check-in and security check procedure took to our surprise a record time since there was only one flight in the morning and the number of passengers was really low: 5 minutes and we were already in the lounge to take a hot tea. We were so jealous of

[148]https://vimeo.com/agilebusinessday/abd17-paolosammicheli

[149]https://www.slideshare.net/xdatap1/tre-metri-sopra-il-cielo-scrum-nellaeronautica-militare

Jörgen's lifestyle, so tailored to man. Upon our arrival in Zurich, the weather was no better than the Swedish one: cold and rain made it a master and it did not seem to be at the end of April. Peter Stevens, a great friend of Joe's, was waiting for us outside the airport with his car. I had met Peter the previous year at the Scrum Gathering[150] in Munich and we had been in touch since I had translated into Italian his article on eXtreme Manufacturing[151], the engineering practices that Joe had devised in the Wikispeed project. While we were in San Diego, Peter invited us to dinner at his home via Twitter for a fondue. So, I met his wife Sabine and, between a chat on Scrum and many laughs, I tasted the most delicious cheese fondue in the world. Peter told us his idea of bringing together the so-called "Second Wave Agile", the pioneering group that is experimenting with agile methods outside software, such as in education, marketing, and clearly in hardware and in the traditional industry. He asked us if we were interested in getting involved and both Joe and I accepted with great enthusiasm.

Peter had just started the first workshop of his new project: Personal Agility System[152]. Peter's idea was to improve productivity and personal work efficiency by applying the Scrum method to themselves. I was interested in this, because I had followed the Self-Coaching course in neuro-linguistic programming, as part of the NLP Coach Diploma I completed a few months before, and I had tried something similar on myself. Peter's idea was even wider than the individual practices I had tried for, so I mentally reminded myself of deepening the topic on his site.

The morning after, Joe and I met in the hotel in the center of Zurich, where the two-day course was held. This time it would not have been a course related to Scrum for Hardware like the previous but a standard CSM ScrumInc course. Despite this, I noticed how the Scrum theme application outside of the software

[150] https://www.scrumalliance.org/courses-events/events/global-scrum-gathering
[151] eXtreme Manufacturing is described in the second part of the book.
[152] https://mypersonalagility.org

was recursive throughout the material. By not including specific engineering practices, however, this course covered the patterns that improve team performance, published on the Scrum Plop[153] website. The pattern of Scrumming the Scrum[154] for example, says that the team considers Sprint Planning as the top priority item, with the improvement action emerged from the last retrospective. In this way you use the Scrum loop to improve Scrum itself and the team improves faster. Interestingly, I found the pattern for managing illegitimus interruptions[155]. This pattern puts a time limit on interruptions that come from urgent assistance requests and bug fixes, allowing the team to focus on Sprint's goals and to be productive.

The evening after the second day of the course, we met Peter again in a bar for the last dinner of that trip. We talked for a long time about the immediate future and the many projects that each of us was about to start. On the door to the café where we had eaten, I greeted these two colleagues with a warm embrace with whom I had strengthened the bond of friendship, esteem and respect and which I felt to be indissoluble. It was a sad moment, my adventure around Europe along with Joe was about to end, but I confided that we would meet again soon.

---

[153]www.scrumplop.org

[154]https://sites.google.com/a/scrumplop.org/published-patterns/retrospective-pattern-language/scrumming-the-scrum

[155]https://sites.google.com/a/scrumplop.org/published-patterns/product-organization-pattern-language/illegitimus-non-interruptus

On the Shoulders of Giants

I took advantage of summer break 2017 to start writing this book and learning Argentine Tango. The idea of learning Tango was born from a workshop that my friend Davide Roitero had organized the year before at the PO Camp[156], an un-conference on the topic of Product Ownership that is annually held in a seaside resort. His speech was titled "Salsa is Waterfall, Tango is Agile". In his workshop, Davide showed us how in Argentine tango – a partner dance in which there is a leader, usually the man, and a follower, the lady – every single step is improvised by the leader. He bases his choices on the dancer herself, on the space available on the dance floor and, of course, on the music. Therefore, improvisation requires the agility to change the dance performance at the same time as the above-mentioned three factors change, while the performance is given. On the opposite, the female dancer has the role of listening and "adjusting" to the leader. It seemed like a perfect metaphor for the relationship between coach and coachee, as well as for the relationship between Product Owner and Scrum Team. So I took the opportunity to learn a new hobby that I thought could enrich me also from a professional point of view.

Lisbon

Towards the end of August, I contacted Peter Stevens[157] to find out whether the idea of bringing together the "Second Wave Agility" in

[156]http://www.pocamp.it/front/?lang=en

[157]https://www.scrumalliance.org/community/profile/pstevens

Lisbon – the ever-increasing number of Agilists who had begun to apply the method outside the software – was taking shape. He told me that the conference was confirmed and that the evening before the event, Sunday at sunset, a mini-cruise had been scheduled for all the speakers on the Lisbon waterfront. We would then talk about the topic. So, he introduced me by email to the event organizer, Hugo Lourenço[158] who included my name among the participants of the mini-cruise. I learned from Peter that Joe was engaged in a Wikispeed event that weekend, so he could not join in. Anyway, Scrum for Hardware would be well represented by Thomas Friend[159], the American coach I had met a few months earlier at the Scrum Gathering in San Diego and Joe's student during Train the Trainer in January 2016. Tom would give a talk in which he would show the uses of Scrum at NASA and, on the day after the conference, he would held a workshop on the topic.

I found a pleasantly summery climate in Lisbon. After lunch in a traditional small restaurant and a stroll in the old town, I headed for the port to meet the other participants of the mini-cruise. First, I met Tom Friend who was having a drink with his wife at the bar in front of the mini-cruise pier. I joined them and little by little, a group of familiar faces gathered around our table. With Peter Stevens there was also Maria Matarelli[160], an American Scrum Trainer specializing in Agile applied to Marketing[161]. I had met her the year before at the Scrum Gathering in Munich and we had made friends because we shared the passion of playing as DJs in our spare time. Maria had recently started collaborating with Peter on the Personal Agility project[162] presented at the conference. Maria would also give a further talk on Agile Marketing together with Alistair Cockburn[163], one of the co-signers of the Agile manifesto

[158]https://www.scrumalliance.org/community/profile/hlouren9o
[159]https://www.scrumalliance.org/community/profile/tfriend2
[160]https://www.scrumalliance.org/community/profile/mmatarelli
[161]http://agilemarketingcertification.com
[162]https://mypersonalagility.org/
[163]https://en.wikipedia.org/wiki/Alistair_Cockburn

and author of the Agile Crystal methods[164]. I immediately liked Alistair – an eccentric and funny person, so clever and intelligent at the same time. We boarded on the yacht that would take us along the Lisbon waterfront and, after taking a glass of prosecco and snacks for everyone, we sat down at a table in a strategic position to admire the view.

Other celebs from the Agile world were arriving on board. I met Steve Denning[165], former director of the World Bank[166] and author of several publications on Leadership and Management. Billy McLaughlin[167] a guitarist with an incredible story also caught my attention. Suffering from a neuromuscular disease that had partially paralyzed his left hand, he had seen his life destroyed in just a year: he had lost his job, he had separated from his wife and many friends had turned their back on him. With great fortitude, he was able to reinvent his profession by learning to play with his other hand in such an original and innovative way[168]. We talked about music and he told me that he would probably visit Italy to

[164]https://en.wikiversity.org/wiki/Crystal_Methods
[165]https://en.wikipedia.org/wiki/Steve_Denning
[166]https://en.wikipedia.org/wiki/World_Bank
[167]http://www.billymclaughlin.com/
[168]http://www.billymclaughlin.com/videos/

participate in a street music event held every year in Perugia. "I do not know this event", I told him "but Perugia is near where I live, if you had to come, please let me know".

The view of Lisbon at sunset was breathtaking.

ScrumDay Portugal 2017

The event took place in the auditorium of the *EDP - Energias de Portugal* headquarters, one of the largest European electricity producers and one of the most important industrial groups in Portugal. I was flabbergasted by the location: a large, comfortable auditorium with perfect acoustics. At the suggestion of Hugo, the event organizer, I arrived well in advance to avoid the crowd at the delivery of the badges. I met Tom Friend who, like me, had arrived very early and, to pass the time, he showed me the material of the workshop he would hold the following day.

As a young man, Tom had made his career as an aircraft pilot in the Navy. In the mid-nineties, he worked as a test pilot in a military aircraft factory in the state of Connecticut. He knew well the OODA Loop[169] by John Boyd and when he began to hear his QA Software Analyst colleagues talking of iterative methods such as Scrum and eXtreme Programming, these topics seemed very familiar to him. After some time, having abandoned the pilot career, he became a QA Software Analyst himself and was able to closely observe the Agile development process of aircraft software. It was the end of the 90s and Agile methods were used by pioneers. He quickly learned that one of the most limiting factors in using an Agile method was the manager's mindset. Tom had a very pragmatic approach to work: when he found problems, he tried to talk directly to the developers in order to find solutions quickly – a too Agile and direct approach, not really liked by the military ranks. Around 2009, retiring from military service as Lieutenant Colonel, he began attending some Agile conferences where he met Jeff Sutherland, who also had a military pilot background. They discussed of the fact that some organizational patterns of the air force could be interesting metaphors in Agile transformations. This common interest led Tom to meet Jeff again and, at another conference, Joe Justice. He immediately established a strong connection with Joe too, as

[169]https://en.wikipedia.org/wiki/OODA_loop

they shared their passion for cars. Tom loves restoring old vintage cars with the help of his four children, 2 sons and 2 daughters, and Wikispeed immediately fascinated him. The two kept in touch and Joe invited him to participate in the first Train the Trainer course in Scrum for Hardware. Tom was intrigued by the idea of teaching Scrum using a vehicle, but he considered Wikispeed a too expensive and heavy project to be used for teaching. Therefore, he began to look for something smaller and with an Agile architecture. He had the idea of using CubeSat[170], a mini-satellite project conceived by some American Universities, and of having it built by students with cardboard, felt-tip pens and glue.

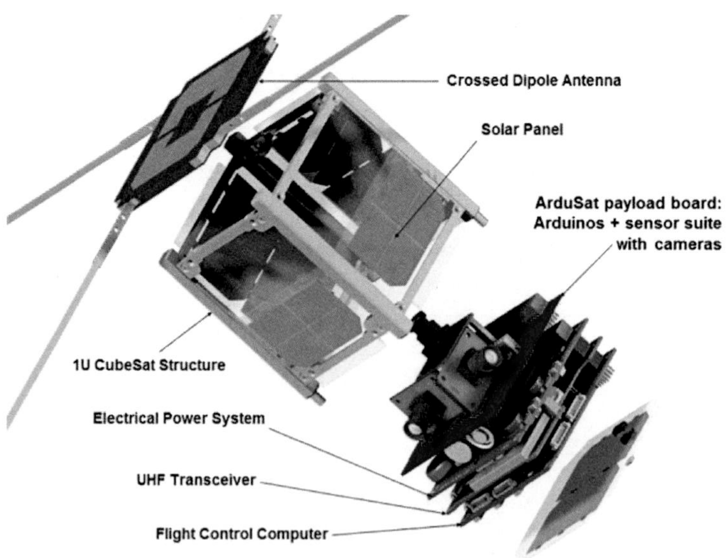

Exploded view of ArduSat - Peter Platzer Wikimedia

Scrum to the Stars

The material[171] that Tom showed me from his PC was as stunning as it was brilliant. Using the CubeSat architecture, he was able to

[170] https://en.wikipedia.org/wiki/CubeSat
[171] http://cubesatscrum.com

explain all the design patterns I knew, with practical examples, going well beyond what had been already published by Hubert Smits and Joe Justice. Scrolling through his slides, I could admire all the creational, structural and behavioral software design patterns[172] described in detail and accompanied by figures with practical examples in the CubeSat architecture.

After the theoretical explanation and the description of how to construct a CubeSat with the images to be cut out of the various layers, a story backlog was presented in which it was requested to incrementally implement the satellite functions. The "lasagna" architecture of the satellite made it possible to iterate rapidly by extending the functionality of the device, simply by adding or modifying the single layers.

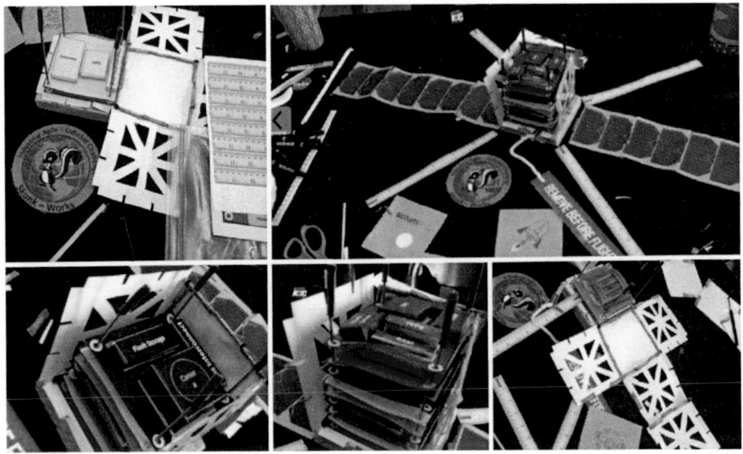

I had a deep admiration for Tom's talent and I was not surprised to learn that he had also started working with Jeff Sutherland and ScrumInc.

[172]https://en.wikipedia.org/wiki/Software_design_pattern

The Conference

Many participants started to arrive; I said goodbye to Tom and went into the auditorium, so that we could pick a good seat before the auditorium got full. International speakers alternated on the stage with their highest quality contents. I really liked Steve Denning's speech, entitled "From Operational Agility to Strategic Agility", in which he showed how some companies were delighting their clients on a large scale, creating an increase in general expectations that put their competitors in serious crisis. This theme was very similar to the one I had dealt with in my articles on the Fourth Industrial Revolution, where I found much affinity with Steve's words. Alistar Cockburn briefly introduced his new creature: Heart of Agile[173], a kind of thinking framework able to evolve companies into Agile Organizations based on four key principles: Collaborate, Deliver, Reflect, Improve.

On stage, there was also Dave Snowden, author of the Cynefin framework[174]. In his presentation, he described his framework by introducing concepts that I already knew well. He insisted on a not too veiled controversy against those in the Agile landscape who confuse correlation with causality, with the belief that specific conditions related to a certain success are in fact the cause of success itself. This phenomenon reminded me of the words Cargo Cult[175], a ritual that appeared in some Melanesian tribal societies following their meeting with the western populations. On that occasion, war materials such as clothes, canned goods, tents, weapons and other useful goods, parachuted into the islands during the Pacific campaign against the Empire of Japan, drastically changed the lifestyle of the natives. These products arrived in large quantities to supply not only the soldiers, but also the islanders who were their guides and hosts. At the end of the war, the air bases were abandoned and the cargos were no longer parachuted, so the is-

[173]http://heartofagile.com/

[174]The description of the Cynefin framework is available in the Appendix of the book.

[175]https://en.wikipedia.org/wiki/Cargo_cult

landers began to imitate the behaviors they had seen in the western service members, in order to keep receiving the supplies. They made wooden headphones, wore them inside fake control towers and waved landing signals in the middle of runways deserted by then. After some time, these cults vanished, but the term remained to indicate a group of people that imitates the superficial aspect of a process, without having an understanding of its deep functioning.

Dublin

Back to Italy from Portugal, I resumed the usual routine that saw me traveling on the roads of Tuscany, Veneto and Lombardy to follow my most important customers. However, I did not get too used to that routine because, after just three weeks, I was back in an airport queuing in front of a gate. This time the destination was Dublin for the Global Scrum Gathering. It would be my third consecutive Scrum Gathering and I was very excited about the idea. Participating in a regular conference, as I had discovered at UDSs, creates a bond between the participants that makes you feel at home as soon as you step in. I felt that feeling immediately, as soon as I met Laura Powers[176] in the lobby. Laura is a very nice American Coach I had met in San Diego by volunteering during her very fun workshop on creating educational games. The intense collaboration we had during the workshop allowed us to make friends immediately. He asked me how my book was going and requested a copy for himself. Shortly after we were joined by Dana Pylayeva[177], a Russian-born coach who lives in New York City and whom I had known in San Diego. The time before, she had told me about her idea of organizing workshops on Self-Forming Teams, which is the practice of spontaneously having the team members creating the compositions of their Teams by themselves. I was glad to know that she would introduce a first version of this workshop

[176]https://www.scrumalliance.org/community/profile/lpowers2
[177]https://www.scrumalliance.org/community/profile/pdana

at that Gathering.

The Gathering in Dublin had a somewhat strange format: all the sessions were organized in one-and-a-half-hour slots. In the previous Gatherings I had attended, one-and-a-half-hour workshops alternated or were held in parallel with 45-minute talks. This allowed having many alternatives in every timetable. I found that having only such long slots, on the contrary, limited the choice as it reduced it to only four slots available each day. Not only that: in case a workshop was not very interesting, it would be difficult to change session in progress, hence nullifying one hour and a half.

I was certainly not disappointed by Laura's Workshop titled "Say "Yes" to "No": The Power of the "No" in Agile". After an enlightening introduction in which she showed how difficult it is for adults to say "No" and how this would be a key skill for effective Product Ownership, she explored the nuances of any possible "No". We discovered that there were variations such as "Not Me", that is, I cannot say Yes because I need to consult others, "Not Yet", that is, I cannot say Yes because I need more information, or "Not Now", that is I cannot say Yes right now. Then, equipped with special playing cards, we played roles in which we had to reply to requests.

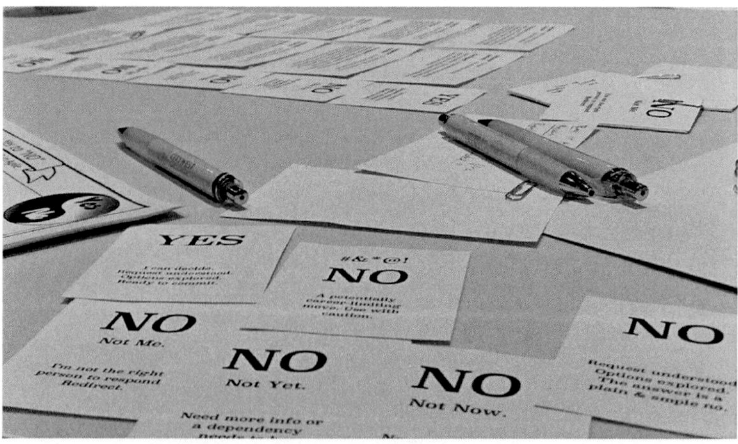

Laura concluded her workshop in an enlightening way with a quote by Tim Ferriss[178]: "What you don't do determines what you can do"

I also took part in Dana's Workshop entitled "Discover Your Dream Teams Through Self-Selection with the Team Ingredients Game". Dana had created a clear handbook on how to organize the team-training event within a company, with particular attention on how to prepare the Management and equip it with the appropriate tools to manage the event itself. We managed to create teams thanks to profile cards that allowed us to easily balance the available talents in the room and highlighting any weaknesses we had to overcome with new staff. I was impressed by the ease with which the workshop took place and we all agreed that teams formed in this way were unquestionably the perfect basis for a harmonious and efficient work. I thought of suggesting this practice to the next customer who would have the same needs.

Moreover, I held great expectations in the "Debunking the Product Owner Role" workshop by Roman Pichler[179], author of some interesting books on Product Management. In his speech, more a talk than a real workshop, he deeply analyzed the nuances in the Product Owner role. There are circumstances in which the Product Owner has extensive responsibilities, from the vision to the individual detail, that Roman calls "Big Product Owner", while in other circumstances the Product Owner simply prioritizes the backlog of a Team with limited autonomy, called "Small Product Owner". In a scaling situation, these two figures coexist and are called, for example, Product Owner and Chief Product Owner in Jeff Sutherland's vision. A first interesting topic was related to the way in which these figures could adjust and collaborate with each other and with the Stakeholders. In support of this, Roman suggested some tools that could be freely downloaded from his site, such as the Product Vision Board[180] and the Go Product Roadmap[181]. Another aspect was related to organizational issues. When is it better to

[178]https://en.wikipedia.org/wiki/Tim_Ferriss
[179]https://www.scrumalliance.org/community/profile/rpichler
[180]https://www.romanpichler.com/tools/vision-board/
[181]https://www.romanpichler.com/tools/product-roadmap/

have a single Product Owner with all responsibility? When is it better to have several Product Owners? What alternatives exist? From a single PO to several different Product Owners for each different product feature, or separating the product in variants with a Product Owner for each variant, up to the classic option with multiple POs, one at a strategic level and others at a tactical level. Roman explored all these options by showing their pros and cons.

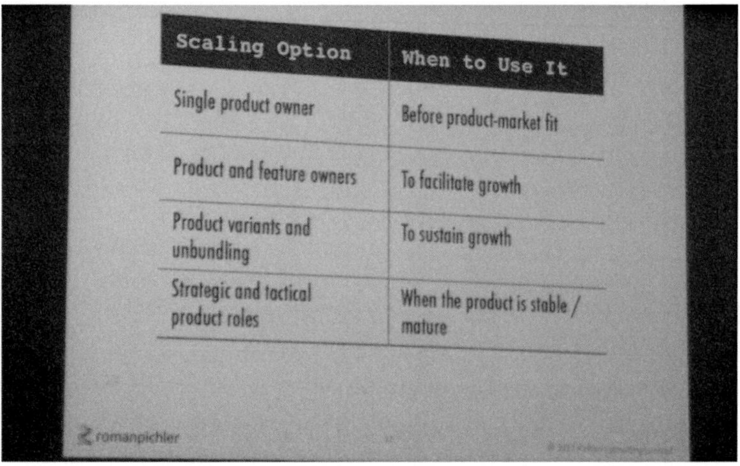

Scaling Option	When to Use It
Single product owner	Before product-market fit
Product and feature owners	To facilitate growth
Product variants and unbundling	To sustain growth
Strategic and tactical product roles	When the product is stable / mature

Its conclusion, as it often happens in these cases, is that there is no approach that always works, but that the level of maturity and complexity of the product must be assessed and its approach adapted during its life cycle.

The second day's keynote was given to Tom Mellor[182], an early Scrum Trainer who had taken part in the Scrum Alliance Board for several years. During his pleasant session, conducted with great humility and humanity, he shared with us his path of maturation towards the most relevant elements of Agile. His final catchphrase made me nearly fall off my chair. He showed us a video clip from the film "Scent of a Woman"[183] in which Al Pacino, in the role of

[182]https://www.scrumalliance.org/community/profile/tmellor2
[183]https://www.youtube.com/watch?v=Fy4c_hLlV1M

Frank Slade[184], a retired blind lieutenant colonel, teaches Tango to a young woman named Dana, starred by Gabrielle Anwar[185]. In the final scene, Tom concluded: "If a blind man can teach Tango, every Scrum Master can teach Scrum to his team" making the whole audience burst into laughter and into a thunderous applause.

The final keynote of the event was reserved to Lyssa Atkins[186], the popular author of Coaching Agile Teams[187]. On the table, we found a sheet printed with drawings on both sides. It summarized the main topics of the talk and included space to add some personal notes. I found this device extremely interesting and I thought of trying it at the first opportunity.

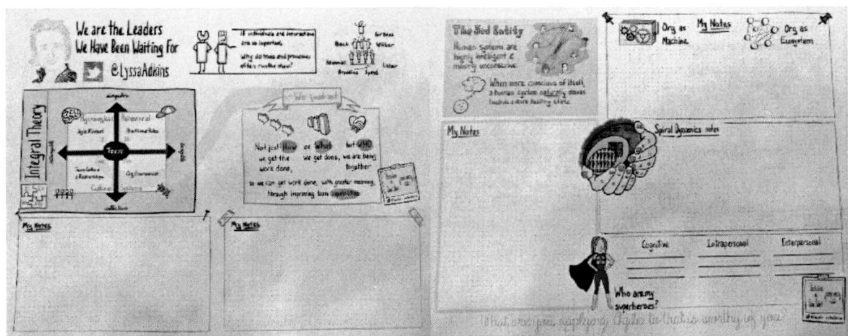

The talk began with a quite inspired rhetorical question: "If individuals and interactions are so important, why processes and tools so often run the show?" And alternating personal stories of her journey in the Amazon rainforest with her daughter, she briefly illustrated the theory of integral thought[188], by Ken Wilber[189], applied to Team Agile coaching and the so-called third entity, that is the relationship that is established between two individuals[190]. In the end, she resumed her story of the Amazon rainforest and of

[184]https://en.wikipedia.org/wiki/Scent_of_a_Woman_(1992_film)
[185]https://en.wikipedia.org/wiki/Gabrielle_Anwar
[186]https://www.scrumalliance.org/community/profile/lclark2
[187]https://www.lyssaadkins.com/coaching-agile-teams-book/
[188]https://en.wikipedia.org/wiki/Integral_theory_(Ken_Wilber)
[189]https://en.wikipedia.org/wiki/Ken_Wilber
[190]https://www.adhdcoaches.org/the-third-entity/

how she had personally realized that minimal climatic variations have devastating impacts on delicate ecosystems like that. Finally, she strongly launched a call to action, claiming that the leaders we were waiting for were exactly us. She asked how we were using our skills. Whom were we teaching how to do twice the work in half the time? Multinational corporations destroying the world, or organizations trying to preserve it and improving the life of our species?

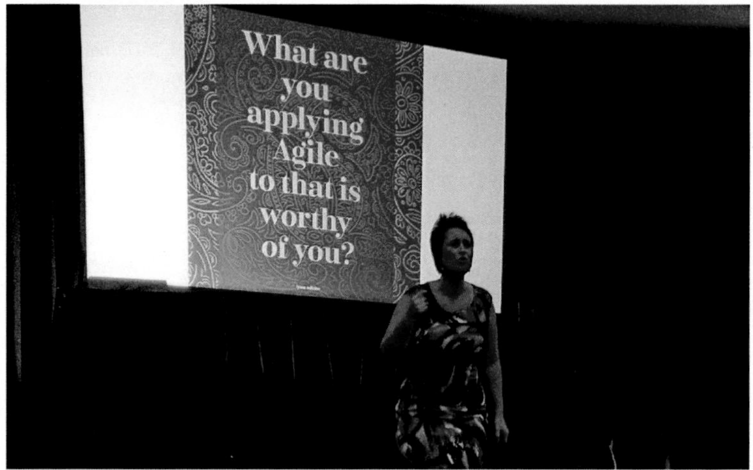

I was deeply impressed by this question. The trigger of this whole book has exactly been Joe's ecological consciousness, which led him to successfully experiment with Scrum in Hardware. Even Henrik Kniberg had started to become a spokesperson[191] of an eco-friendly lifestyle and in a small part I had also contributed to this, translating the subtitles of his video into Italian. However, Lyssa's call to action tasted so intense. It created a sense of urgency that generated a feeling of guilt in those who decided to ignore it. I tried to talk about it with Joe as I recognized a connection between all these initiatives.

I left the Gathering full of thoughts, but I had no time to waste: a

[191]https://www.youtube.com/watch?v=3CM_KkDuzGQ

great friend was waiting for me in the center of Dublin: Claudio Perrone[192].

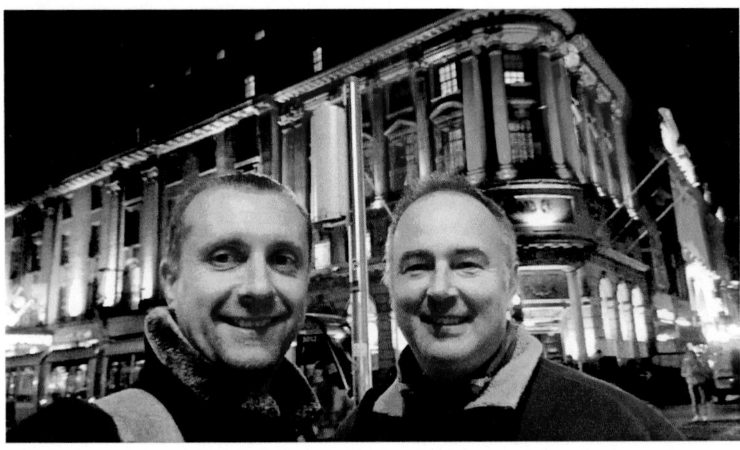

I had known Claudio since the end of 2014, when we used to meet online at the Lean Agile Round Tables LART[193], video conferences about Agile themes. We had met in person at the Mini IAD of Savona[194] and since then, we had kept in touch regularly. Claudio is known for having created an Agile method called Popcorn Flow[195]. He had started holding workshops where he taught the method and he was writing a book about it. He was definitely the friend who could give me more suggestions than anyone else, to help me with my current activities. We met in the city center, in front of a pastry shop. After a short tour of the city to see some typical places, such as Trinity College and Temple Bar, we stopped to dine in a typical Irish restaurant. Claudio gave me a lot of advice on how to set up my Scrum for Hardware workshop and I asked him an interview to include it in this book, in which he explained Popcorn Flow[196]. He accepted immediately and we decided to meet online one evening in the following weeks: it was late and we both had to wake up

[192]https://agilesensei.com
[193]https://plus.google.com/communities/105716988525004834486
[194]https://www.agileday.it/mini/2016/savona/
[195]https://popcornflow.com
[196]The description of the Popcorn Flow method is available in the Appendix.

early the morning after.

Joe

Back to Italy, I just had time to repack my suitcase: the last planned trip for that year awaited me. Joe had his Scrum for Hardware course in Stockholm and I had found a way to adjust my schedule and join him.

I flew to Stockholm with a flight from Bologna that stopped in Frankfurt; the direct Ryanair flight that I had taken the previous time in Padua did not exist anymore and so I went back to an airport a little closer to my home. I arrived in Stockholm in the early afternoon and headed for a hotel just in front of the Crisp offices, where the course would be held.

I was curious to see this hotel[197], as Joe had recommended it to me enthusiastically by email: it was equipped with a small supermarket of organic products and the ristobar was known for its food, which was healthy and special at the same time. At the check-in, I found a very youthful environment. There were students sitting at the tables or on the sofas all over the place talking or working at the computer. Downstairs, thanks to the magnetic card of my room, I could access a reserved area for hotel guests: sofas and lots of space where I could work or spend my time. It was amazing: this area was exactly in the basement of the building, so in theory the group of rooms without windows would have seemed depressing. Instead, the colors of the numerous doors, the carpet with strange patterns and the various murals created a pleasant and attractive environment. The room was then enriched with futuristic technical solutions, like a soft light that illuminated the floor automatically to the movement. This allowed going to the bathroom at night without having to turn on the light and avoiding any discomfort for the eyes. I had shared my arrival in Sweden on Facebook and I soon

[197]http://hotelwith.se/en/

discovered that Henrik and Sophia Kniberg were traveling abroad. Too bad, I thought, it would have been nice to meet them again.

When I returned to the lobby, I found Joe waiting for me. It had been almost six months since we last met and we had many things to tell. My book had already been released electronically and Joe had read the first chapters. While we were having dinner, he announced me that, the day after, he would give me even more space, asking me to present two sets of slides for each half-day and to facilitate all the games. This ultimately corresponded to dealing with almost half the contents, a considerable quantity! This did not intimidate me; however, at that point I knew his material very well.

The following day, I discovered that the course contained several news. Joe had added new case studies, including that of the Tesla-3M project on solar panel roof tiles, which made it possible to transform every roof into a photovoltaic system, without changing its aesthetics. In a break, I showed Joe the slides I had created to explain eXtreme Manufacturing: starting from Peter Stevens' descriptions, I explained every principle with examples and footage from both Joe's material and photos and examples taken from my clients' experience with Festo Consulting[198]. Joe liked those slides

[198]http://www.festocte.it/

very much and he asked me whether I wanted to introduce them the day after. I was happy to accept and, the same evening, I converted them to the ScrumInc format. Joe filmed me with his smartphone while I was presenting the material and asked if I agreed to upload it to the YouTube Wikispeed channel[199]. Of course, I was proud an honored to give my consent to it.

The following evening, after dining together, I asked Joe to record with my phone an interview with him that would help me to improve the chapter with his story. We sat on the hotel's sofas and talked for over an hour.

He answered my numerous questions on Wikispeed and we ended up talking about very personal topics, our childhood and the values we believed in. He told me how he felt his family upbringing as strongly related to the values of Scrum. "When you're the youngest of five children," he told me, "you get an education that's very much about respect and fairness." For example, a pair of new shoes can be cause for jealousy in someone else, so when someone's shoes were to be renewed, this was the moment when everyone received a pair of new shoes. At the table, in some families there is the idea that "the first who arrive wins". In my family, it did

[199]https://www.youtube.com/watch?v=Zq1IcVMImvE

not work this way; everyone received their share of food and only after everyone had eaten their portion, they could have a second one, in equal parts. This spirit of respect for siblings is also found in Scrum, in the team spirit that derives from it and in its five values". I perfectly identified with Joe's experience. Growing up in a family where I was the eldest of three children, I had received the same kind of education. Joe continued with his confidences: "Everything I learned from Jeff Sutherland, Ken Schwaber, even though I have not spent so much time with him as with Jeff, Peter Stevens and even from you is so important!" "From me too?" I asked, surprised, "Sure. For example, everything you wrote about Open Source communities would have been really helpful when I started Wikispeed. After all, "*we are all standing on the shoulders of giants*" and it is important to understand how much we depend on each other and how much each one is the fruit of the contribution of others. I remember an event, in 2011, when I was in the Detroit area for the International Auto Show. It was a very intense cultural experience. The town where I stayed was called Hillsdale and its economy was based on car-related companies. These were going through the most critical moment of the crisis: three companies had already declared bankruptcy and the fourth was about to do it. All the small businesses in the town that worked for them had gone bankruptcy or moved elsewhere and there were several thousands of unemployed people, who lived for the day doing odd jobs and recurring to their savings. While I was having breakfast in a semi-deserted bar, I could overhear the conversation at a table next to mine. A businessman was boasting about how things went well for him, so much that he had just changed his car buying a new sports one. He was the owner of one of the two city's grain milling plants. Taking advantage of the crisis, he had bought the other plant, he had closed it and he had fired the employees so as not to have competitors in the area. Still in the same conversation, shortly after, he started complaining about how depressing the city was with the crisis, since they had not even hung up the Christmas decorations, and he was eventually wondering whether he should move elsewhere. That was a key moment for me, as the conviction that I had had since childhood had now strengthened. In order to get rich, that man had contributed to damaging the city and at the same time was thinking of moving elsewhere because it had become an unpleasant place to live in. On the opposite, if he had helped to improve it, his life would have improved too as his perception of wealth and quality of life depended on the environment around him." Joe had it clear that improving the lowest common denominator was the way to improve our lives. We realized how our values were similar and how they mirrored our profession: it was not by chance that both of us had showed such a genuine passion for what we did, well above what people normally feel for their job. I asked him if he had any advice for me, for my future. What could the next step be? Joe stopped for a second and said: "I think it's time for you to learn directly from Jeff Sutherland." We checked his European training schedule and I found two courses the following month in Munich and Stockholm. "If I were you, I would put this among my priorities", he told me, "among other things, the Monaco course is on Scrum@Scale and I am sure you will find a lot of useful material for your work."

Jeff

When I was back to Italy, I started organizing for this new adventure. The day before the course, I would be in Turin for work and fortunately, there was a flight after dinner that allowed me to get to Monaco in time.

I arrived at the classroom early in the morning and found one of the organizers, Jean Pierre Berchez[200], to welcome me. Jean Pierre had participated in the Scrum for Hardware course in Monaco six months before and, remembering me, he greeted me warmly. I was one of the first comers and he introduced me to Jeff, who was

[200]https://www.scrumalliance.org/community/profile/jberchez

connecting his laptop to the projector. Jean Pierre began to ask me about my book, as he had seen my announcement on LinkedIn and Jeff immediately showed his interest. "Jeff I have already published a first version in English, would you like a copy?" I held my breath, Jeff Sutherland was definitely a busy man – how could he find the time to read my stories? "Of course, send me a copy, please". I immediately turned on my laptop, created a free coupon and sent it to him by email. The classroom slowly filled with people and the course started in perfect time. Later, during lunch break, I checked my inbox via smartphone and found the notification that Jeff had downloaded the file during a morning break.

Scrum@Scale

I fell immediately in love with Scrum@Scale. It was so different from the other Agile Scaling methods I knew. It was not a *Framework*, an organizational design to be implemented completely or in part, but rather a *Process Framework*, which you could design your organization with. In this, I recognized a great affinity with the Scrum of the Scrum Guide. Just like Scrum, Jeff was planning to publish a guide and release it under a Creative Commons license[201].

According to Jeff, the method consisted of using Scrum himself to scale up Scrum to the whole organization. The approach was therefore, exactly like Scrum, iterative and incremental, and provided a list of 12 components to be implemented, paying attention to the context and culture of the organization.

[201]The Scrum@Scale guide is available in the Appendix of the book.

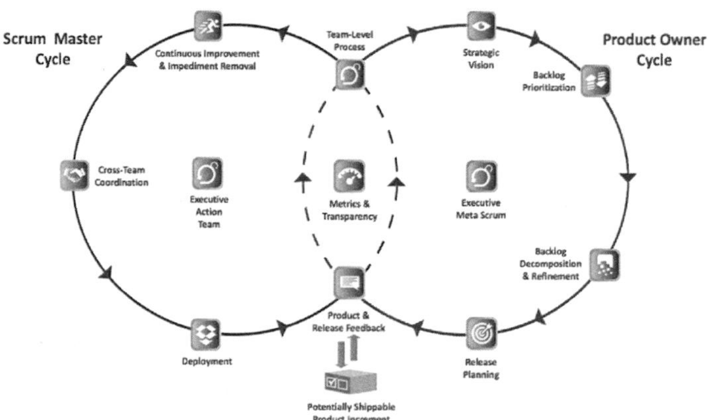

For each described component, examples from 3 different domains were shown: an American Defense vendor, whose name could not be disclosed[202], which represented a kind of authoritarian and very bureaucratic organization, Autodesk[203], a CAD software company founded in 1982, with a push towards modernization, and Spotify[204], an online music company founded with Scrum, which was trying not to lose its original agility while growing up with well over 1000 employees. It seemed unthinkable that three such different companies could follow the same organizational framework, yet it was so.

The other aspect that immediately struck me was linked to the fact that, contrary to other Frameworks, Scrum@Scale regulated only human relations, abstracting from the context of the carried-out work, and could therefore be applied to any field, not just to product development. Clearly, I immediately began to think that all this could be useful for my Scrum projects in Hardware, since it was almost always involving more teams and many external suppliers.

At the beginning of the course, we were asked to refer to an

[202]https://en.wikipedia.org/wiki/Non-disclosure_agreement
[203]https://en.wikipedia.org/wiki/Autodesk
[204]https://en.wikipedia.org/wiki/Spotify

organization we knew, and as each component was shown, we had to make a judgment on a rectangular post-it, following Toyota's signals for continuous improvement: *green* no problem, *yellow* some impediments under control, *red* serious impediments with a tendency to improve, stagnant or worsening and *purple* completely stuck. The goal was getting to the end of the two days with a post-it wall full of ideas about where we could start scaling Scrum in our organization. This would constitute the first transformation backlog.

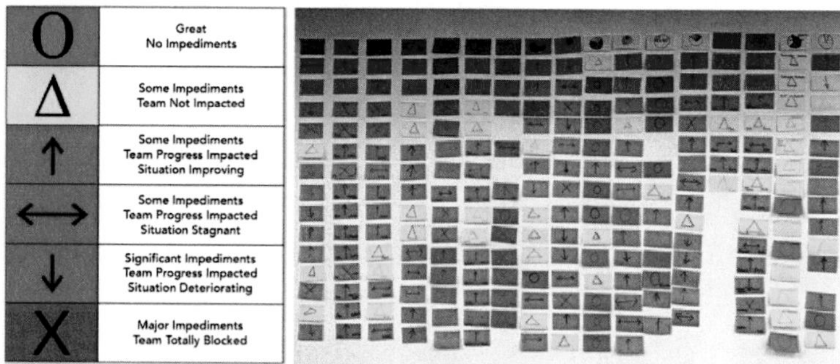

I really liked this approach because it immediately linked what we were learning with our personal reality. The Scrum@Scale Framework strongly emphasized the role and responsibilities of Product Owner and Scrum Master. These were responsible for interfacing the other teams with a series of events mimicking those of the Scrum. This extended the typical Scrum spirit and attitude throughout the organization creating an extremely cohesive, pragmatic and goal-oriented system.

On the morning of the second day, I arrived early, hoping to be again among the first comers and to exchange a few ideas with Jeff. I discovered that one hour before the start of the course he followed a ritual that allowed him to adapt his material to any unanswered questions reported on a poster in the classroom, and to introduce other examples. I was struck by the maniacal care that this person, even at the peak of a global success, continued to reserve for small things: in my work experience, I had met many people who, after obtaining the first weak successes, "sat down" and relaxed their style.

Almost jokingly, I asked him if he had started reading my book. He replied that he had read the first chapter and that he liked it. I was on top of the world! The most flattering comment I could ever dream of.

I told him that I would also take part in the Stockholm course the following Monday and Tuesday, and I suggested having dinner together one evening at the weekend, if he had no other commitments. He replied that he would talk to his wife who was accompanying him on the journey.

One more time, this reinforced the belief I had already confirmed knowing Joe Justice, Henrik Kniberg and, years ago, Mark Shuttleworth[205] in Ubuntu: really great people are those which, despite having an incredible success, maintain their simplicity and naturalness. I was greatly appreciating this, also in Jeff Sutherland.

At the end of the course, in order to review the themes lectured in the two days, we made a game with a software that I had already experimented with my students: Kahoot[206]. Using our mobile phones, we had to choose the correct answer to the questions that appeared on the screen. You earned points not only by answering correctly, but also based on the speed of the answers. After each question, a temporary ranking was shown. The fight was tremendous, a very close competition, but in the end I turned out to be the winner! I loudly cheered like a child, among the general laughter of the other participants, and ran in front of the screen to take a selfie with Jeff and my name on the gold medal podium.

[205]https://en.wikipedia.org/wiki/Mark_Shuttleworth
[206]https://kahoot.com/

My cheerfulness caused some commotion in the classroom and Jean Pierre had to struggle a little to bring the silence back and accomplish the course, while Jeff was amusedly laughing.

Traveling with Jeff

I landed in Stockholm around lunchtime and shared it all on Facebook: "Stockholm again! Third time this year. Am I qualified for citizenship?" An amused Sophia Kniberg replied saying that my grey cap and non-exciting-blue clothes, so far from the Italian stereotype, qualified me perfectly. She and her husband had not returned from their trip yet and asked me to say hi to everyone. I took advantage of the free evening to go dance Tango in a club near my hotel and the morning after, I went to Nobel Museum. At lunchtime, there would be the Nobel Peace Prize ceremony and I did not want to miss it. In the museum, they had set up a room in which they showed the event and I watched the whole ceremony there.

In the afternoon, while I was relaxing in a Pub after a long walk in the center, I received a call from Jeff: his wife had reserved in a restaurant not far from my hotel and they were inviting me to join them. I was also excited to meet Arline, Jeff's wife. I had read a paper in which they told their experience of Scrum in church[207] and I wanted to understand how many similarities there were with what I had experienced in the open source community.

We dined at a Spanish restaurant and talked a lot. Arline wanted to know everything about me: how I had discovered Scrum, how I had come to do Scrum with Hardware and about my voluntary activities. She told me about her children, about her life and I told her how beautiful a holiday on the Tuscan hills could be, hoping she would force her husband to visit me in Italy. I asked Jeff to tell me his stories about his military pilot career in Vietnam, the beginnings of the Scrum and also of Scrum@Scale.

He told me that he was organizing to create a first handful of trainers to help him teach Scrum@Scale globally and asked if I was interested. "Of course I am!" I answered enthusiastically.

We ended up talking about even more conceptual subjects, such as the relationship between Scrum and Cynefin. I had presented this theme a few months before at the Italian Agile Day and I was fascinated by that[208]. "Scrum was born to solve complex problems, but personally, I have experimented with *naïve* uses of Scrum even in Complicated and Obvious systems," I told Jeff "and many of Joe's experiences reinforce this idea". Jeff stared at me deeply with his blue eyes: "We have examples of Scrum even in Chaotic systems, to be honest. Certainly, not exactly as in the Scrum Guide, but it is always Scrum. There are experiences of military operations with Scrum". "Jeff, I'll show you my winning battle: losing weight with Scrum," I said jokingly. I showed him my smartphone with the image of my diet's Burn Down Chart and he exclaimed to Arline: "It's really an impressive Burn Down Chart!" "What do you think, Jeff, could this be the idea for my next book?" "It sounds like a great idea," he told me as he raised his glass of red wine. I took the opportunity for a toast. Both Jeff and Arline love red wine and we ended up talking about the wines produced around Siena.

---

[207]https://www.scruminc.com/scrum-in-church/

[208]"Agile Everywhere" November 2017, University of Urbino: https://vimeo.com/247726104

The morning after, I showed up at Crisp's offices very early, knowing Jeff's habits. The door was opened by Reza Farhang[209], the Scrum Trainer I had already met before. He told me he would spend some time with us, as he was Jeff's co-trainer. I found Jeff transcribing the backlog of the course on post-it notes. I asked him: "Can I help you in some way? Even simple tasks, I did 4 trainings with Joe". Jeff handed me the marker: "Would you do the Backlog, please?" I did not miss the chance: "Of course I would!" After completing the backlog, I started drawing the Burn Down Chart, as I had learned from Joe, and ended up keeping it updated during the two days. Some students asked questions that were related to Scrum for Hardware and Jeff asked me to answer. In the second half of the course, Reza was on the phone with some clients and asked me to help Jeff facilitate games. What a thrill to hear the Certified Scrum Master course from the creator of Scrum! Helping him in the classroom, moreover, is one among the greatest professional fulfillments that I remember.

These two days flew and soon it was time to say goodbye. However, it was actually a "See you soon". I knew that a few months later, I would fly to the States to be back in the classroom with Jeff, but

[209]https://www.crisp.se/konsulter/reza-farhang

this time to become a Scrum@Scale Trainer.

The Method

Scrum

Scrum is an Agile framework designed to develop complex software projects, created by Jeff Sutherland and Ken Schwaber and presented for the first time at the OOPSLA 1995 Conference[210]. The definition of Scrum and the rules are described in the **Scrum Guide**, available in Appendix. To those who are not familiar with the concepts of Scrum, I recommend a careful reading of the Scrum Guide to better understand this chapter.

The Basic Rules

Scrum rules use **3 Roles, 5 Ceremonies and 3 Key Artifacts**. Any implementation lacking even just one of these elements cannot be called Scrum.

The 3 **Roles** in Scrum are *Scrum Master*, *Product Owner* and *Development Team* and these 3 roles together are defined **Scrum Team**. The Scrum Master is responsible for Scrum to be fully understood and acted upon by the whole Scrum Team. The Product Owner has the task of maximizing the value of the product and the work of the Development Team. The Development Team is a group of minimum three and maximum nine people, with the role of producing, during each Sprint, a product increment that works and that is potentially shippable.

---

[210]http://agilix.nl/resources/scrum_OOPSLA_95.pdf

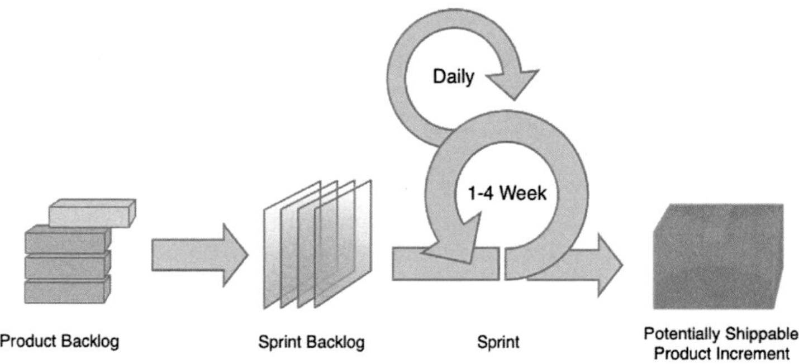

The 3 Scrum **Artifacts** are *Product Backlog, Sprint Backlog* and *Potentially Shippable Product Increment.* Product Backlog is a list of *items* sorted by value, containing all the information about the product to be developed. The Product Owner is solely responsible for its prioritization. The Sprint Backlog is a list of *items* that have to be developed during the Sprint. The Potentially Shippable Product Increment is a product increment that is potentially deliverable, created during the Sprint and analyzed at the end of the same, during the Sprint Review.

The Scrum Team works in iterations of constant duration, called Sprint; every Sprint has a maximum duration of 4 weeks and acts as a container for all Scrum events.

During the Sprint, the following *events* take place:

- *Sprint Planning*, a meeting that takes place at the beginning of the Sprint and where the Development Team negotiates with the Product Owner about the list of tasks to be carried out in the Sprint.
- *Daily Meeting*, a meeting of up to 15 minutes that takes place every day in the same place and at the same time, in which the members of the Development Team are updated on the work of the previous day, on the work to be carried out the same day and on possible difficulties.

- *Sprint Review*, a meeting that takes place at the end of the Sprint, open to the entire Scrum Team and to any concerned stakeholders, inspecting the work produced during the Sprint.
- *Retrospective*, a meeting that takes place immediately after the Review and concluding the Sprint, in which the Scrum Team takes into consideration any improvements and organizes accordingly.
- *Backlog refinement*, an event detailed by the Team during the Sprint and a moment when the Team improves and estimates the items of the Product Backlog that will be tackled in the subsequent sprints.

A Healthy Tension

The reason why it is appropriate that the three Scrum roles are embodied by three different people is clearly explained in the video by Henrik Kniberg "PO in a NUTSHELL[211]".

In developing a product of any type there are three objectives we want to achieve.

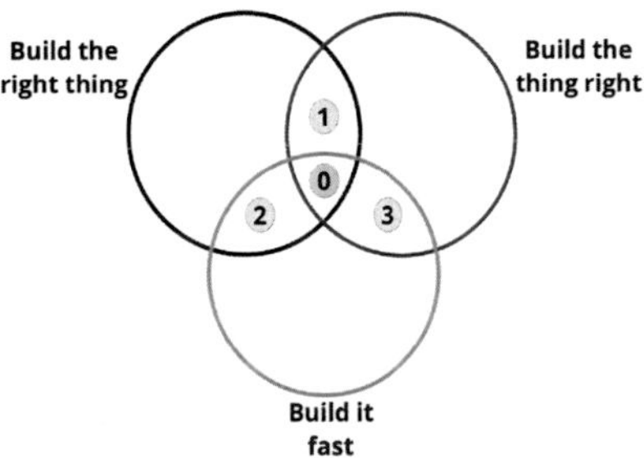

Build the right thing: we want to build the right and actually useful product functionality for our clients.

[211] https://www.youtube.com/watch?v=502ILHjX9EE

Build the thing right: we want to build the right product from an engineering point of view.

Build it fast: we want to get to the market as quickly as possible.

Ideally, everyone wants to be at point **0** of the diagram, perfectly balanced between the three elements. What happens if we find ourselves at point **1**? We built the right product and we did it technically very well. However, we have been too slow and our competitors have already conquered the best customers. The road is uphill and we will hardly manage to make up for lost time. What happens if we find ourselves at point **2** instead? We built the right product quickly. However, our product is technically very weak, customers complain and medium term correction of defects and maintenance cost kill the company's profits. Certainly not a good deal. Finally, what happens if we find ourselves at point **3**? We built a beautiful cathedral in record time. Unfortunately, our clients did not want a cathedral – they just wanted a tent. Our expensive product will remain on the shelves gathering dust. Scrum's organization seeks to keep the projects close to point **0** by dividing priorities between the three roles. The *Product Owner* will focus primarily on understanding what features are really useful, that is, they are "*the right thing*"; the members of the *Development Team* will focus on building the product in a technically effective way, or building "*the thing right*"; and the *Scrum Master* will focus on the process, so productivity increases and reduces the feedback loop. The faster the learning cycle, the more the Scrum Team will be able to understand how to maintain a stability near point **0**. This *Healthy Tension* is one of the reasons why the three so divided Scrum roles are the best way to organize a working group.

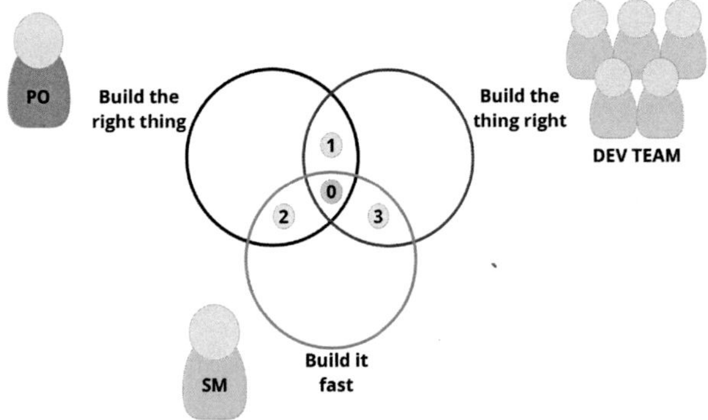

Feedback Loop

The reason behind having a Potentially Shippable Product Increment at the end of each Sprint is, in addition to getting an incremental value, generating Feedback that can reduce the inherent risks in the design of a new product or service. If the scope is the so-called cognitive work, that is immaterial work as it is formed by ideas, the task is not easy, but the required change is limited to the mindset, methods and tools. Having to work with tangible objects, that is *atoms* instead of ideas, this is even more difficult. However, just because it is more difficult, it may represent an important competitive advantage, so much that many companies invest a lot in this respect. How to proceed? Let us look at some ways.

Hardware Compiler

We talked about it in Chapter 4. If there were a machine that would allow a single person to draw a complex object and view it created and mounted with its parts in seconds, designing physical objects would not be so different from software. Every designer's idea could take shape quickly generating a rapid feedback loop, which would make it possible to innovate faster and better. 3D printing technology comes close to this in many cases. There are YouTube videos[212] that show how you can print everything now: from clothes, to jewelry, human implants, cars and even buildings. The technologies behind 3D printers are evolving very quickly and become cheaper and cheaper every day. To print electronic cards, for example, Wikispeed uses a machine that costs only 2,700 usd[213] whose construction patterns are available free of charge at buildyourcnc.com[214]. Thus, if during the Sprint a Team Member has an idea on how to improve the car's electronics, the Team can quickly print a card and assess whether this produces improvement within the review, without having to wait weeks to receive it from external suppliers.

At an industrial level, we are experiencing more and more insistently[215] the so-called "*Batch Size 1*", that is programmable assembly lines that can produce limited editions, up to a single piece, at prices not too far from series production, allowing quick experimentation.

---

[212]https://www.youtube.com/watch?v=FSu19nz7NlE

[213]http://wikispeed.org/2013/03/rapid-prototyping-circuit-boards/

[214]https://buildyourcnc.com

[215]https://www.festo.com/PDF_Flip/trends_in_automation/2_2017/GB/html5/index.html#17/z

Application Report Stama Maschinenfabrik GmbH
Milling-turning centres from Stama are fully focused on flexibility

FESTO

Batch size 1 - setup time 0

Many users of milling-turning centres from the Stama brand re reporting time savings of up to 70% and unit cost reductions of 50%. The reason for this is the high flexibility of the machines and their virtually negligible setup times. This enables small batch sizes and high-volume series to be processed one after the other in almost any combination. The integrated automation solution from Festo for loading and unloading the workpieces as well as the tool changer in the additional magazine play their part in this success.

HiTech Anticipation

In the software world, this practice is already in use. For example, if you ask a professional to build a website for you, he will start to sketch a model on paper with sharpies asking your opinion — a preliminary feedback. After a few days, he will show you some drawings, called a *mock up*, representing a fairly faithful picture of what he understood from your requests. And on these pictures, which are sometimes even dynamic so that pressing on some areas they animate the model, the discussion will continue allowing the professional to reduce the risk of designing something that does not reflect your wishes. One of the technologies that make up the Industry 4.0 package is specifically the Virtual and Augmented Reality. Giants such as Microsoft, Google, Sony and Epson are devoting to research in this area. For example, Microsoft Hololens[216] promises to satisfy the needs to anticipate the feedback while designing a physical complex object. In a promotional video[217],

[216] https://www.microsoft.com/en-us/hololens
[217] https://www.youtube.com/watch?v=u4o0zsJ-S44

there is a designer who, after drawing the hull of a motorcycle on her computer, wears glasses and is able to interact with it in augmented reality: her project appears around a real bike without hull, allowing her to observe and interact immediately with her creation.

Industrial design products such as Maya[218] of Autodesk, have already been integrated[219] with Hololens. Another video[220] shows in detail the operation of this technology, so that even Ford[221] has announced that they have adopted this tool in their design process.

Test Driven Development

The method originates in Extreme Programming[222] and is one of the 12 principles described by Peter Stevens in the article in Chapter 7, reported in next chapter. The idea is to take the development process on three looping phases:

- Writing an automatic test that represents the meeting of a requirement.

218 https://www.autodesk.com/products/maya/overview

219 https://www.autodesk.com/products/fusion-360/blog/future-of-design-with-microsoft-hololens-and-fusion-360/

220 https://www.youtube.com/watch?v=q0K3n0Gf8mA

221 https://www.youtube.com/watch?v=3QyA7HhIYkg

222 https://it.wikipedia.org/wiki/Extreme_programming

- Implementing the feature the easy way in order to pass the test.
- Improved functionality, while maintaining the test success.

This usually occurs with a two-color light message: red and green. For the first step, when you write your test, you get a red light. A test is carried out and it fails for lack of capability. In the second step, you are working to get a green light as simply as possible. In the third step, you wonder if the solution can be improved. The operation is carried out without fear, because in case of error the light will be red, warning us immediately.

For example, the same approach was used by Joe Justice in the Wikispeed project. He knew that the car had to pass the crash test, so he simulated a test with his team. Red light. They created an aluminum parallelepiped and tried it in the simulator. Green light. At this point, they began to empty the parallelepiped trying to make the frame as light as possible, keeping the green light. As soon as they were satisfied with the outcome, they tried a physical test, which provided them with real values, enriching the coefficients of the simulator and making it more realistic. After a few iterations, the simulator was so accurate that there was no need to repeat any real tests.

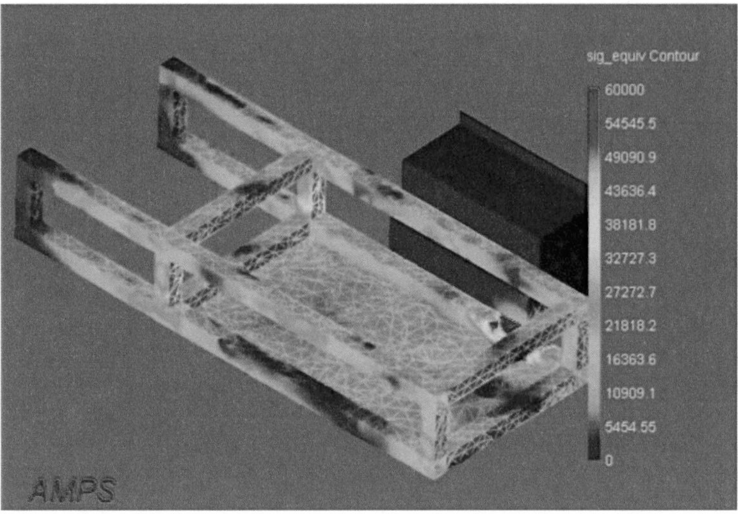

The same approach is used by Saab Aeronautics[223] to design their own military aircraft. Each engineer in the team can experience his idea in the design of the aircraft and see the results quickly in a simulator. This puts all the staff in the best position to be creative and experiment with new ideas.

The Genius

Mario Monicelli's movie "Amici Miei[224]" contains my favorite definition about genius.

> «What is genius? It is imagination, intuition, decision and execution speed".

Getting a feedback loop is always easier and less expensive, for example. If you want this to be a competitive advantage, you will require you to use a little imagination, intuition, decision and execution speed.

[223]http://saab.com/air/gripen-fighter-system/gripen/gripen/

[224]https://en.wikipedia.org/wiki/My_Friends_(film)

At Saab, they told us how, having to test a new radar planned for the Gripen fighter jet and well before the plane could fly, they used the Gripen D, the two seater previous model. After fitting the new radar on the back seat, connecting it to the aircraft sensors through adapters, they sent it to cruising altitude with a pilot only for the necessary recordings. Tying material to a seat through seatbelts is something that you might have made to fix the grocery shopping on the backseat of your car, but I had never seen that on a military plane!

Remember how the volunteers of WIKISPEED, spending only $800 and three days of work against the 36,000 dollars and three months demanded by specialist suppliers, managed to create an attractive car that could take part into the trade show in Detroit of 2011.

You must therefore equip your teams with the freedom and confidence needed to create a climate in which creative problem solving emerges, thanks to the contribution of all and looking for unconventional solutions.

Develop competencies

Scrum requires the development team to be cross-functional, meaning that all the skills necessary to create the product reside in the team, so that all the processing steps are carried out during the sprint. It may be that people with specialized skills, employed in a non-continuous way during the development cycle, are underutilized in some phases of the sprint. To prevent this from happening, and to allow team self-organization, Scrum encourages the development of T-Shaped Skills in all team members. In this case, the T represents the form of a competence matrix in which each team member has a basic skill in each area required by product development, and at the same time, he has an advanced level of knowledge in one of the sectors. What does it mean? If we represent the various skills on a matrix, we can see a T-shaped diagram, where each basic skill is placed in a corresponding area involving the product and an advanced knowledge is placed in one of them.

	Skill 1	Skill 2	Skill 3	Skill 4	Skill 5	
Level 0						
Level 1						
Level 2						
Level 3						
Level 4						

T-Shaped Skills

However, in LeSS - Large Scale Scrum, Craig Larman asserts that, in order to obtain really performing teams, it is necessary to create the conditions for people to develop pi-shaped skills, i.e. in the form of π (pi), with a very strong primary skill, a secondary discrete skill and a basic skill on all other aspects.

	Skill 1	Skill 2	Skill 3	Skill 4	Skill 5	
Level 0						
Level 1						
Level 2						
Level 3						
Level 4						

Pi-Shaped Skills

Larman also asserts that, in this situation, people should act as mentors in their primary skill and carry out most of the activities in the secondary skill, in order to continue to deepen the lesser-known subject.

How is it better to behave, therefore, to ensure that the team develops and grows steadily over time?

Pairing

The practice of pair programming[225] was born within eXtreme Programming[226] already in the mid-nineties. In *pair programming*, two programmers work together at the same workstation, alternating in the roles of driver and navigator: a metaphor derived from rally racing, in which a navigator signals the curves to the pilot looking at them on the map, so that he can concentrate on driving. In the Wikispeed project, volunteers experimented that the practice of working in pairs is very useful even in the context of manual work.

[225]https://en.wikipedia.org/wiki/Pair_programming
[226]https://en.wikipedia.org/wiki/Extreme_programming

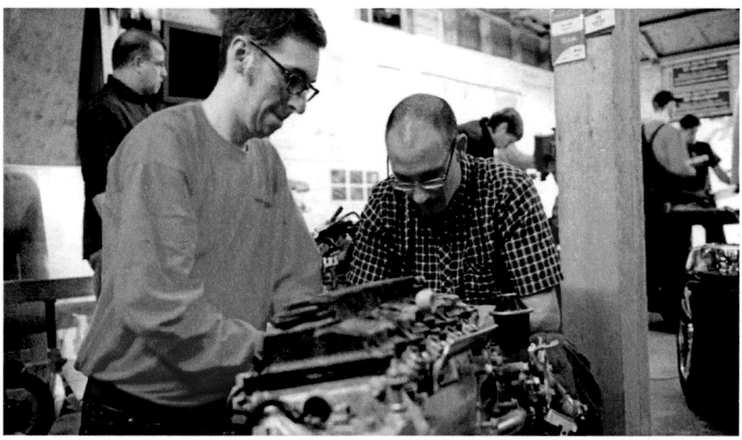

Working in pairs reduces the need for detailed documentation, allows learning from each other and it has been noticed that, working together, makes people feel more secure. In addition, working in pairs allows adding new staff to the team without slowing down the work of the more experienced. The Wikispeed team believes that working in pairs has enormous value, so much so that it has adopted the rule of *aggressive pairing*, according to which all work is organized in pairs.

Swarming

The English word Swarming refer to the action performed by the bees when they move together for a certain reason, forming a swarm. In software development teams, this is commonly associated with mob programming[227] or the practice where the whole team is dedicated to solving the same problem using a computer only and a projector, or a very large screen, so that everyone can see the same part of the project and can collaborate. Hardware teams spontaneously use this practice, for example to move very heavy objects or to integrate the final product. Swarming, however, is also very useful in the act of design and in troubleshooting.

[227]https://en.wikipedia.org/wiki/Mob_programming

When should we use pairing, swarming or simply work alone? Some teams use a very interesting working agreement, displayed as follows:

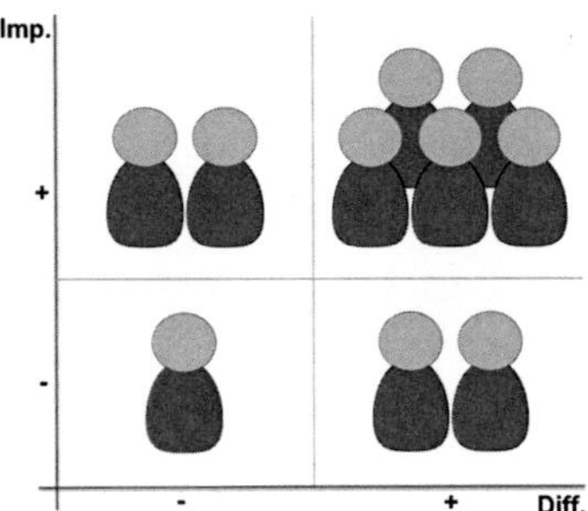

The two axes represent the *difficulty* and *importance* of the activities to be performed. Easy and unimportant things are done individually. Activities that are important or difficult are carried out by a pair. Those that are important *and* difficult are tackled by the whole team at the same time, in order to obtain an appropriate balance between the learning of the team members and the efficiency in carrying out the activities.

Motivate Learning

To ensure that learning is considered a value for the whole organization, it is necessary to create the rules and conditions that allow it to be perceived as such. With this goal, the Wikispeed team has adopted name tags with a special color key.

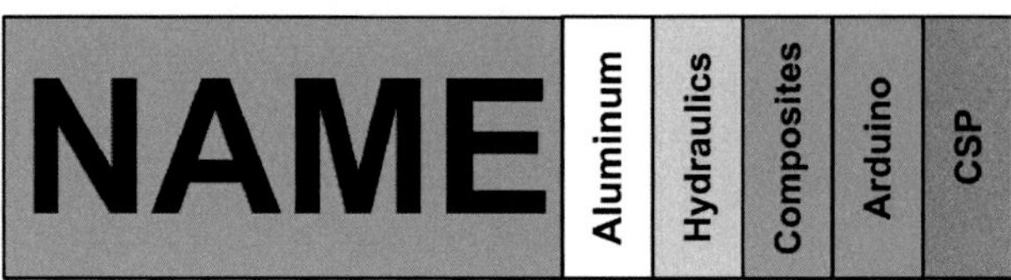

The *white* Aluminum skill refers to the design, construction, installation and testing skills of the aluminum components of the car, such as the frame and the racks of the interior and engine modules.

The *yellow* Hydraulics skill includes tubes, gaskets, joints and everything needed to transport liquids into the vehicle.

Composites *blue* materials include the carbon fiber of the body and the eco-leather of the seats. This material also requires the ability to design, cut, assemble and test.

With the *green* Arduino tag, we indicate the electronic skills related to the various systems in the car. On Wikispeed, a circuit called Ruggeduino[228] is mounted. Although based on a very well-known and easy to learn hobby-programming language, it has the certifications to be used in civil and industrial projects. The last *orange* skill is the Certified Scrum Professional certification, which is the ability to start new teams and teach Scrum to others. Those who in the Wikispeed project have all the colors in their color label are called *black belt* and are the most important people in the company.

This way of representing, and to some extent *gamifying*, one's own skills is also found in Ubuntu. Membership in the various working groups (development, documentation, translations, etc.) was represented in the personal profile of the volunteer with icons, called badges, and created a kind of tension to want to "collect" them all.

[228]https://www.rugged-circuits.com/microcontroller-boards/

User information

Launchpad Id:
xdatap1

Email:
Log in for email information.

Jabber:
<email address hidden>

Member since:
2005-06-15

← BADGES

Signed Ubuntu Code of Conduct:
Yes

IRC:
xdatap1 on irc.freenode.net

SSH keys:
x@bwing

Time zone:
Europe/Rome (UTC+0100)

OpenPGP keys:
D278DC5A1AD5AF14BE60B13F1B5A76DF41999AEA,
FF87AA65EAC7BF034D532B9758FE51B63EF806B1

Languages:
English, Italian

Karma:
0

How to choose the Scrum Master

The selection of the Scrum Master is not defined anywhere in the Scrum Guide. Who chooses him? With which criteria?

Different methods can be observed: in some cases, the Scrum Master offers voluntarily and is then appointed by the management; in others, he was born as a member of the Team and is elected within it, and often partly continues to carry out development activities, as a team member.

One of my clients was in the need to reorganize the development department to harmonize his teams. His Scrum Masters, elected among the team members, carried out their part-time role and continued to work on development as well. Various problems were emerging: in some teams, there was an overabundance of aspiring Scrum Masters while in others the role had been played by the person with more seniority of service, without however manifesting a great enthusiasm. The fact of playing the role in a partial way also reduced the focus and provided an alibi on not devoting time to the study of coaching practices.

I suggested taking advantage of the reorganization to experiment a different method of choosing the Scrum Master, taking inspiration from Craig Larman's LeSS method.

Considering the existing constraint, which required to maintain the number of people employed (*head count*), that of Scrum Master would become a full time assignment and each Scrum Master would be assigned two teams. Those wishing to become Scrum Masters should apply to an internal Job Posting and pass an assessment interview held by the Coaches who led the transformation. After that, the teams would indicate their preferences among the selected people and the management would finalize the pairings, trying to satisfy as many people as possible.

The idea of having full-time and professionalized Scrum Masters convinced everyone in the company and the managers decided to experiment with this different method. The top management assured me that Scrum Master would be a role and not a *job title*, and with the mantra "Job and Salary safety, Role unsafety", the new organization was announced to the whole company development department.

Selection Criteria

I began to think about what could be a good way to select candidates. Scrolling back to the book by Lyssa Atkins "Coaching Agile Teams"[229] I pondered on the multiplicity of roles that the Agile Coach must play, and in particular on its three main functions:

- Trainer
- Facilitator
- Coach

I also had a look at "Succeeding with Agile" by Mike Cohn[230] with his acronym *ADAPT*[231], which is about Awareness, Desire, Ability, Practice and Transfer and I had a crazy intuition: if ADAPT works for organizations, why should not it be good for a single individual?

[229] https://www.goodreads.com/book/show/8337919-coaching-agile-teams

[230] https://www.goodreads.com/book/show/6707987-succeeding-with-agile

[231] The ADAPT model is described in the chapter "Other Ingredients" in the Getting Started section.

Therefore, I tried to place the meaning of each letter within the context of an aspiring Scrum Master:

- Awareness of the role and of oneself.
- Desire of the role and how we see ourselves.
- Ability to read coaching situations.
- Practice, practical skills as a facilitator.
- Transfer, ability to transfer concepts, to teach.

This skill *checklist* seemed to cover well the roles of trainer, facilitator and coach of the book "Coaching Agile Teams"[232].

The Interview

The interview was held in a dedicated room and, with the permission of the candidates, it was audio recorded, so that the interviewer would not need to take notes during the interview and could focus on the candidate.

The **Awareness** component was explored with two questions:

1) What characteristics should a Scrum Master have?

2) What characteristics, among those you have listed, do you think you have and on which do you think you have to work harder?

While for question 1 there were correct and well-documented answers even in the Certified Scrum Master courses, question 2 aimed at understanding how people were aware of the personal growth path required by the role.

For the **Desire** part, the questions were:

3) Why do you want to be a Scrum Master?

4) Think about yourself tomorrow, you are a Scrum Master. What has changed in you and what do others say about you?

[232]https://www.goodreads.com/book/show/8337919-coaching-agile-teams

Question 3 aimed at understanding if the motivation was related to the role, career and prestige or if it also derived from the presence of soft relational skills, perhaps developed outside of the working context, with hobbies, sports and voluntary activities. Question 4 sought to explore how the candidates saw themselves in the role; any awareness of the difficulties would be considered favorably.

The **Ability** part was conducted with two situational questions:

5) In a team of four developers, one person always does solo work. Others suffer from this but do not openly say anything. You are their Scrum Master, what will you do?

6) A manager who has not fully understood Scrum enters the team room and complains that a feature he had promised a client has not been completed yet, and the relative story has dragged for a further 2 sprints beyond what expected. He alludes to the fact that the Team does not commit itself. You are the Scrum Master and you are in the room at that moment, what will you do?

These questions evaluated the compliance with the principles of the Scrum Guide, the quantity and quality of options that people listed and an approach in line with systemic thinking and complexity, described later in the paragraphs Agile Management and Cynefin.

The **Practice** component aimed at evaluating facilitation and visualization capabilities. The candidate was asked to visualize on a flipchart the concepts that were read from a book [233], as if they were dialogues that emerged in a meeting. Just like in meetings, the facilitator can intervene to ask a question, but certainly cannot monopolize the speech. It was then explained to the candidate that it was not a dictation but a way to visualize the key concepts and that he could interrupt the reading by asking questions, without exaggerating. This test aimed at evaluating the spelling, the order and the use of color.

[233]In the case described here, I read to the candidates the chapter The Fourth Industrial Revolution of this same book, which I had already completed at thattime. Using a piece of this book to try out a practice published here for the first time is a tribute to recursion so loved by the Free Software Hacker community.

Finally for the **Transfer** part, it was asked to explain what Agile was in a first question and how Scrum worked in a second one. The candidate had the possibility to use the flipchart if he thought it useful. The questions were always asked in a situational way (e.g.: I am a consultant for a foreign branch, I am traveling in development and meeting you I ask you to explain what Agile means, the term I heard at a meeting the same morning). Moreover, it was assessed how much the answer strove to adapt to the context and vocabulary of the person who posed the question in the imagined situation.

Evaluation

The evaluation of the candidates' responses was carried out later, listening to the audio recordings and analyzing the photos of the artifacts produced in the Practice and Transfer questions. At first, the key aspects of the answers were noted and then a vote was assigned, on a scale similar to the Italian scholastic one, from 4 to 8. A second evaluation tried to harmonize the judgments once all the interviews were listened to, in order to have a balanced vote between the candidates. A summary table was then created in which there was a single vote for each individual component of ADAPT. The individual votes, however, were not added to get the final ranking; instead, in order to try to absorb the complexity of the choice of a suitable Scrum Master, those with serious fails were first discarded. Then, the remaining ones were ordered case by case, trying to evaluate the candidate in its entirety and not based on the mere algebraic sum of votes. The goal was to build a list of ordered people to be able to enter the role with the aim of selecting those who had the smallest gap to fill.

Outcomes

The development department involved in the process had about 100 employees distributed between groups of systems engineers, support groups and 10 Scrum teams. The goal was to identify 5 Scrum Master candidates.

As stated to the management before starting the interviews, I would consider this process a success if it were able to surprise me; that is, if suitable people emerged from it who had not already seemed such since the beginning of the Agile transition. Of the 5 new Scrum Masters selected, two were former team members who, despite not having held this role previously, had managed to overcome in the rankings of people who acted as Scrum Masters for about two years; and this showed how much potential and hidden talent there were in them. Many people excluded from the final choice, however, had shown that they had characteristics of suitability, and this was reassuring in the possible future prospect of having to repeat the process for an enlargement of the workforce or in case of refusals. The new Scrum Masters all showed great enthusiasm and the first feedback after some Sprints are very encouraging. The same method was used later with another client, on a more limited staff, and has again received positive feedback and allowed to start tasks with enthusiasm. It will be interesting to see how other colleagues can use it and provide confirmation or denial about its validity.

Pattern of Performance

In software engineering, the concept of *design pattern* can be defined as "a general design solution to a recurring problem". It is a description or a logical model applied for the resolution of a problem that may frequently occur, even before the definition of the solving algorithm for the computational part. It is often an effective approach to contain or reduce technical debt.[234]

ScrumPlop[235] is the community that meets annually since 2010 to collect, catalog and publish the patterns that the performing teams

[234]Adaptation of the definition of Design pattern from Wikipedia: https://en.wikipedia.org/wiki/Design_pattern

[235]http://www.scrumplop.org

adopt using Scrum. The first Scrum patterns had already been published in 1997 by Mike Beedle, together with Devos, Sharon, Schwaber and Sutherland, in the paper SCRUM: An extension pattern language for hyperproductive software development[236], while the nine most common patterns – those that Jeff Sutherland suggests to use first in order to create stable and performing teams – were presented at the Agile Alliance 2013 in Nashville[237] and they are:

- Stable Teams
- Yesterday's Weather
- Swarming: One Piece Continuous Flow
- Interrupt Pattern: Illegitimus Non Interruptus
- Daily Clean Code
- Emergency Procedure
- Scrumming the Scrum
- Happiness Metric
- Teams that Finish Early Accelerate Faster

While the Scrum Guide provides basic Scrum rules, patterns amplify it by showing how teams can solve problems in particular contexts. According to the authors, Scrum should be simple, fast and fun. For many new Scrum Masters, Scrum is difficult, slow and painful instead. Performance patterns are designed as a remedy for the various headaches encountered by the Scrum Masters in their professional career.

Stable Teams

This pattern suggests keeping the teams stable, avoiding moving people continuously from one team to another. Stable teams tend

[236]http://jeffsutherland.org/scrum/scrum_plop.pdf

[237]https://www.agilealliance.org/resources/sessions/coaching-simple-patterns-that-avoid-common-pitfalls-for-scrum-teams/

to agree and learn more about their skills, making estimates more reliable and allowing the business to be predictable. In traditional organizations, often, workgroups change when the project changes; in Agile organizations, work flows towards stable teams, and not vice versa.

Yesterday's Weather

In many cases, the number of Story Points[238] completed in the previous sprint is the best indicator of how many points will be completed in the following sprint. With this pattern, the team plans sprint stories based on the velocity average of the last three sprints. In the event that the team completes the work before the end of the sprint, another story ready at the head of the backlog will be *pulled* in agreement with the PO.

Swarming: One Piece Continuous Flow

When a team is struggling to complete the work of the Sprint, it is often because there are too many things started simultaneously (*work in progress*) and the team is not focused on finishing first the most valuable item. *Swarming* all on one item in order to complete it quickly increases the performance of the entire Sprint. How does it work? Whoever takes charge of the highest priority item is considered the "captain" of the team: everyone has to help him and nobody should interrupt him. As soon as the captain finishes the first item, anyone taking the next item is the new captain.

Interrupt Pattern: Illegitimus Non Interruptus

This pattern allows the allocation of a time buffer for any unplanned work and prevents it from exceeding. It is based on three simple

[238]https://en.wikipedia.org/wiki/Planning_poker

rules that allow the company to organize itself to avoid losing the production rhythm:

1. The team creates a buffer for interruptions based on historical data. For example, if it turns out that 30% of a team's work comes from unplanned work, with a velocity of 60 points, 20 are reserved for the interruption buffer.
2. All requests must go through the Product Owner, who will consider whether to insert them in the backlog to do them in the next sprints, reject them completely or insert them into the interruption buffer of the current Sprint. The team starts working on the new activity only after completing the current one.
3. If the buffer exceeds the maximum size, the Product Owner calls the Sprint Abort procedure and notifies the management that all release dates are postponed by a Sprint.

This last rule means that the buffer does not exceed except in extreme circumstances, and that its size gradually levels to the minimum possible, if used in conjunction with the Yesterday's Weather pattern. A reducing buffer increases the Sprint capacity accordingly and allows the team to accelerate.

Daily Clean Code

The correction of problems by the same day in which they are detected aims at getting a flawless project every day and reduces the maintenance costs. In fact, it is already known in Lean practices that immediate correction of root problems improves production capacity.

Emergency Procedure

When burndown does not show progress towards the Sprint Goal, we suggest this procedure, similar to the one used for a long time by the pilots of airplanes: when a problem emerges, immediately execute the specific emergency procedure, without trying to understand what does not work. It is the responsibility of the Scrum Master to ensure that the procedure is carried out immediately, preferably within half of the Sprint. Here are some steps of the emergency procedure. Use the necessary ones:

1. Change the way the work is done. Do something differently.
2. Ask for help, usually by transferring some of the work to someone else.
3. Reduce the Sprint scope.
4. Abort the Sprint and plan again.
5. Inform the management of any impact on the release dates.

Scrumming the Scrum

Identify the single most important impediment and remove it within the next sprint. To do this, the impediment removal item is placed in the Sprint Backlog as a higher priority user story, provided with acceptance criteria that determine when it is completed. Then evaluate the state of the story during the Sprint Review along with the others. This pattern has been included in the description of the retrospective in the 2017 version of the Scrum Guide.

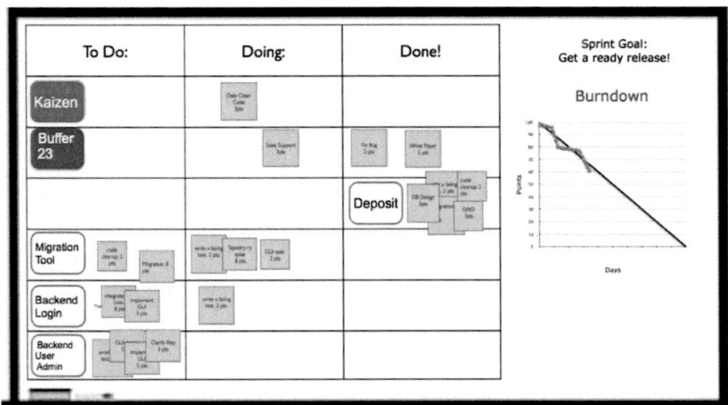

Scrum Board example, by ScrumInc

Happiness Metric

Happiness is one of the best metrics because it is a predictive indicator. When people think about how happy they are, they are actually projecting the way they feel in the future. If they feel that the company is in trouble, or that they are doing something wrong, they will feel sad. If there are any impediments or a frustrating rule system, they will feel sad. A very powerful way to understand the status of a team is to understand how happy they are. The Scrum Master asks two questions:

- How happy are you about the company?
- How happy are you about your role?

Team members answer questions with a scale of 1 to 5. These numbers are kept in a spreadsheet and tracked weekly. If the numbers change significantly, it is important to talk with the team to find ways to make them happier. By monitoring the morale of the Team, the Scrum Master succeeds in anticipating the drops in velocity and acting proactively.

Teams that Finish Early Accelerate Faster

Teams often accept an excessive workload in the Sprint and cannot finish it. Recognizing failure and being always under pressure are elements that prevent the Team from improving. It is therefore advisable to take less work, maximizing the chances of success, using for example, the Yesterday's Weather pattern. Then, the other Patterns of the list that reduce the impediments in the Sprint must be implemented and this will allow managing the interruptions and finishing the Sprint Backlog in advance. When the team completes the work in advance, it can take the most valuable item from the backlog. This will ensure that the value of Yesterday's Weather grows in the following sprints. To increase the probability of accelerating, it is good to apply Scrumming the Scrum to identify the improvement action in the retrospective and place it as the top priority in the next sprint.

The full list of Scrum Patterns published by the ScrumPlop[239] group can be consulted in the A Scrum Book[240] website.

[239]http://www.scrumplop.org
[240]http://scrumbook.org/

Extreme Manufacturing

One of the most challenging things for many Scrum teams is to create a real **Potentially Shippable Product Increment (PSPI)** at the end of every Sprint. We want a feedback and learn as much as possible from it. What if the product is technically very complex? How to build a PSPI in just one or two weeks?

Software teams use a set of engineering practices, known under the name of eXtreme Programming[241], like the Test Driven Development, Pair Programming and Continuous Integration; but those are contextual to Software development. What if you have to deal with complex tangible products?

Extreme Manufacturing is a set of principles created by Joe Justice during the WIKISPEED project. Those principles have been publishes by Peter Stevens[242], a Certified Scrum Trainer who lives in Zurich, Switzerland. The verbatim copy of his articles Extreme Manufacturing Explained[243], published in June 2013, is available in this chapter, enriched with photos, links and additional notes.

Extreme Manufacturing Explained

In 2008, Joe Justice responded to a challenge from the X-Prize competition to create a road-legal 100mpg automobile. Despite having little time, hardly any budget, competition from over 100 well-funded competitors from companies and universities around the world, and changing requirements from the awards committee, his company's WIKISPEED entry placed 10th in the Mainstream

[241] https://en.wikipedia.org/wiki/Extreme_programming

[242] https://saat-network.ch/about-saat-network/about-peter-stevens-cst/

[243] http://www.scrum-breakfast.com/2013/06/extreme-manufacturing-explained.html

class. Joe not only created a great car, he also developed an Agile approach to creating physical products.

As a software developer, Joe was an "Agile native." He had only worked with methods like Scrum and Extreme Programming, so his engineering practices drew heavily on his software experience. Today, WIKISPEED is selling prototypes, and the WIKISPEED approach to manufacturing is turning heads worldwide at companies like Boeing and John Deere. "Our technology is more sophisticated than yours, but your culture is light-years ahead of ours!"

Joe calls his approach "Extreme Manufacturing." XM emphasizes the ability to create products quickly and integrate changes rapidly into existing products. XM is collection of principles and patterns to help you create and adapt products quickly.

The list of the principles is the following:

1. Optimize for change
2. Object-Oriented, Modular Architecture
3. Test Driven Development
4. Contract-First Design
5. Iterate the Design
6. Agile Hardware Design Patterns
7. Continuous Integration Development
8. Continuously Deployed Development
9. Scaling Patterns
10. Partner Patterns

These principles and patterns do not represent the final wisdom on Agile manufacturing, but rather a work-in-progress, on the discovery of better ways to manufacture things.

1. Optimize for change

What happens if an engineer comes up with a way to build a safer car door? Can that new door be deployed right away? No.

A stamping machine and a custom made die produce that door. Together they cost over 10 million US dollars and they must first be amortized before the new door can be economically produced. Given the high costs, it can take 10 years or more before that better door can enter production. You can see the impact of the need to amortize huge investments in the slow, incremental changes in automobiles from year to year, even from decade to decade!

WIKISPEED can change their design every seven days. They employ tools like value stream mapping not merely to reduce the variance of products produced or to optimize the flow through the production line, but first and foremost to reduce the cost of change. It does not cost them more to use a new design than to use an existing design. So if they have a safer way to build the door today, they start using it next week.

Welcoming and responding to change represent core Agile values and principles (see the Agile Manifesto and the Principles behind the Agile Manifesto). So by adopting this principle, you take a huge step towards becoming an Agile organization.

2. Object-Oriented, Modular Architecture

n the software industry until the 1980's, programs were developed on a procedural model. This led to extremely complex, unmaintainable solutions. A change to one part of the program usually required changes throughout the program.

This 'tight-coupling' is still pervasive in automotive designs. A change to the suspension requires a change to the chassis, which requires a change to something else, with eventually impacts the design of the entire car.

Today software developers use "information hiding" and object-oriented design patterns to create loosely coupled, highly modular solutions. So you can change for instance the login process without having to modify other parts of your system.

At the X-Prize competition, many of the competitors dropped out. Why? As it became clear that there would be many entrants, the organizers planned to hold a race on city streets to determine the overall winner. This was changed to a coast-to-coast rally, and finally they settled on a race over a very demanding, closed course racetrack. Each acceptance scenario posted very different demands on the suspension. These changes posed huge challenges for teams that could not embrace change rapidly.

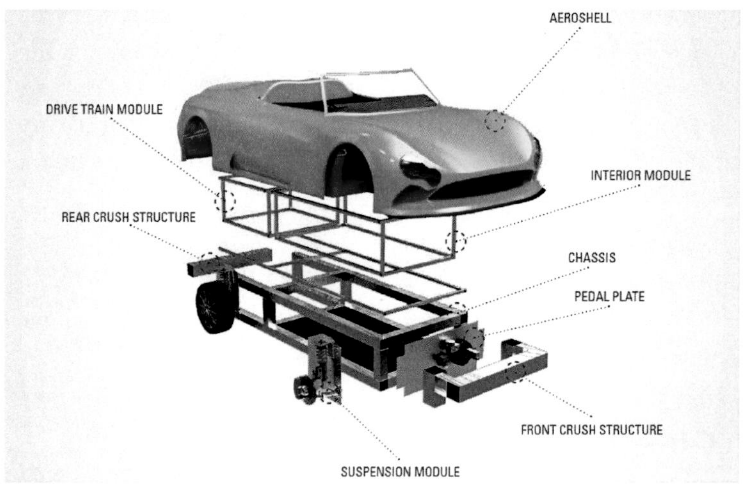

The WIKISPEED car is designed as 8 modules, with simple interfaces between the modules. Due to its modular architecture, WIKISPEED was able to switch suspension systems with a minimum of fuss. WIKISPEED has also discovered it can apply related patterns, like inheritance and code reuse, to its advantage.

Embracing change is a core agile value. The ability to adapt rapidly meant WIKISPEED did better in the X-Prize competition than the nearly 100 entrants who dropped out without producing a car.

How do you achieve an object-oriented, modular architecture? The next two principles, 3 - Test-Driven Development and 4 - Contract-first Design will help you.

3. Test-Driven Development

Before Joe started building a car, he created a model for predicting fuel economy. He identified over 100 well known, freely available parameters, like weight, drag coefficients, engine power, tire size, etc. Based on these parameters he could predict the EPA fuel economy of the car within a few percent.

Armed with this model, he was able to calculate the characteristics the WIKISPEED entrant must have in order to achieve not only 100 miles per gallon, but also to achieve performance characteristics worthy of a high-end sports car.

Team WIKISPEED wanted to achieve five-star crashworthiness according to the specifications of the NHTSA and IIHS. These specify impacts under multiple conditions to evaluate the crashworthiness of the cars. These tests are quite expensive, US$10'000 per test, plus the costs of the vehicle itself, transport and disposal of the test vehicle and the travel costs for the people involved. How can they update their designs every week, when each change requires retesting? Step one was to use Finite Element Analysis to simulate the crashes. When they believed their car would pass the test, they ran an actual test.

Lateral Crash Test of Wikispeed

Of course they did not pass the test, but that was not the purpose. They wanted real crash data so they could better model crashes in their simulations. They updated their simulations based on the actual crash data. After a few iterations, their simulations became so good, that the authorities now accept the results of their simulations in lieu of actual tests. Since they can now do (almost) fully automated tests, they can simulate crash tests every week.

When designing new components,

1. Create the test it is expected to pass. That can be very high level, like emissions tests or crash standards, or it might be more component level. If it is possible to automate the test (or create an automated proxy for the test), do so, as this reduces the cost of repeating the test after future design changes.
2. Create the simplest design possible that enables the test to pass.
3. Iterate on the design, improving it until it is more valuable to work on another portion of the product.

In software, this process is known as "Red-Green-Refactor." To implement something, first create a test, which by definition fails immediately ("goes red"). Then implement functionality to make it pass (go green). Then improve the design for better maintainability, efficiency, etc. This is called refactoring.

4. Contract First Design

The initial design decision of the WIKISPEED car was that it should consist of eight modules – body, chassis, motor, suspension, interior, etc. Before Team WIKISPEED even started to design individual components, they designed the interfaces between those modules.

Joe did not know what suspension would be used on his car, but he was able identify the external parameters and boundary conditions of the suspension. After researching the subject, he found that that if the suspension mounting could withstand 8 gees, it would more than meet all the necessary requirements, even for Formula One racing applications. So the team identified a suitably sized block of aluminum that could carry that load. Any suspension that could be attached to that block could be used on the WIKISPEED car without modification to the rest of the car.

Wikispeed Suspension

So when designing a solution,

- Design the interfaces based on outside parameters, e.g. load factors, or communication and power requirements.
- Only architect the connections up front, not the individual components.
- Leave room to grow, i.e. over engineer these interfaces, because changing these fundamental contracts may be expensive.

P.S. Be sure to check out the Wrapper pattern to ensure independence between your design and the design of any component suppliers.

5. Iterate the Design

One frequently asked question for hardware or embedded projects considering Scrum is, "How can we get stuff done every sprint? It takes longer to develop a piece of hardware than could ever fit in a two-week sprint!" Hardware development needs to take a slightly different view on iterations and iterating than software development.

When the WIKISPEED engineers were first working on the interior, they realized that the lack of an emergency brake was slowing down their progress. The brake handle sits between the seats, close to the gearshift and to the attach points for the seats and seat belts. Because no one knew what the emergency brake handle looked like, they were unwilling to commit to design decisions on these nearby components.

The solution was "version 0.01" of the emergency brake: a cardboard box that said, "the brake handle will fit in this box." That was enough functionality that the team could move forward on nearby components, even though nobody had any illusions that this cardboard box would actually hold the car in place!

When working with hardware, you will iterate on your designs:

1. Create the test that your design should pass.
2. Create the simplest design possible that enables the test to pass.
3. Improve the design to be simpler or more elegant.
4. Repeat this process ("Iterate on the design") until improving this component is no longer the highest value work you can do.

In the case of v0.01 of the emergency brake, the acceptance test was "Can the engineers design the surrounding components with confidence?" The cardboard box satisfied this test. Other components were judged to be of higher value, so they stayed with the cardboard box until the other components were finished enough.

When developing software with Agile, each iteration should produce potentially deliverable functionality. That may not be possible when working with hardware, so you may need to iterate on a particular item many times before the design is satisfactory. In the case of the WIKISPEED X-Prize entrant, those subsequent iterations included, "An emergency brake to hold the car in place," and "An emergency brake which produces no resistance when the car is in motion."

You may also need to iterate on your acceptance tests, especially as you strive to automate them. Before WIKISPEED performed a real crash test, they had done many Finite Element simulations. These are cheap and repeatable, because all they need is computer time. Then they had a real crash test performed. That crash produced results that were different from their simulation, so they iterated. They used the real crash data to improve their simulation. Eventually their simulations became close enough to reality that they no longer needed the expensive physical tests.

6. Agile Hardware Design Pattern

A pattern is an old idea. A pattern is simple way to represent implicit knowledge about well-known solutions to well-known problems. Patterns were pioneered in architecture by Christopher Alexander[244] to facilitate the understanding of good solutions to common challenges in building houses and other structures. Software developers picked up on the idea to communicate solutions to typical challenges in computer systems. WIKISPEED has identified a number of patterns to help design good hardware. For example:

1. Wrapper – Use a wrapper to adapt a third party part to your contract. If you use the supplier's interface as your contractual interface, any change in either product or supplier will probably cause you to redesign the interface, a potentially expensive undertaking.
2. Facade – Use a façade, a connector of connectors with a simple interface, whenever multiple wires (like data & power) need to go to the same place.
3. Singleton – Every component needs power, data and ground. The first thing every engineer wants to create when designing a new component is the power, data and ground bus. The singleton pattern says for each basis component, there is just one in use. So if you need a power-data-ground bus - use ours!

Sometimes the patterns have a cost. The wrapper pattern added 8 kg to the weight of a WIKISPEED car, for example by adding an extra slab of aluminum between the chassis and the suspension.

Was the design pattern worth the extra weight? Yes, because that pattern allowed Team WIKISPEED to a) reduce several hundred pounds from the weight of the car by steady optimization, and b) react easily and cheaply to the changing suspension requirements. Had they not been able to do that, they would not have been able to participate in the final selection round.

---

[244]https://wikipedia.org/wiki/Christopher_Alexander

7. Continuous Integration Development

WIKISPEED has team members contributing in 20+ different countries, any time of the day, with variable availability. How does they produce a cohesive, salient product? The answer has two parts, the first part is about engineering practices, and the second about how to scale.

At the engineering level, Extreme Manufacturing employs Continuous Integration Development (CID) to run their test suite frequently (see principle 3 - Test Driven Development). Continuously Deployed Development (see principle 8) ensures a tight collaboration between product creation and product manufacturing, so the goal of never being more than 7 days from releasing an improved product can be achieved.

Continuous Integration Development (CID) ensures that the test suite is automated as much as practical, so that every time a team member sends in an updated design, an extensive test suite is run automatically.

Every time a team member uploads a new 3d drawing to DropBox, Box.net, Windows SkyDrive, or any of the file sharing technologies in use, WIKISPEED run tests. WIKISPEED can simulate crash tests and stress tests on the part using FEA (Finite Element Analysis)[245] and a software package like LS Dyna[246] or AMPStech[247]. WIKISPEED can simulate airflow, aerodynamics, fluid flow, heat transfer, and electrical propagation using CFD (Computational Fluid Dynamics[248]).

[245] https://en.wikipedia.org/wiki/Finite_element_method
[246] https://en.wikipedia.org/wiki/LS-DYNA
[247] http://www.ampstech.com/
[248] https://en.wikipedia.org/wiki/Computational_fluid_dynamics

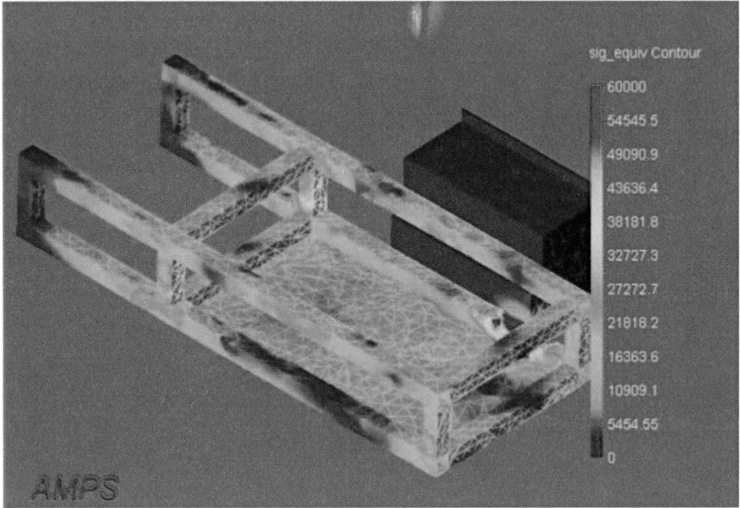

These tests can be run automatically whenever a new CAD shows up, and write out a 1 page report with a list of red or green lights. Green lights mean the test is same or better than the current version, or passes an explicit test for that part or module.

In this way, team members from all over the world can simultaneously contribute in parallel with very different ideas for improvements to each module. And it's easy to know what the current best part is; the version of record is whatever part in CAD has passed all tests with the most green lights.

WIKISPEED includes tests for simplicity and low cost, along with user ergonomics, maintainability, manufacturability, and conformance to interface(s) of the module they are a part of.

8. Continuously Deployed Development

Extreme Manufacturing requires going from an idea to a deliverable, working product or service in 7 days or less. How do you produce a new design in volume in such a compressed timeline?

Let's look at how traditional companies address the problem of new product creation: When a traditional car manufacturer designs a new transmission, they build a new factory. Step one is to negotiate with various political districts for optimal conditions, e.g. access to roads & power, conditions for taxation, etc. Then they acquire the land, build the facility, hire and train the workforce, and configure the line. After many years of preparation, their customers can finally order a product for delivery.

How do you compress years of lead time down to a one week delivery cycle?

This Principle involves making the mass-manufacturing line flexible, so it can produce different products within a 7 day sprint. These products might be existing products, modified products or completely new products.

Achieving this operational flexibility might mean additive or subtractive rapid prototyping machines, or both. It might mean some machines or lean cells are placed on lockable casters so they can be wheeled in or out of the flow depending on the sprint goal. This often means that the team reconfigures the machinery following daily Scrum each morning. And this always means test fixtures connected to andon lights[249] at all stages of the line.

R&D belongs at the head of the line. If the new product design team is within earshot of the volume manufacturing line, bi-directional communication occurs. If the R&D group deploys to the production line every sprint, both teams can work together to reconfigure the line to test and produce the new product. As cross functional skill grows, any separation between the R&D and manufacturing team dissolves and we simply have the cross-functional product team. Each individual has specializations, welding certifications for example, but through pairing they work on every aspect of the product flow from idea to customer delivery and support.

How are you going to get a truly marketable product, if you only

[249]https://en.wikipedia.org/wiki/Andon_(manufacturing)

have seven days to create a new product? See XM Principle 5: Iterate the Design. The objective is to create a first version within a week. Then iterate on the design to improve it as needed. Use the intermediate results to get feedback from customers, users and other stakeholders. Early designs will be big and clunky, making use of off-the-shelf components, but as you iterate the design and get feedback on it, you will zero in on your target.

For services, the story is exactly analogous. Ideally the service providers are the advanced marketers and innovators of new services, and within a sprint they interact with customers to improve the service and make the improvements available to the customers.

9. Scaling Patterns

XM scales as Scrum scales, by adding teams. Coordination can occur through the Product Owners, Scrum Masters or Team Members, depending on the scope of the issues involved.

When multiple teams work on the same module, they each own a sub-module, which will require another finer pass of Contract-First Design to create interfaces for sub-modules before those teams can be created. For example, within the engine module there is the fuel system module, the engine electronics module, the exhaust system module. Each module has an interface that loosely couples it the other modules and clear tests of their value and technical excellence. Creating Teams

Applied at WIKISPEED, the first design decision is the fundamental architecture of the product being created, in their case a car. What are the main modules, e.g. engine, body, drive train, cockpit, etc., and what are the interfaces between them? Once the modules have been identified and the contacts between them created (see XM Principle 4: Contract-First Design), sub-teams can be created on each side of an interface to develop that module.

If capacity allows and velocity and quality metrics indicate adding more teams per module will improve velocity and quality, then multiple teams can work in parallel per module.

Each team owns their own integration and tests, no team is "done" with an increment of their module until all tests pass, including tests that it complies with their module's interface and no additional connections have been introduced.

Team Coordination

In XM Scrum of Scrums, teams consist of 4 to 5 people, including a Product Owner and Scrum Master. Each product owner is responsible for pulling stories from the Portfolio Product Backlog (or simply "Backlog"), and getting clarity when their team needs it on the customer visible value and Net Present Value each story is intended to deliver.

This clarity comes from the Chief Product Owner (CPO) who sequences and refines the Portfolio Product Backlog continuously. The CPO is not a senior role in pay or experience, but is simply the person available enough to keep backlog ready for the teams, answer questions, and have the most clear understanding of the customer visible value the Portfolio Product Backlog is aiming to produce. Ideally, the CPO is the customer, and the one paying for the product or service the backlog is aiming to produce.

On each team, each Scrum Master is responsible for accelerating the velocity of the team, i.e. the amount of work sustainably delivered each sprint. Sustainable implies that the teams are happy and that all work completed satisfies the quality metric called the Definition of Done. Scrum Masters have an additional job here, too: they collaborate with the Scrum Masters of other teams to negotiate the shared resources like space, tools, and modules, across teams.

In this way, a team of 5 has clear expectations for themselves on how to resolve the most common types of impediments: lack of clarity is handled ASAP by the product owner, lack of backlog is handled ASAP by the product owner, lack of visibility into team delivery trend/quality/happiness is handled as a matter of course each week by the Scrum Master, and resource constraints and coordination are handled ASAP by the Scrum Master."

10. Partner Patterns

Deliveries often rely on third party suppliers, and often they are not yet able to deliver a new product that meets our new specification within a single sprint. So what can we do in order to go from an idea to a new product or service in a customer's hands in less than 7 days?

WIKISPEED first designs a wrapper, usually a plate of aluminum with pre-defined bolt patterns, around the third party supplied part to create a known "interface" that won't change, even if that third party part changes. You might see how this is enforced by principle 2: Object-Oriented, Modular Architecture and 4: Contract-First Design, and then sped up by principle 6: Agile Hardware Design Patterns.

Once each third party part is wrapped in a known interface, you can iterate between suppliers and in-house prototypes or volume parts at very low cost. The only marginal cost is that of changing the wrapper itself.

Then, to expedite suppliers, ask them to deliver a certain set of performance characteristics as opposed to an engineering specification. "Do you have a transmission suitable for 100hp motor?", not "Here is our design for a transmission, can you build it?" Why should you wait months for a supplier to build a device to your specifications when they have a device that will satisfy your needs already in the catalog or in stock?

Many engineers are quick to design their own solution, which works to the team's advantage when the design team is also the volume manufacturing team. But in cases where some production is outsourced, sending a list of values and tests to the outsourced vendor and not sending an engineering specification gives the supplier the most room to innovate. This allows the vendor to do what they do best, that part, which is why you are partnering with them in the first place. Team WIKISPEED finds they get higher quality parts faster, often from within the vendor's existing stock.

The Other Ingredients

Important Things

In my experience, confirmed by what I have learned from my colleagues' experience, two things are necessary first to Scrum for Hardware.

First, it is necessary that **Scrum is understood** with the principles and values of the Agile manifesto at all levels in the company **especially in top management**. We will discuss this in more detail in the next section, Agile Management, but I can already anticipate that all the managers I have observed understanding Scrum correctly had a common feature: they needed it. There was an "urgency for change" determined by a real, compelling reason. Sometimes the needs were technical, other times they were business-oriented; but the driver was always there, and it was strong. I do not want to suggest that this is necessary a rule, but I have not observed a single manager yet approaching Scrum and making the effort to understand it without an urgent **need** of the benefits that this brings.

Secondly, it is necessary to finance a continuous research and development **process** (not an office) that identifies better ways to implement eXtreme Manufacturing principles every day. This requires the adoption of engineering practices, tools and machinery that at the time of writing the book fall under the name of Industry 4.0[250] as well as creative expedients to shorten the Feedback Loop, such as those described in the chapter on Scrum[251]. In the industry, these tools can be very expensive, even if their cost decreases every

[250]What Industry 4.0 includes is described in chapter 4

[251]See Chapter 6 - Scrum, Feedback Loop paragraph.

day and many countries grant tax deductions and incentives to companies that invest in this sense.

Doing Scrum for Hardware is not so different from doing it in Software, but it is certainly harder and more expensive. If a software team realizes that it has accumulated technical debt, in most cases all it needs is to convince its Product Owner about it. If that same Scrum Team in software invests a part of the Sprint in the recovery of technical debt – with refactoring for example – this is not so obvious to a large company's top management, in which maybe there are dozens of other teams. In Scrum for Hardware, however, a team that starts evolving and experimenting existing pieces of a product with something new will produce scraps of material and prototypes that will be immediately noticed by anyone who passes through the work area. Any *wasted* material is clearly visible and does not only cost time, as in software, but also money, and it takes up space. In this case, instead of minimizing the processing and waste material, typical optimization of literally interpreted Lean Manufacturing, it will be necessary to find an intelligent way to recycle, reuse or dispose of it effectively. Other times, to shorten the feedback loop it will be necessary to change supplier or renegotiate contracts; but rarely, in an industrial company, a single team has the autonomy to renegotiate or change a supplier. Often this task is assigned to a special office, called *procurement*, or at a level of Management away from the team. How to proceed? It will also be necessary for the people in charge of the purchases to understand the principles underlying production to be able to skillfully negotiate details that enhance the company's agility.

Agile Management

An Agile Manager does not do a different job than a traditional manager: like all managers, he *takes difficult decisions*. The difference lies in the way he does it. An Agile Manager has understood and metabolized the concept of Complexity, as defined in the

Cynefin model described in the appendix of the book, and he "knows not to know": as Peter Stevens once told me "**complicated** is when I know the questions but not the answers, **complex** is when I do not even know the questions". An Agile Manager makes decisions by prioritizing the ability to cope with change. He knows that nothing is definitive and this is the reason why he explores, with the rest of the organization, a world that is a continuous discovery. Agile is a style of Management closer to the definition of Leadership and acquiring it requires going through a long and winding path. A list of practical suggestions can be found in the Management 3.0[252] material by Jurgen Appelo[253], for which I report a small excerpt.

Guidelines for Managers in Complexity

1. Address complexity with complexity
2. Use a diversity of perspectives
3. Assume subjectivity and coevolution
4. Steal and tweak
5. Assume dependence on context
6. Anticipate, adapt, explore
7. Reduce the feedback cycle
8. Keep options open

Address complexity with complexity

The most complex tool available to you is your brain. To make sense of complex problems you can use tools such as storytelling, metaphors and visualization. **A system's complexity must be adjusted to the complexity of the system it is in**, says Michael R. Lissack in the book "The Interaction of Complexity and Management[254]"

[252]https://management30.com/

[253]http://jurgenappelo.com

[254]https://www.goodreads.com/book/show/4852736-the-interaction-of-complexity-and-management

Use a diversity of perspectives

Complexity per se is an anti-methodology, as opposed to the concept of the silver bullet, functional in every context, which instead the methodologies tend to propose. Combining a set of different perspectives, even if not perfectly positioned, produces a better point of view than a single well-defined point of view. This is the purpose, for example, of the collaboration between the Product Owner, who has a business focus, with the Development Team, which has a technical focus, in the Scrum Team itself with a single objective.

Assume subjectivity and coevolution

Complex systems are often also adaptive: their complexity is not only intrinsic but also due to a natural and unpredictable evolution of the system. In this context, the observer influences the observed system, just as the system in turn influences the observer. When cause and effect are interdependent, one can solve a situation even by focusing on another.

Steal and tweak

Successful systems spend much of their time copying and adapting ideas from others. Innovation is often imagined as a process of creating new things from scratch; often, however, innovation passes from the transposition of a good idea from one domain to another or from an unprecedented combination of existing ideas.

Assume dependence on context

Be skeptical: it is not sure that what worked in the past or for other functions will work today for you too. "Any relationship that anyone identifies between a management action and an obtained result may have more to do with time and place than with the action itself," says Ralph Stacey for example in the book "Complexity and Organizational Reality[255]".

Anticipate, adapt, explore

Explore a situation by imagining improvements (anticipate), trying something (explore) and responding to the change you get (adapt). In the book "The Toyota Way[256]" we read, in fact, "An evolving and improving system requires by its nature a continuous experimentation".

Reduce the feedback cycle

"The only way to win is to learn faster than others" says Eric Ries in the book "The Lean Startup[257]". Systems that have a slower feedback loop have a higher extinction rate. It is necessary to iterate, every day faster and faster.

Keep options open

In the book The Interaction of Complexity and Management[258] we read, "The absorption of complexity involves creating risk hedging options and strategies", even outside your expectations. Get ready for any kind of surprise.

In Detail

Another aspect to take into consideration is the ability of systems theory[259]. We need to make decisions that involve and consider the

[255] https://www.goodreads.com/book/show/9927574-complexity-and-organizational-reality
[256] https://www.goodreads.com/book/show/161789.The_Toyota_Way
[257] https://www.goodreads.com/book/show/10127019-the-lean-startup
[258] https://www.goodreads.com/book/show/4852736-the-interaction-of-complexity-and-management
[259] https://en.wikipedia.org/wiki/Systems_theory

whole system, to avoid actions that locally appear to be good but that do not improve, or in the worst cases, degrade the performance at the system level. Peter Senge extensively explores this theme, for example, in the book "The fifth discipline[260]". The theme of Agile Management is very broad and a complete discussion is beyond the scope of this book. Those who wish to further explore the subject are advised to read the following:

- The Leader's Guide to Radical Management: Reinventing the Workplace for the 21st Century[261] - Stephen Denning
- The Fifth Discipline: The Art & Practice of The Learning Organization[262] - Peter Senge
- Management 3.0: Leading Agile Developers, Developing Agile Leaders[263] - Jurgen Appelo
- The Interaction of Complexity and Management[264] - Michael Lissack
- Complexity and Organizational Reality[265] - Ralph D. Stacey

Well begun is half done

I am not a lover of proverbs, but I think this is appropriate in our context. Especially if you are about to start your first project with Scrum for Hardware, what you need is to start with a well done Liftoff.

[260]https://en.wikipedia.org/wiki/The_Fifth_Discipline

[261]https://www.goodreads.com/book/show/8873049-the-leader-s-guide-to-radical-management

[262]https://www.goodreads.com/book/show/255127.The_Fifth_Discipline

[263]https://www.goodreads.com/book/show/10210821-management-3-0

[264]https://www.goodreads.com/book/show/4852736-the-interaction-of-complexity-and-management

[265]https://www.goodreads.com/book/show/9927574-complexity-and-organizational-reality

The word Liftoff in English indicates a phase of rocket take-off: this is the moment in which the maximum amount of energy is needed, when adequate force is necessary to overcome gravity in order to launch the vehicle into orbit. The book "Liftoff - Start and Sustain Successful Agile Teams" by Diana Larsen and Ainsley Nies introduced the Liftoff concept for project launches. That is an event to be held before the start of a project or the start of the development of a new product, with the aim of instilling the team with the impetus that will lead it to success. The duration of the Liftoff can vary from half a day for the easiest activities on already run-in teams, up to a few weeks. It is unwise to go beyond the duration of a sprint.

Participants

Participants are numerous: there is the presence of a facilitator who takes care of the process and that of all the teams involved, complete with leadership figures (SM and PO in case of Scrum team or Coordinators for teams of other methodologies or frameworks). It is also important that the product manager and the key sponsors participate, above all in the strategic alignment activities. Optionally trainers and coaches can take part in training, if foreseen during the event.

Logistics

It takes a lot of space, well organized with large free walls to display produced artifacts, in order to always have them available. For the Liftoffs, some companies choose equipped, pleasant and comfortable spaces inside congress centers; others prefer quiet places, perhaps outdoors, in the green with spas, swimming pool and other amenities. Changing the scene helps to focus attention and to break the patterns of continuous distraction to which we are continuously exposed in the working environment. Furthermore, having plenty of space in nature reduces stress, facilitates concentration and creativity and serves as a motivating element. The conversations that take place in the breaks become precious and open the chances to serendipity[266]. It is also important that there are some kinds of comfort items, such as drinks and snacks, available for the whole duration of the event.

Never Too Late

Events like this bring such a benefit, that some companies organize them even for already started projects: in situations where conflicts arise due to the lack of alignment of the key figures of a project, the execution of a Liftoff allowed bringing the activities back to the right track by saving the project from being wrecked. Liftoff repetitions are frequent even in cases where they substantially change the composition of the core team, the focus or the product area. In similar cases, designing the activities described later in the

[266]https://en.wikipedia.org/wiki/Serendipity

Agile Chartering section, it is necessary to select the most relevant ones.

The Agenda

The agenda consists of three main parts:

- Setting the Stage
- Agile Chartering
- Retrospective and Closing

Setting the Stage serves to create the appropriate climate and prepare the ground for the next part of *Agile Chartering*, which will actually produce the artifacts useful to start the project. The final *Retrospective* is aimed at examining how the Liftoff itself has been carried out and is used to identify any problems to be faced quickly before the start of the project and to capitalize on the learning process, also in view of a future Liftoff.

Setting the Stage

The first activities aim at creating a climate of collaboration and creativity useful to make the Liftoff a successful event. The "One Word Check-In[267] method" consists of having each participant tell a term that represents his or her expectations concerning the event. In this way, everyone will speak at the very beginning of the meeting; and this is encouraged on the basis of studies that show that, if we intervene in the first 5 minutes of a meeting, we are predisposed to participate, differently from passive listening. It goes without saying that what we want from a Liftoff is that everyone makes his or her own contribution. Another suggested activity at this stage, in cases where there is a history of previous events, could be a retrospective from which to bring out common

[267]http://www.funretrospectives.com/one-word/

learning, usable as a starting point. Further introduction events, especially if the subject matter of the Liftoff is new, can be a Lean Coffee[268] or something longer like an Open Space. If the Liftoff lasts several days, it may be appropriate to think about a social event at dinnertime or later, recommended if you are offsite and there are people on the road. It is useful to keep in mind that, depending on the origin of the participants, the uses may vary (in Italy, I have generally seen organizing meeting at the pizzeria, while in Germany we inexorably ended up in beer halls). If possible, also include this kind of meetings in the event budget: very productive conversations often emerge with good food and alcohol and can be considered a safe investment.

Agile Chartering

For Agile Chartering we mean a high-level summary of the key success factors of a project or product, typically elaborated in the form of posters on the walls of the team room for the duration of the project. According to the Agile Chartering model of the Liftoff book, there are three phases to complete: *Purpose, Alignment, Context.*

Purpose

Purpose is the reason why a project is carried out; the activity with this name offers support and inspiration in trying to understand what drives us to create a given product. It consists of three artifacts: Product Vision, Team Mission and Mission Test.

Product Vision is the vision of what you want to achieve in the finished state, the guiding image in the search for resources that fund the initiative. It is usually presented by a manager at the beginning of the chartering and is extended and clarified with the collaboration of all those present. There are many ways to get a

[268]http://leancoffee.org

product vision from a group; what I prefer is a Lego® Serious Play®[269] workshop.

Team Mission is the way the team intends to reach the Vision. To bring out the Mission, a good method could be to create a Canvas, for example on the model of Lean Canvas[270] by Ash Maurya, of Product Canvas[271] by Roman Pichler or also of Opportunity Canvas[272] by Jeff Patton.

Mission Tests can also be defined as critical criteria through which we can determine our success. If not all the people involved in the initiative are aligned with each other, they will hardly get the desired success. The Mission Tests can already appear in the Canvas designed for the Mission, or they can be generated explicitly with an activity like the Futurspective Path to Nirvana[273].

Alignment

The Alignment phase has the objective to create the alliance that leads to the result described in the Purpose phase. To create an alliance, the objective of the initiative must be aligned with the personal objectives of the people who take part into it. We all win if we win together; or, as stated in the slogan of the Liftoff book, "Came As Individuals, Left As a Team". The activities envisaged in the Alignment are the identification of the core teams, if necessary, the definition of working agreements and the definition of values. In Scrum, there are several Working Agreements:

- The Working Agreement, understood as the set of simple rules that govern the life of the team.
- The Definition of Done, a set of criteria that must be respected to consider a job as complete.

[269]https://en.wikipedia.org/wiki/Lego_Serious_Play
[270]https://blog.leanstack.com/why-lean-canvas-vs-business-model-canvas-af62c0f250f0
[271]http://www.romanpichler.com/tools/product-canvas/
[272]http://jpattonassociates.com/opportunity-canvas/
[273]http://www.funretrospectives.com/path-to-nirvana/

- The Definition of Ready, a criterion that establishes when the items of a Product Backlog are sufficiently clear to be eligible for Sprint Planning.

The last described activity is that of identifying team values. Some teams adopt Scrum values: Respect, Courage, Commitment, Openness and Focus; others prefer to choose their own. It depends a lot on the context: my advice as a coach is to leave the team in full autonomy.

Context

No man is an island... let alone a team in a company. It is necessary to identify how the nascent initiative is placed in the company context and which interactions it must have with the Single Matter Experts, with the Stakeholders and with other teams. To do this, it is useful to create a chart that illustrates the relationships.

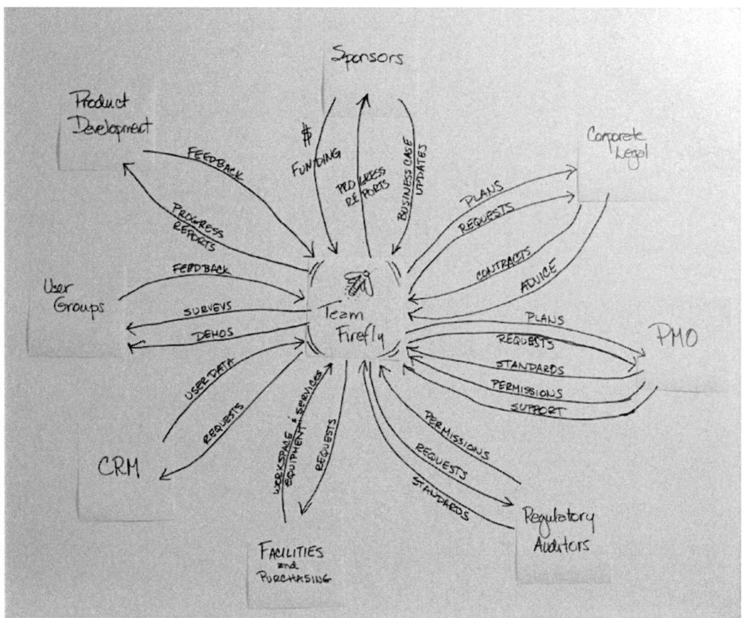

Example of "Team Boundaries" from the Liftoff book

Other activities of this last phase are the identification and discussion of available resources (time, external media, budget, workspaces, suppliers and equipment, tools, training, etc.). Another fundamental aspect is the discussion of the product's starting architecture, its modules and interfaces: these, as seen in the previous chapter, are the basis of an Agile Architecture. To finish, it is necessary to proceed to a risk analysis activity, for example listing a FUD backlog[274] and then categorizing the items one by one in a ROAM scheme: Resolved, Owned, Accepted, Mitigated[275].

The final phase consists in the creation of the initial Product Backlog, for example through the method of User Story Mapping[276] created by Jeff Patton, which can also be used with tangible prod-

[274]"Fear, Uncertainty and Doubts".

[275]Resolved, Owned, Accepted, Mitigated. Each activity is discussed and classified in one of these four categories.

[276]http://jpattonassociates.com/user-story-mapping/

ucts.

Image from jpattonassociates.com

All the artifacts discussed so far, composing Agile Chartering, are to be considered emerging. They need to be reviewed periodically and updated according to the evolution of the team; retrospectives will be a good time for this review.

Retrospective and Closing

At the end of all the activities, it will be appropriate to collect the material (I absolutely recommend taking many pictures), to list the subsequent steps and to close with a Liftoff Retrospective. The book also suggests a session of 360° appreciation[277], useful to get out from the event with the right mood.

All Hands

An organization that has achieved a fair degree of agility or has extended the use of Scrum beyond the boundaries of mere product development, will find itself having a release cycle that "beats the

[277]http://www.funretrospectives.com/360-degrees-appreciation/

time" of the entire company. For example, we had two releases per year in Ubuntu, while the cycle is quarterly or four times a year in many other companies. On the releases, or at least no more than once a year, it is advisable to find a moment in which the entire organization ponders on what has been produced until then, shares successes and failures, reinforces the vision and drives enthusiastically all the collaborators towards the new goal. Many companies also use this time to meet the most important customers and organize socializing moments that encourage the corporate culture while creating new business opportunities and reinforcing the brand perception. These events are known as "user conference" or "user group" or "developer summit" or "all hands" depending on whether the emphasis is on the user or on the internal staff. Some perform the two events on different days of the same week, in order to have specific moments to talk about the topics that they want to keep restricted only to the circle of collaborators. The duration of these events varies a lot, from a couple of days up to even a week or two.

Generally all companies, but especially those that have offices distributed in different countries, find it very useful to meet everyone in person, as face-to-face communication, topped with moments of socialization, makes interpersonal relationships easier, informal and direct for the rest of the year.

Open Space

Beyond the typical conference format, in which the whole program is decided and formalized before the event, a free and emerging format is increasingly being applied to companies traditionally more inclined to structure any situation, such as banks. The best-known format for organizing a congress free space is called Open Space Technology[278]. It is based on four principles and one rule:

1. Whoever comes is the right people

[278]https://en.wikipedia.org/wiki/Open_Space_Technology

2. Whatever happens is the only thing that could have
3. Whenever it starts is the right time
4. When it's over, it's over

The only rule is called the "law of two feet", that is:

- If at any time during our time together you find yourself in any situation where you are neither learning nor contributing, use your two feet and go someplace else where you can be more productive.

It is easy to understand how these principles and this simple rule create a dynamic and spontaneous environment.

A facilitator directs the event or more than one if the conference is particularly large.

How does it work? Before the conference begins, an empty program grid is prepared, showing the available spaces and the time slots for the planning. The grid is generally analogical, set up on a wall covered in sticky notes; in crowded conferences, you can use software that is accessible from PC and mobile.

At the beginning of the Open Space, a "market" moment is organized in which all the participants gather in a single room and the facilitator explains the principles, the law and the practical rules to use the tools and the available spaces. Then you leave some time to allow the schedule to fill up for at least the first day of the event. If you use an analog schedule on a wall, normally every proponent presents his or her session in a few words (less than 1 minute).

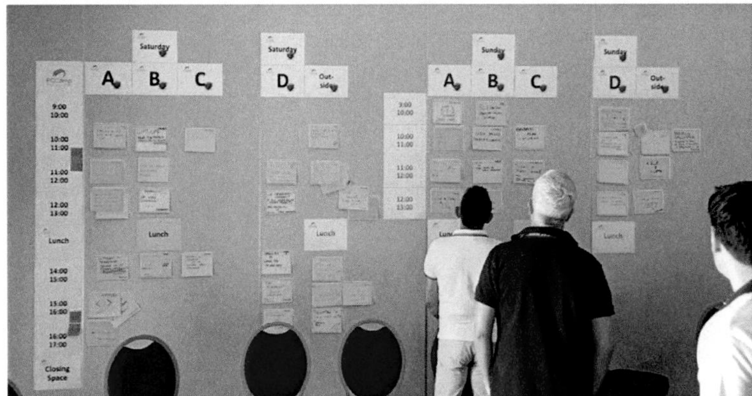

Program of POCamp 2016

At that point, the event begins, and a sort of "organized chaos" creates magic, generating interesting and productive conversations.

The proponents of each session act as facilitators of the sessions themselves and have to worry that the times are strictly respected to avoid that the sessions overlap, and collect the synthesis of the produced material.

Usually, a collective final space is used to share in rotation all the things that they liked the most and the feedback to better organize it the following time.

POCamp 2016 final retrospective

Practices used in UDS

As stated in the second chapter, the Ubuntu Developer Summit was a sort of open conference extended for five days, from Monday to Friday, with a participation that has also reached 800 people. In this section, I will list the practices that have been refined over the years in this event.

The **schedule** was kept on a proprietary software product, called summit.ubuntu.com[279]. The schedule was divided in Tracks (example: Desktop, Server, Mobile, Community, etc.), each Track had a leader, clearly identifiable by a special shirt, which served as session facilitator. To avoid duplication of sessions, he received notification of each new session and all participants were invited to speak with the single track leader to make sure that the topic was not already present in other sessions. The insertion of the proposals began a few

[279]Unfortunately this website is not maintained online anymore.

days before the event itself, so that at the opening of the conference there was already material to cover the first days. The rest of the days were filled with new proposals that gradually emerged during the works.

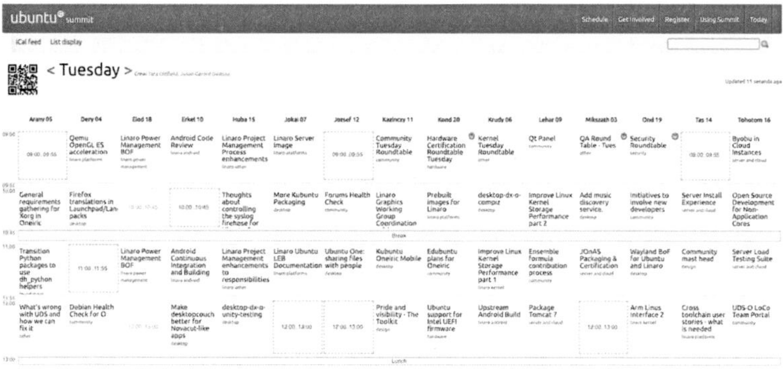

Half Day Program of UDS, May 2011

The **spaces** were organized in a manic way. In each room where the sessions were held there were two projectors, one available to project something from the proponent's PC, such as slides or other material, the other to project the **minutes** of the session itself. Each session aimed at having actions at its end, so the approach was very pragmatic. All participants, using tools that allowed the simultaneous editing of a file, collaboratively updated the report of what was discussed with the list of actions. The tools that were used were Gobby[280] at first and then the most modern Etherpad[281]. Thanks to the projection of the minutes of the current session, all the participants, even those who did not have the PC with them, could see in real time what was transcribed, and suggest changes or ideas. Furthermore, those who arrived when the session had already started would immediately see what had been discussed up to that point.

The actions emerged from each session were tracked on Launch-

[280]http://gobby.github.io/

[281]http://etherpad.org/

pad[282], another software developed internally within Ubuntu to manage the development of the project, in a component called Blueprint[283]. These tasks were voluntarily taken on by the participants and a burn-down chart[284] was automatically generated on them indicating the progress on a site called status.ubuntu.com[285].

It was also possible to participate remotely in each session. The session's audio was broadcasted in streaming and distant participants could ask questions and intervene through a chat IRC[286].

Each session could have different objectives: some were of consideration and discussion about past things, to suggest actions for improvement; others discussed the future instead, in order to plan the works to come.

Particularly interesting from the point of view of the spirit of the project was an initiative called Ubuntu Free Culture Showcase[287]. It was a session in which we were trying to coordinate a collection of material that could be included in the subsequent release and better represent the essence of the Ubuntu word. The material consisted of images, sounds, music or even short movies and animations. A jury took care to choose the most representative items that were included in a package that the users could then install in their PC. From a certain moment on, the most significant image was also included in the background images of the system's default installation.

The opening slot of the first day was reserved to Mark Shuttleworth's Keynote in which the vision for the next release was emphasized. After-lunch slots, however, were reserved to various kinds of Keynote Speeches. The fact of having a motivating talk in the most critical slot, just after lunch, was an intelligent practice as it allowed us to be more focused on the work. The community

[282]https://launchpad.net/

[283]https://launchpad.net/+tour/feature-tracking

[284]https://en.wikipedia.org/wiki/Burn_down_chart

[285]Unfortunately this website is not maintained online anymore.

[286]https://en.wikipedia.org/wiki/Internet_Relay_Chat

[287]https://wiki.ubuntu.com/UbuntuFreeCultureShowcase

manager Jono Bacon traditionally animated the closing slot of the last day that is the feedback and greetings moment.

How to start

In Mike Cohn's book "Succeeding with Agile[288]", he talks about a model of adoption of Scrum, which has always fascinated me, represented with the acronym ADAPT. The first letter stands for **Awareness**. To start a successful agile transformation, we begin by conveying to people the awareness that there is a different way of working and that this makes work very productive and even fun. This can be done in different ways: training, workshops, conferences, stories of other companies, etc. It is then necessary to wait for the **Desire** to experience this new way. The best way to do this is to suggest starting a pilot project that people voluntarily decide to be part of. In this way, the **Skill** is developed to work with Scrum, thanks also to targeted training, coaching and team building initiatives and through the **Practice**, you acquire the mastery of the method, so you can **Transfer** these skills to new teams by extending their adoption across the organization. The most common mistake in many companies is the rush to extend the new method to the whole organization without having understood and successfully practiced it yet. The secret to overcoming a certain reticence and the normal resistance to change is to build success starting from success itself: to demonstrate that the adoption of Scrum allows better work in a tangible way, amplifying people's learning and making work easier and fun.

---

[288]https://www.mountaingoatsoftware.com/books/succeeding-with-agile-software-development-using-scrum

Appendix

Scrum Guide

In this chapter you'll find the verbatim copy of the Scrum Guide, version released in November 2017. The Scrum Guide is available on the scrumguides.org[289] website and released under the Creative Commons BY-SA license, which is described on the creativecommons.org[290] website.

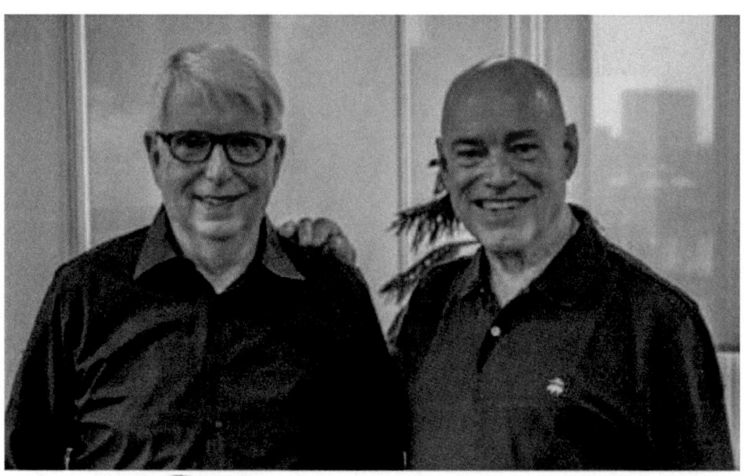

[289]http://scrumguides.org/

[290]https://creativecommons.org/licenses/by-sa/4.0/

Purpose of the Scrum Guide

Scrum is a framework for developing, delivering, and sustaining complex products. This Guide contains the definition of Scrum. This definition consists of Scrum's roles, events, artifacts, and the rules that bind them together. Ken Schwaber and Jeff Sutherland developed Scrum; the Scrum Guide is written and provided by them. Together, they stand behind the Scrum Guide.

Definition of Scrum

Scrum (n): A framework within which people can address complex adaptive problems, while productively and creatively delivering products of the highest possible value.

Scrum is:

- Lightweight
- Simple to understand
- Difficult to master

Scrum is a process framework that has been used to manage work on complex products since the early 1990s. Scrum is not a process, technique, or definitive method. Rather, it is a framework within which you can employ various processes and techniques. Scrum makes clear the relative efficacy of your product management and work techniques so that you can continuously improve the product, the team, and the working environment.

The Scrum framework consists of Scrum Teams and their associated roles, events, artifacts, and rules. Each component within the framework serves a specific purpose and is essential to Scrum's success and usage.

The rules of Scrum bind together the roles, events, and artifacts, governing the relationships and interaction between them. The rules of Scrum are described throughout the body of this document.

Specific tactics for using the Scrum framework vary and are described elsewhere.

Uses of Scrum

Scrum was initially developed for managing and developing products. Starting in the early 1990s, Scrum has been used extensively, worldwide, to:

1. Research and identify viable markets, technologies, and product capabilities;
2. Develop products and enhancements;
3. Release products and enhancements, as frequently as many times per day;
4. Develop and sustain Cloud (online, secure, on-demand) and other operational environments for product use; and,
5. Sustain and renew products.

Scrum has been used to develop software, hardware, embedded software, networks of interacting function, autonomous vehicles, schools, government, marketing, managing the operation of organizations and almost everything we use in our daily lives, as individuals and societies.

As technology, market, and environmental complexities and their interactions have rapidly increased, Scrum's utility in dealing with complexity is proven daily.

Scrum proved especially effective in iterative and incremental knowledge transfer. Scrum is now widely used for products, services, and the management of the parent organization.

The essence of Scrum is a small team of people. The individual team is highly flexible and adaptive. These strengths continue operating in single, several, many, and networks of teams that develop, release, operate and sustain the work and work products of thousands of people. They collaborate and interoperate through sophisticated development architectures and target release environments.

When the words "develop" and "development" are used in the Scrum Guide, they refer to complex work, such as those types identified above.

Scrum Theory

Scrum is founded on empirical process control theory, or empiricism. Empiricism asserts that knowledge comes from experience and making decisions based on what is known. Scrum employs an iterative, incremental approach to optimize predictability and control risk. Three pillars uphold every implementation of empirical process control: transparency, inspection, and adaptation.

Transparency

Significant aspects of the process must be visible to those responsible for the outcome. Transparency requires those aspects be defined by a common standard so observers share a common understanding of what is being seen.

For example:

- A common language referring to the process must be shared by all participants; and,
- Those performing the work and those inspecting the resulting increment must share a common definition of "Done".

Inspection

Scrum users must frequently inspect Scrum artifacts and progress toward a Sprint Goal to detect undesirable variances. Their inspection should not be so frequent that inspection gets in the way of the work. Inspections are most beneficial when diligently performed by skilled inspectors at the point of work.

Adaptation

If an inspector determines that one or more aspects of a process deviate outside acceptable limits, and that the resulting product will be unacceptable, the process or the material being processed must be adjusted. An adjustment must be made as soon as possible to minimize further deviation.

Scrum prescribes four formal events for inspection and adaptation, as described in the Scrum Events section of this document:

- Sprint Planning
- Daily Scrum
- Sprint Review
- Sprint Retrospective

Scrum Values

When the values of commitment, courage, focus, openness and respect are embodied and lived by the Scrum Team, the Scrum pillars of transparency, inspection, and adaptation come to life and build trust for everyone. The Scrum Team members learn and explore those values as they work with the Scrum events, roles and artifacts.

Successful use of Scrum depends on people becoming more proficient in living these five values. People personally commit to achieving the goals of the Scrum Team. The Scrum Team members have courage to do the right thing and work on tough problems. Everyone focuses on the work of the Sprint and the goals of the Scrum Team. The Scrum Team and its stakeholders agree to be open about all the work and the challenges with performing the work. Scrum Team members respect each other to be capable, independent people.

The Scrum Team

The Scrum Team consists of a Product Owner, the Development Team, and a Scrum Master. Scrum Teams are self-organizing and cross-functional. Self-organizing teams choose how best to accomplish their work, rather than being directed by others outside the team. Cross-functional teams have all competencies needed to accomplish the work without depending on others not part of the team. The team model in Scrum is designed to optimize flexibility, creativity, and productivity. The Scrum Team has proven itself to be increasingly effective for all the earlier stated uses, and any complex work.

Scrum Teams deliver products iteratively and incrementally, maximizing opportunities for feedback. Incremental deliveries of "Done" product ensure a potentially useful version of working product is always available.

The Product Owner

The Product Owner is responsible for maximizing the value of the product resulting from work of the Development Team. How this is done may vary widely across organizations, Scrum Teams, and individuals.

The Product Owner is the sole person responsible for managing the Product Backlog. Product Backlog management includes:

- Clearly expressing Product Backlog items;
- Ordering the items in the Product Backlog to best achieve goals and missions;
- Optimizing the value of the work the Development Team performs;
- Ensuring that the Product Backlog is visible, transparent, and clear to all, and shows what the Scrum Team will work on next; and,
- Ensuring the Development Team understands items in the Product Backlog to the level needed.

The Product Owner may do the above work, or have the Development Team do it. However, the Product Owner remains accountable.

The Product Owner is one person, not a committee. The Product Owner may represent the desires of a committee in the Product Backlog, but those wanting to change a Product Backlog item's priority must address the Product Owner.

For the Product Owner to succeed, the entire organization must respect his or her decisions. The Product Owner's decisions are visible in the content and ordering of the Product Backlog. No one can force the Development Team to work from a different set of requirements.

The Development Team

The Development Team consists of professionals who do the work of delivering a potentially releasable Increment of "Done" product at the end of each Sprint. A "Done" increment is required at the Sprint Review. Only members of the Development Team create the Increment.

Development Teams are structured and empowered by the organization to organize and manage their own work. The resulting synergy optimizes the Development Team's overall efficiency and effectiveness.

Development Teams have the following characteristics:

- They are self-organizing. No one (not even the Scrum Master) tells the Development Team how to turn Product Backlog into Increments of potentially releasable functionality;
- Development Teams are cross-functional, with all the skills as a team necessary to create a product Increment;
- Scrum recognizes no titles for Development Team members, regardless of the work being performed by the person;
- Scrum recognizes no sub-teams in the Development Team, regardless of domains that need to be addressed like testing, architecture, operations, or business analysis; and,
- Individual Development Team members may have specialized skills and areas of focus, but accountability belongs to the Development Team as a whole.

Development Team Size

Optimal Development Team size is small enough to remain nimble and large enough to complete significant work within a Sprint. Fewer than three Development Team members decrease interaction and results in smaller productivity gains. Smaller Development Teams may encounter skill constraints during the Sprint, causing the Development Team to be unable to deliver a potentially releasable Increment. Having more than nine members requires too much coordination. Large Development Teams generate too much complexity for an empirical process to be useful. The Product Owner and Scrum Master roles are not included in this count unless they are also executing the work of the Sprint Backlog.

The Scrum Master

The Scrum Master is responsible for promoting and supporting Scrum as defined in the Scrum Guide. Scrum Masters do this by helping everyone understand Scrum theory, practices, rules, and values.

The Scrum Master is a servant-leader for the Scrum Team. The Scrum Master helps those outside the Scrum Team understand which of their interactions with the Scrum Team are helpful and which aren't. The Scrum Master helps everyone change these interactions to maximize the value created by the Scrum Team.

Scrum Master Service to the Product Owner

The Scrum Master serves the Product Owner in several ways, including:

- Ensuring that goals, scope, and product domain are understood by everyone on the Scrum Team as well as possible;
- Finding techniques for effective Product Backlog management;
- Helping the Scrum Team understand the need for clear and concise Product Backlog items;
- Understanding product planning in an empirical environment;
- Ensuring the Product Owner knows how to arrange the Product Backlog to maximize value;
- Understanding and practicing agility; and,
- Facilitating Scrum events as requested or needed.

Scrum Master Service to the Development Team

The Scrum Master serves the Development Team in several ways, including:

- Coaching the Development Team in self-organization and cross-functionality;
- Helping the Development Team to create high-value products;
- Removing impediments to the Development Team's progress;
- Facilitating Scrum events as requested or needed; and,
- Coaching the Development Team in organizational environments in which Scrum is not yet fully adopted and understood.

Scrum Master Service to the Organization

The Scrum Master serves the organization in several ways, including:

- Leading and coaching the organization in its Scrum adoption;
- Planning Scrum implementations within the organization;
- Helping employees and stakeholders understand and enact Scrum and empirical product development;
- Causing change that increases the productivity of the Scrum Team; and,
- Working with other Scrum Masters to increase the effectiveness of the application of Scrum in the organization.

Scrum Events

Prescribed events are used in Scrum to create regularity and to minimize the need for meetings not defined in Scrum. All events are time-boxed events, such that every event has a maximum duration. Once a Sprint begins, its duration is fixed and cannot be shortened or lengthened. The remaining events may end whenever the purpose of the event is achieved, ensuring an appropriate amount of time is spent without allowing waste in the process.

Other than the Sprint itself, which is a container for all other events, each event in Scrum is a formal opportunity to inspect and adapt something. These events are specifically designed to enable critical transparency and inspection. Failure to include any of these events results in reduced transparency and is a lost opportunity to inspect and adapt.

The Sprint

The heart of Scrum is a Sprint, a time-box of one month or less during which a "Done", useable, and potentially releasable product Increment is created. Sprints have consistent durations throughout a development effort. A new Sprint starts immediately after the conclusion of the previous Sprint.

Sprints contain and consist of the Sprint Planning, Daily Scrums, the development work, the Sprint Review, and the Sprint Retrospective.

During the Sprint:

- No changes are made that would endanger the Sprint Goal;
- Quality goals do not decrease; and,
- Scope may be clarified and re-negotiated between the Product Owner and Development Team as more is learned.

Each Sprint may be considered a project with no more than a one-month horizon. Like projects, Sprints are used to accomplish something. Each Sprint has a goal of what is to be built, a design and flexible plan that will guide building it, the work, and the resultant product increment.

Sprints are limited to one calendar month. When a Sprint's horizon is too long the definition of what is being built may change, complexity may rise, and risk may increase. Sprints enable predictability by ensuring inspection and adaptation of progress toward a Sprint Goal at least every calendar month. Sprints also limit risk to one calendar month of cost.

Cancelling a Sprint

A Sprint can be cancelled before the Sprint time-box is over. Only the Product Owner has the authority to cancel the Sprint, although he or she may do so under influence from the stakeholders, the Development Team, or the Scrum Master.

A Sprint would be cancelled if the Sprint Goal becomes obsolete. This might occur if the company changes direction or if market or technology conditions change. In general, a Sprint should be cancelled if it no longer makes sense given the circumstances. But, due to the short duration of Sprints, cancellation rarely makes sense.

When a Sprint is cancelled, any completed and "Done" Product Backlog items are reviewed. If part of the work is potentially releasable, the Product Owner typically accepts it. All incomplete Product Backlog Items are re-estimated and put back on the Product Backlog. The work done on them depreciates quickly and must be frequently re-estimated.

Sprint cancellations consume resources, since everyone regroups in another Sprint Planning to start another Sprint. Sprint cancellations are often traumatic to the Scrum Team, and are very uncommon.

Sprint Planning

The work to be performed in the Sprint is planned at the Sprint Planning. This plan is created by the collaborative work of the entire Scrum Team.

Sprint Planning is time-boxed to a maximum of eight hours for a one-month Sprint. For shorter Sprints, the event is usually shorter. The Scrum Master ensures that the event takes place and that attendants understand its purpose. The Scrum Master teaches the Scrum Team to keep it within the time-box.

Sprint Planning answers the following:

- What can be delivered in the Increment resulting from the upcoming Sprint?
- How will the work needed to deliver the Increment be achieved?

Topic One: What can be done this Sprint?

The Development Team works to forecast the functionality that will be developed during the Sprint. The Product Owner discusses the objective that the Sprint should achieve and the Product Backlog items that, if completed in the Sprint, would achieve the Sprint Goal. The entire Scrum Team collaborates on understanding the work of the Sprint.

The input to this meeting is the Product Backlog, the latest product Increment, projected capacity of the Development Team during the Sprint, and past performance of the Development Team. The number of items selected from the Product Backlog for the Sprint is solely up to the Development Team. Only the Development Team can assess what it can accomplish over the upcoming Sprint.

During Sprint Planning the Scrum Team also crafts a Sprint Goal. The Sprint Goal is an objective that will be met within the Sprint through the implementation of the Product Backlog, and it provides guidance to the Development Team on why it is building the Increment.

Topic Two: how will the chosen work get done?

Having set the Sprint Goal and selected the Product Backlog items for the Sprint, the Development Team decides how it will build this functionality into a "Done" product Increment during the Sprint. The Product Backlog items selected for this Sprint plus the plan for delivering them is called the Sprint Backlog.

The Development Team usually starts by designing the system and the work needed to convert the Product Backlog into a working product Increment. Work may be of varying size, or estimated effort. However, enough work is planned during Sprint Planning for the Development Team to forecast what it believes it can do in the upcoming Sprint. Work planned for the first days of the Sprint by the Development Team is decomposed by the end of this meeting, often to units of one day or less. The Development Team self-organizes to undertake the work in the Sprint Backlog, both during Sprint Planning and as needed throughout the Sprint.

The Product Owner can help to clarify the selected Product Backlog items and make trade-offs. If the Development Team determines it has too much or too little work, it may renegotiate the selected Product Backlog items with the Product Owner. The Development Team may also invite other people to attend to provide technical or domain advice.

By the end of the Sprint Planning, the Development Team should be able to explain to the Product Owner and Scrum Master how it intends to work as a self-organizing team to accomplish the Sprint Goal and create the anticipated Increment.

Sprint Goal

The Sprint Goal is an objective set for the Sprint that can be met through the implementation of Product Backlog. It provides guidance to the Development Team on why it is building the Increment. It is created during the Sprint Planning meeting. The Sprint Goal gives the Development Team some flexibility regarding the functionality implemented within the Sprint. The selected Product Backlog items deliver one coherent function, which can be the Sprint Goal. The Sprint Goal can be any other coherence that causes the Development Team to work together rather than on separate initiatives.

As the Development Team works, it keeps the Sprint Goal in mind. In order to satisfy the Sprint Goal, it implements functionality and technology. If the work turns out to be different than the Development Team expected, they collaborate with the Product Owner to negotiate the scope of Sprint Backlog within the Sprint.

Daily Scrum

The Daily Scrum is a 15-minute time-boxed event for the Development Team. The Daily Scrum is held every day of the Sprint. At it, the Development Team plans work for the next 24 hours. This optimizes team collaboration and performance by inspecting the work since the last Daily Scrum and forecasting upcoming Sprint work. The Daily Scrum is held at the same time and place each day to reduce complexity.

The Development Team uses the Daily Scrum to inspect progress toward the Sprint Goal and to inspect how progress is trending toward completing the work in the Sprint Backlog. The Daily Scrum optimizes the probability that the Development Team will meet the Sprint Goal. Every day, the Development Team should understand how it intends to work together as a self-organizing team to accomplish the Sprint Goal and create the anticipated Increment by the end of the Sprint.

The structure of the meeting is set by the Development Team and can be conducted in different ways if it focuses on progress toward the Sprint Goal. Some Development Teams will use questions, some will be more discussion based. Here is an example of what might be used:

- What did I do yesterday that helped the Development Team meet the Sprint Goal?
- What will I do today to help the Development Team meet the Sprint Goal?
- Do I see any impediment that prevents me or the Development Team from meeting the Sprint Goal?

The Development Team or team members often meet immediately after the Daily Scrum for detailed discussions, or to adapt, or replan, the rest of the Sprint's work.

The Scrum Master ensures that the Development Team has the meeting, but the Development Team is responsible for conducting the Daily Scrum. The Scrum Master teaches the Development Team to keep the Daily Scrum within the 15-minute time-box.

The Daily Scrum is an internal meeting for the Development Team. If others are present, the Scrum Master ensures that they do not disrupt the meeting.

Daily Scrums improve communications, eliminate other meetings, identify impediments to development for removal, highlight and promote quick decision-making, and improve the Development Team's level of knowledge. This is a key inspect and adapt meeting.

Sprint Review

A Sprint Review is held at the end of the Sprint to inspect the Increment and adapt the Product Backlog if needed. During the Sprint Review, the Scrum Team and stakeholders collaborate about what was done in the Sprint. Based on that and any changes to the Product Backlog during the Sprint, attendees collaborate on the next things that could be done to optimize value. This is an informal meeting, not a status meeting, and the presentation of the Increment is intended to elicit feedback and foster collaboration.

This is at most a four-hour meeting for one-month Sprints. For shorter Sprints, the event is usually shorter. The Scrum Master ensures that the event takes place and that attendees understand its purpose. The Scrum Master teaches everyone involved to keep it within the time-box.

The Sprint Review includes the following elements:

- Attendees include the Scrum Team and key stakeholders invited by the Product Owner;
- The Product Owner explains what Product Backlog items have been "Done" and what has not been "Done";
- The Development Team discusses what went well during the Sprint, what problems it ran into, and how those problems were solved;
- The Development Team demonstrates the work that it has "Done" and answers questions about the Increment;
- The Product Owner discusses the Product Backlog as it stands. He or she projects likely target and delivery dates based on progress to date (if needed);
- The entire group collaborates on what to do next, so that the Sprint Review provides valuable input to subsequent Sprint Planning;
- Review of how the marketplace or potential use of the product might have changed what is the most valuable thing to do next; and,
- Review of the timeline, budget, potential capabilities, and marketplace for the next anticipated releases of functionality or capability of the product.

The result of the Sprint Review is a revised Product Backlog that defines the probable Product Backlog items for the next Sprint. The Product Backlog may also be adjusted overall to meet new opportunities.

Sprint Retrospective

The Sprint Retrospective is an opportunity for the Scrum Team to inspect itself and create a plan for improvements to be enacted during the next Sprint.

The Sprint Retrospective occurs after the Sprint Review and prior to the next Sprint Planning. This is at most a three-hour meeting for one-month Sprints. For shorter Sprints, the event is usually shorter. The Scrum Master ensures that the event takes place and that attendants understand its purpose.

The Scrum Master ensures that the meeting is positive and productive. The Scrum Master teaches all to keep it within the time-box. The Scrum Master participates as a peer team member in the meeting from the accountability over the Scrum process.

The purpose of the Sprint Retrospective is to:

- Inspect how the last Sprint went with regards to people, relationships, process, and tools;
- Identify and order the major items that went well and potential improvements; and,
- Create a plan for implementing improvements to the way the Scrum Team does its work.

The Scrum Master encourages the Scrum Team to improve, within the Scrum process framework, its development process and practices to make it more effective and enjoyable for the next Sprint. During each Sprint Retrospective, the Scrum Team plans ways to increase product quality by improving work processes or adapting the definition of "Done", if appropriate and not in conflict with product or organizational standards.

By the end of the Sprint Retrospective, the Scrum Team should have identified improvements that it will implement in the next Sprint. Implementing these improvements in the next Sprint is the adaptation to the inspection of the Scrum Team itself. Although improvements may be implemented at any time, the Sprint Retrospective provides a formal opportunity to focus on inspection and adaptation.

Scrum Artifacts

Scrum's artifacts represent work or value to provide transparency and opportunities for inspection and adaptation. Artifacts defined by Scrum are specifically designed to maximize transparency of key information so that everybody has the same understanding of the artifact.

Product Backlog

The Product Backlog is an ordered list of everything that is known to be needed in the product. It is the single source of requirements for any changes to be made to the product. The Product Owner is responsible for the Product Backlog, including its content, availability, and ordering.

A Product Backlog is never complete. The earliest development of it lays out the initially known and best-understood requirements. The Product Backlog evolves as the product and the environment in which it will be used evolves. The Product Backlog is dynamic; it constantly changes to identify what the product needs to be appropriate, competitive, and useful. If a product exists, its Product Backlog also exists.

The Product Backlog lists all features, functions, requirements, enhancements, and fixes that constitute the changes to be made to the product in future releases. Product Backlog items have the attributes of a description, order, estimate, and value. Product Backlog items often include test descriptions that will prove its completeness when "Done".

As a product is used and gains value, and the marketplace provides feedback, the Product Backlog becomes a larger and more exhaustive list. Requirements never stop changing, so a Product Backlog is a living artifact. Changes in business requirements, market conditions, or technology may cause changes in the Product Backlog.

Multiple Scrum Teams often work together on the same product. One Product Backlog is used to describe the upcoming work on the product. A Product Backlog attribute that groups items may then be employed.

Product Backlog refinement is the act of adding detail, estimates, and order to items in the Product Backlog. This is an ongoing process in which the Product Owner and the Development Team collaborate on the details of Product Backlog items. During Product Backlog refinement, items are reviewed and revised. The Scrum Team decides how and when refinement is done. Refinement usually consumes no more than 10% of the capacity of the Development Team. However, Product Backlog items can be updated at any time by the Product Owner or at the Product Owner's discretion.

Higher ordered Product Backlog items are usually clearer and more detailed than lower ordered ones. More precise estimates are made based on the greater clarity and increased detail; the lower the order, the less detail. Product Backlog items that will occupy the Development Team for the upcoming Sprint are refined so that any one item can reasonably be "Done" within the Sprint time-box. Product Backlog items that can be "Done" by the Development Team within one Sprint are deemed "Ready" for selection in a Sprint Planning. Product Backlog items usually acquire this degree of transparency through the above described refining activities.

The Development Team is responsible for all estimates. The Product Owner may influence the Development Team by helping it understand and select trade-offs, but the people who will perform the work make the final estimate.

Monitoring Progress Toward Goals

At any point in time, the total work remaining to reach a goal can be summed. The Product Owner tracks this total work remaining at least every Sprint Review. The Product Owner compares this amount with work remaining at previous Sprint Reviews to assess progress toward completing projected work by the desired time for the goal. This information is made transparent to all stakeholders.

Various projective practices upon trending have been used to forecast progress, like burn-downs, burn-ups, or cumulative flows. These have proven useful. However, these do not replace the importance of empiricism. In complex environments, what will happen is unknown. Only what has already happened may be used for forward-looking decision-making.

Sprint Backlog

The Sprint Backlog is the set of Product Backlog items selected for the Sprint, plus a plan for delivering the product Increment and realizing the Sprint Goal. The Sprint Backlog is a forecast by the Development Team about what functionality will be in the next Increment and the work needed to deliver that functionality into a "Done" Increment.

The Sprint Backlog makes visible all the work that the Development Team identifies as necessary to meet the Sprint Goal. To ensure continuous improvement, it includes at least one high priority process improvement identified in the previous Retrospective meeting.

The Sprint Backlog is a plan with enough detail that changes in progress can be understood in the Daily Scrum. The Development Team modifies the Sprint Backlog throughout the Sprint, and the Sprint Backlog emerges during the Sprint. This emergence occurs as the Development Team works through the plan and learns more about the work needed to achieve the Sprint Goal.

As new work is required, the Development Team adds it to the Sprint Backlog. As work is performed or completed, the estimated remaining work is updated. When elements of the plan are deemed unnecessary, they are removed. Only the Development Team can change its Sprint Backlog during a Sprint. The Sprint Backlog is a highly visible, real-time picture of the work that the Development Team plans to accomplish during the Sprint, and it belongs solely to the Development Team.

Monitoring Sprint Progress

At any point in time in a Sprint, the total work remaining in the Sprint Backlog can be summed. The Development Team tracks this total work remaining at least for every Daily Scrum to project the likelihood of achieving the Sprint Goal. By tracking the remaining work throughout the Sprint, the Development Team can manage its progress.

Increment

The Increment is the sum of all the Product Backlog items completed during a Sprint and the value of the increments of all previous Sprints. At the end of a Sprint, the new Increment must be "Done," which means it must be in useable condition and meet the Scrum Team's definition of "Done". An increment is a body of inspectable, done work that supports empiricism at the end of the Sprint. The increment is a step toward a vision or goal. The increment must be in useable condition regardless of whether the Product Owner decides to release it.

Artifact Transparency

Scrum relies on transparency. Decisions to optimize value and control risk are made based on the perceived state of the artifacts.

To the extent that transparency is complete, these decisions have a sound basis. To the extent that the artifacts are incompletely transparent, these decisions can be flawed, value may diminish and risk may increase.

The Scrum Master must work with the Product Owner, Development Team, and other involved parties to understand if the artifacts are completely transparent. There are practices for coping with incomplete transparency; the Scrum Master must help everyone apply the most appropriate practices in the absence of complete transparency. A Scrum Master can detect incomplete transparency by inspecting the artifacts, sensing patterns, listening closely to what is being said, and detecting differences between expected and real results.

The Scrum Master's job is to work with the Scrum Team and the organization to increase the transparency of the artifacts. This work usually involves learning, convincing, and change. Transparency doesn't occur overnight, but is a path.

Definition of "Done"

When a Product Backlog item or an Increment is described as "Done", everyone must understand what "Done" means. Although this may vary significantly per Scrum Team, members must have a shared understanding of what it means for work to be complete, to ensure transparency. This is the definition of "Done" for the Scrum Team and is used to assess when work is complete on the product Increment.

The same definition guides the Development Team in knowing how many Product Backlog items it can select during a Sprint Planning. The purpose of each Sprint is to deliver Increments of potentially releasable functionality that adhere to the Scrum Team's current definition of "Done".

Development Teams deliver an Increment of product functionality every Sprint. This Increment is useable, so a Product Owner may choose to immediately release it. If the definition of "Done" for an increment is part of the conventions, standards or guidelines of the development organization, all Scrum Teams must follow it as a minimum.

If "Done" for an increment is not a convention of the development organization, the Development Team of the Scrum Team must define a definition of "Done" appropriate for the product. If there are multiple Scrum Teams working on the system or product release, the Development Teams on all the Scrum Teams must mutually define the definition of "Done".

Each Increment is additive to all prior Increments and thoroughly tested, ensuring that all Increments work together.

As Scrum Teams mature, it is expected that their definitions of "Done" will expand to include more stringent criteria for higher quality. New definitions, as used, may uncover work to be done in previously "Done" increments. Any one product or system should have a definition of "Done" that is a standard for any work done on it.

End Note

Scrum is free and offered in this Guide. Scrum's roles, events, artifacts, and rules are immutable and although implementing only parts of Scrum is possible, the result is not Scrum. Scrum exists only in its entirety and functions well as a container for other techniques, methodologies, and practices.

Acknowledgements

People

Of the thousands of people who have contributed to Scrum, we should single out those who were instrumental at the start: Jeff

Sutherland worked with Jeff McKenna and John Scumniotales, and Ken Schwaber worked with Mike Smith and Chris Martin, and all of them worked together. Many others contributed in the ensuing years and without their help Scrum would not be refined as it is today.

History

Ken Schwaber and Jeff Sutherland worked on Scrum until 1995, when they co-presented Scrum at the OOPSLA Conference in 1995. This presentation essentially documented the learning that Ken and Jeff gained over the previous few years, and made public the first formal definition of Scrum.

The history of Scrum is described elsewhere. To honor the first places where it was tried and refined, we recognize Individual, Inc., Newspage, Fidelity Investments, and IDX (now GE Health).

The Scrum Guide documents Scrum as developed, evolved, and sustained for 20-plus years by Jeff Sutherland and Ken Schwaber. Other sources provide you with patterns, processes, and insights that complement the Scrum framework. These may increase productivity, value, creativity, and satisfaction with the results.

[291]http://creativecommons.org/licenses/by-sa/4.0/legalcode
[292]http://creativecommons.org/licenses/by-sa/4.0/

Scrum@Scale Guide

In this chapter you'll find the verbatim copy of the Scrum@Scale Guide, version 1.02 updated the August 21, 2018. The Scrum@Scale Guide is available online at www.scrumatscale.com[293] and it is released under the Creative Commons BY-SA license, described on the creativecommons.org[294] website.

Purpose of the Scrum Scale Guide

Scrum, as originally outlined in the Scrum Guide, is a framework for developing, delivering, and sustaining complex products by a single team. Since its inception, its usage has extended to the creation of products, processes, services, and systems that require the efforts of multiple teams. Scrum@Scale was created to efficiently coordinate this new ecosystem of teams in a way that optimizes the overall strategy of the organization. It achieves this goal through setting up a "minimum viable bureaucracy" via a scale-free architecture, which naturally extends the way a single Scrum team functions across the organization.

This guide contains the definitions of the components that make up the Scrum@Scale framework, including its scaled roles, scaled events, and enterprise artifacts, as well as the rules that bind them together.

Dr. Jeff Sutherland developed Scrum@Scale based on the fundamental principles behind Scrum, Complex Adaptive Systems theory, game theory, and object-oriented technology. This guide was

[293]http://www.scrumatscale.com

[294]https://creativecommons.org/licenses/by-sa/4.0/

developed with the input of many experienced Scrum practitioners based on the results of their field work. The goal of this guide is for the reader to be able to implement Scrum@Scale on their own.

Why Scrum@Scale?

Scrum was designed for a single team to be able to work at its optimal capacity while maintaining a sustainable pace. In the field, it was found that as the number of Scrum teams within an organization grew, the output (working product) and velocity of those teams began to fall (due to issues like cross-team dependencies and duplication of work). It became obvious that a framework for effectively coordinating those teams was needed in order to achieve linear scalability. Scrum@Scale is designed to accomplish this goal via its scale-free architecture.

By utilizing a scale-free architecture, the organization is not constrained to grow in a particular way determined by a set of arbitrary rules; rather it can grow organically based on its unique needs and at a sustainable pace of change that can be accepted by the groups of individuals that make up the organization. The simplicity of the Scrum@Scale model is essential to a scale-free architecture and carefully avoids introducing extra complexity that will cause productivity per team to decrease as more teams are created.

Scrum@Scale is designed to scale across the organization as a whole: all departments, products and services. It can be applied across multiple domains in all types of organizations in industry, government, or academia.

Definition of Scrum@Scale

Scrum: A framework within which people can address complex adaptive problems, while productively and creatively delivering viable products of the highest possible value.

The Scrum Guide is the minimal feature set that allows inspection and adaptability via radical transparency to drive innovation, customer satisfaction, performance, and team happiness.

Scrum@Scale: A framework within which networks of Scrum teams operating consistently with the Scrum Guide can address complex adaptive problems, while creatively delivering products of the highest possible value.

NOTE: These "products" may be hardware, software, complex integrated systems, processes, services, etc., depending upon the domain of the Scrum teams.

Scrum@Scale is:

- Lightweight - the minimum viable bureaucracy
- Simple to understand - consists of only Scrum teams
- Difficult to master - requires implementing a new operating model

Scrum@Scale is a framework for scaling Scrum. It radically simplifies scaling by using Scrum to scale Scrum.

In Scrum, care is taken to separate accountability of the "what" from the "how". The same care is taken in Scrum@Scale so that jurisdiction and accountability are expressly understood in order to eliminate wasteful organizational conflict that keep teams from achieving their optimal productivity.

Scrum@Scale consists of components that allow an organization to customize their transformational strategy and implementation. It gives them the ability to target their incrementally prioritized change efforts in the area(s) they deem most valuable or most in need of change and then progress on to others.

In separating these two jurisdictions, Scrum@Scale contains two cycles: the Scrum Master Cycle (the "how") and the Product Owner

Cycle (the "what"), each touching the other at two points. Taken together, these cycles produce a powerful framework for coordinating the efforts of multiple teams along a single path.

The Components of the Scrum@Scale Framework

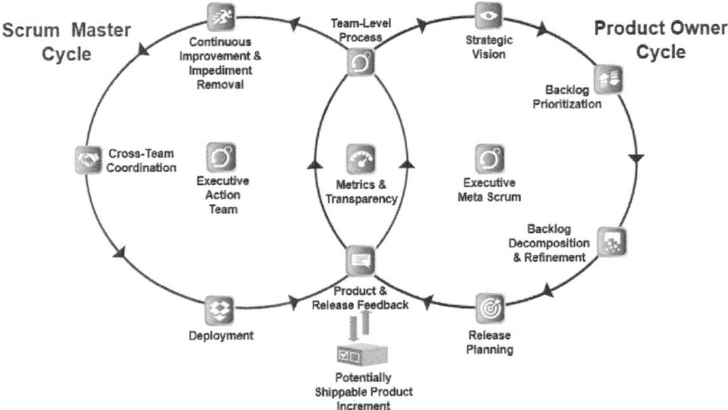

Values-Driven Culture

Besides separating accountability of the "what" and the "how," Scrum@Scale further aims to build healthy organizations by creating a values-driven culture in an empirical setting. The Scrum values are: Openness, Courage, Focus, Respect, and Commitment. These values drive empirical decision making, which depend on the three pillars of transparency, inspection, and adaptation.

Openness supports transparency into all of the work and processes, without which there is no ability to inspect them honestly and attempt to adapt them for the better. Courage refers to taking the bold leaps required to deliver value quicker in innovative ways.

Focus and Commitment refer to the way we handle our work obligations, putting customer value delivery as the highest priority.

Lastly, all of this must occur in an environment based on respect for the individuals doing the work, without whom nothing can be created.

Scrum@Scale helps organizations thrive by supporting a transformational leadership model which fosters a positive environment for working at a sustainable pace and putting commitment to deliver customer-facing value at the forefront of our efforts.

Getting Started with Scrum@Scale

When implementing large networks of teams, it is critical to develop a scalable **Reference Model** for a small set of teams. Any deficiencies in a Scrum implementation will be magnified when multiple teams are deployed. Many of the initial scaling problems will be organizational policies and procedures or development practices that block high performance and frustrate teams.

Therefore, the first challenge is to create a small set of teams that implements Scrum well. This is best accomplished by the creation of an **Executive Action Team (EAT)**, which is accountable for the development and execution of the transformation strategy. The EAT must be comprised of individuals who are empowered, politically and financially to ensure the existence of the Reference Model. This set of teams works through organizational issues that block agility and creates a Reference Model for Scrum that is known to work in the organization and can be used as a pattern for scaling Scrum across the organization.

As the Reference Model of teams accelerates, impediments and bottlenecks that delay delivery, produce waste, or impede business agility become apparent. The most effective way to eliminate these problems is to spread Scrum across the organization so that the entire value stream is optimized.

Scrum@Scale achieves linear scaling in productivity by saturating the organization with Scrum and distributing velocity and quality organically, consistent with the organization's specific strategy, product, and services.

Scrum Master Cycle

Team-Level Process

The **Team-Level Process** constitutes the first touch point between theScrum Master and Product Owner Cycles, and is laid out clearly in the Scrum Guide. It is composed of three artifacts, five events, and three roles. The goals of the team level process are to:

- maximize the flow of completed and quality tested work.
- increase performance of the team over time.
- operate in a way that is sustainable and enriching for the team.
- accelerate the customer feedback loop.

Coordinating the "How" - The Scrum of Scrums

A set of the teams that need to coordinate in order to deliver value to customers comprise a "**Scrum of Scrums**" **(SoS)**. This team is itelf a Scrum Team, which is responsible for a fully integrated set of potentially shippable increments of product at the end of every Sprint from all participating teams. A SoS functions as a Release Team and must be able to directly deliver value to customers. To do so effectively, it needs to be consistent with the Scrum Guide; that is, have its own roles, artifacts, and events:

Roles:

The SoS needs to have all of the skills necessary to deliver a fully integrated potentially shippable Product Increment at the end of every Sprint. (It may need experienced architects, QA Leaders, and other operational skill sets.) It has Product Owner representation to resolve prioritization issues. The Scrum Master of the Scrum of Scrums is called the **Scrum of Scrums Master (SoSM)**.

Events:

The SoSM should facilitate a Backlog Refinement event wherein impediments are identified as "ready" to be removed, and the team determines how best to remove them and how they will know when they are "done.'' Particular attention should be paid to the SoS Retrospective in which the teams' representatives share any learnings or process improvements that their individual teams have succeeded with, in order to standardize those practices across the teams within the SoS. Since the SoS needs to be responsive in real-time to impediments raised by participating teams, at least one representative (usually the team's Scrum Master) of each of the participating teams need to attend a **Scaled Daily Scrum (SDS)**. The SDS event mirrors the Daily Scrum in that it optimizes the collaboration and performance of the network of teams. Any person or number of people from participating teams may attend as needed.

Additionally, the SDS:

- is time-boxed to 15 minutes or less.
- must be attended by a representative of each team including the Product Owner team.
- is a forum where team representatives discuss what is going well, what is getting done, and how teams can work together more effectively. Some examples of what might be discussed are:
  - What impediments does my team have that will prevent them from accomplishing their Sprint Goal (or impact the upcoming release)?

- Is my team doing anything that will prevent another team from accomplishing their Sprint Goal (or impact their upcoming release)?
- Have we discovered any new dependencies between the teams or discovered a way to resolve an existing dependency?
- What improvements have we discovered that can be leveraged across teams?

The Scrum of Scrums Master (SoSM)

The Scrum of Scrums Master (SoSM) is accountable for the release of the joint teams' effort and must:

- make progress visible.
- make an impediment backlog visible to the organization.
- remove impediments that the teams cannot address themselves.
- facilitate prioritization of impediments, with particular attention to cross-team dependencies and the distribution of backlog.
- improve the efficacy of the Scrum of Scrums.
- work closely with the Product Owners to deploy a potentially releasable Product Increment at least every Sprint.
- coordinate the teams' deployment with the Product Owner's Release Plans.

Scaling the SoS

Depending upon the size of the organization or implementation, more than one SoS may be needed to deliver a very complex product. In those cases, a **Scrum of Scrum of Scrums (SoSoS)** can be created out of multiple Scrums of Scrums. The SoSoS is an organic pattern of Scrum teams which is infinitely scalable. Each

SoSoS should have SoSoSM's and scaled versions of each artifact & event.

Scaling the SoS reduces the number of communication pathways within the organization so that complexity is encapsulated. The SoSoS interfaces with a SoS in the exact same manner that a SoS interfaces with a single Scrum team which allows for linear scalability.

Sample Diagrams:

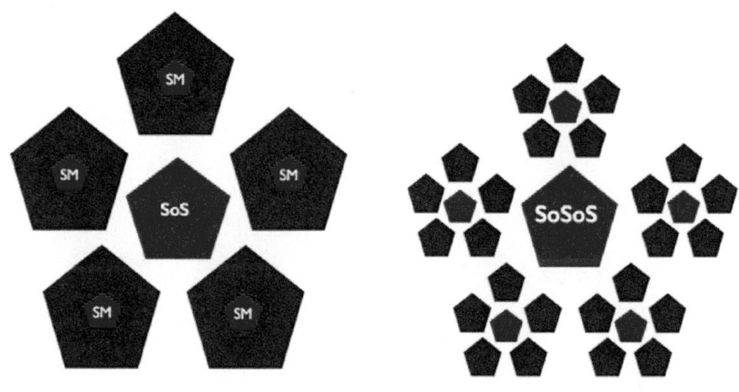

SoS of 5 Teams

SoSoS of 25 Teams

Note: While the Scrum Guide defines the optimal team size as being 3 to 9 people, Harvard research determined that optimal team size is 4.6 people.[295] Experiments with high performing Scrum teams have repeatedly shown that 4 or 5 people doing the work is the optimal size. It is essential to linear scalability that this pattern be the same for the number of teams in a SoS. Therefore, in the above and following diagrams, pentagons were chosen to represent a team of 5. These diagrams are meant to be examples only, your organizational diagram may differ greatly.

[295]Hackman, J Richard, Leading teams: Setting the stage for great performances, Harvard Business Press, 2002

The Executive Action Team

The Scrum of Scrums for the entire agile organization is called the **Executive Action Team (EAT)**. The leadership team creates an agile bubble in the organization where the Reference Model operates with its own guidelines and procedures that integrates effectively with any part of the organization that is not agile. It owns the agile ecosystem, implements the Scrum values, and assures that Scrum roles are created and supported.

The EAT is the final stop for impediments that cannot be removed by the SoS's that feed it. Therefore, it must be comprised of individuals who are empowered, politically and financially, to remove them. The function of the EAT is to coordinate multiple SoS's (or SoSoS's) and to interface with any non-agile parts of the organization. As with any Scrum team, it needs a PO and SM. It would be best if the EAT met daily as a Scrum team. They must meet at least once per Sprint and have a transparent backlog.

Sample Diagram showing an EAT coordinating 5 groupings of 25 teams:

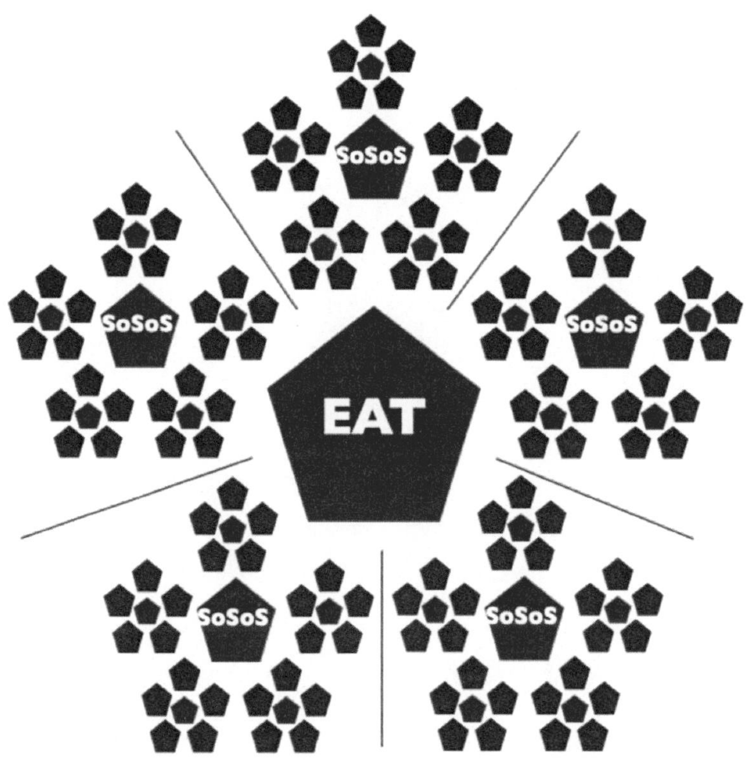

The EAT's Backlog & Responsibilities

Scrum is an agile operating system that is different from traditional project management. The entire SM organization reports into the EAT, which is responsible for implementing this agile operating system by establishing, maintaining, and enhancing the implementation in the organization. The EAT's role is to create an Organizational Transformation Backlog (a prioritized list of the agile initiatives that need to be accomplished) and see that it is carried out. For example, if there is a traditional Product Development Life Cycle in the old organization, a new agile Product Development Life Cycle needs to be created, implemented, and supported. It will typically support quality and compliance issues better than the old method but be implemented in a different way with different rules and guidelines. The EAT ensures that a Product Owner organization is created and funded and that this organization is represented on the EAT to support these efforts.

The EAT is accountable for the quality of Scrum within the organization. Its responsibilities include but are not limited to:

- creating an agile operating system for the Reference Model as it scales through the organization, including corporate operational rules, procedures, and guidelines to enable agility.
- measuring and improving the quality of Scrum in the organization.
- building capability within the organization for business agility.
- creating a center for continuous learning for Scrum professionals.
- supporting the exploration of new ways of working.

Finally, the EAT must set up and support a corresponding Product Owner organization through associations of PO's that mirror the SoS's and scale their PO functions. These teams of PO's and key stakeholders are known as **MetaScrums**.

Outputs/Outcomes of the Scrum Master Cycle

The SM organization (SoS, SoSoS, and EAT) work as a whole to complete the other components of the Scrum Master Cycle:

Continuous Improvement and Impediment Removal, Cross-Team Coordination, and Deployment.

The goals of Continuous Improvement and Impediment Removal are to:

- identify impediments and reframe them as opportunities.

- maintain a healthy and structured environment for prioritizing and removing impediments, and then verifying the resulting improvements.
- ensure visibility in the organization to effect change.

The goals of Cross-Team Coordination are to:

- coordinate similar processes across multiple related teams.
- mitigate cross-team dependencies to ensure they don't become impediments.
- maintain alignment of team norms and guidelines for consistent output.

Since the goal of the SoS is to function as a release team, the deployment of product falls under their scope, while what is contained in any release falls under the scope of the Product Owners. Therefore, the goals of the Deployment are to:

- deliver a consistent flow of valuable finished product to customers.
- integrate the work of different teams into one seamless product.
- ensure high quality of the customer experience.

Product Owner Cycle

Coordinating the "What" - The MetaScrum

A group of Product Owners who need to coordinate a single backlog that feeds a network of teams are themselves a team called a **MetaScrum**. For each SoS there is an associated MetaScrum. A MetaScrum aligns the teams' priorities along a single path so that they can coordinate their backlogs and build alignment with stakeholders to support the backlog. A team's product owner is accountable for the composition and prioritization of the team backlog and may pull backlog from the shared metascrum backlog into the team backlog or generate independent backlog at his or her discretion.

MetaScrums hold a scaled version of Backlog Refinement, the **Scaled Backlog Refinement Meeting**

- Each team PO (or proxy) must attend
- This event is the forum for Leadership, Stakeholders, or other Customers to express their preferences

This event occurs as often as needed, at least once per Sprint, to ensure a Ready backlog.

The main functions of the MetaScrum are to:

- create an overarching vision for the product & make it visible to the organization.
- build alignment with key stakeholders to secure support for backlog implementation.
- generate a single, prioritized backlog; ensuring that duplication of work is avoided.
- create a minimally uniform "Definition of Done" that applies to all teams in the SoS.
- eliminate dependencies raised by the SoS.
- generate a coordinated Release Plan.
- decide upon and monitor metrics that give insight into the product.

MetaScrums, just like SoS's, function as Scrum teams on their own. As such, they need to have someone who acts as a SM and keeps the team on track in discussions. They also need a single person who is responsible for coordinating the generation of a single Product Backlog for all of the teams covered by the MetaScrum. This person is designated as the **Chief Product Owner**.

The Chief Product Owner (CPO)

Through the MetaScrums, Chief Product Owners coordinate priorities among Product Owners who work with individual teams. They align backlog priorities with Stakeholder and Customer needs. Just like a SoSM, they may be an individual team PO who chooses to play this role as well, or they may be a person specifically dedicated to this role. Their main responsibilities are the same as a regular PO's, but at scale:

- Setting a strategic vision for the whole product.
- Creating a single, prioritized backlog of value to be delivered by all of the teams.
  - these items would be larger Product Backlog Items than that for a team PO.
- Working closely with their associated SoSM so that the Release Plan that the MetaScrum team generates can be deployed efficiently.
- Monitoring customer product feedback and adjusting the backlog accordingly.

Scaling the MetaScrum

Just as SoS's can grow into SoSoS's, MetaScrums can also expand by the same mechanism. There is no specific term associated with these expanded units, nor do the CPO's of them have specific expanded titles. We encourage each organization to develop their own. For the following diagrams, we have chosen to add an additional "Chief" to the title of those PO's as they magnify out.

Some sample diagrams:

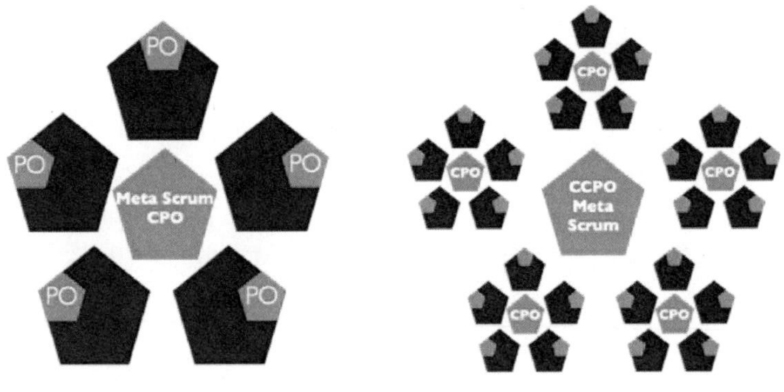

MetaScrum of 5 Teams MetaScrum of 25 Teams

NOTE: As mentioned above, these pentagons represent the ideal sized Scrum teams and ideal sized MetaScrums. These diagrams are meant to be examples only, your organizational diagram may differ greatly.

The Executive MetaScrum (EMS)

The MetaScrums enable a network design of Product Owners which is infinitely scalable alongside their associated SoS's. The MetaScrum for the entire agile organization is the **Executive MetaScrum**. The EMS owns the organizational vision and sets the strategic priorities for the whole company, aligning all the teams around common goals.

Sample diagram showing an EMS coordinating 5 groups of 25 teams:

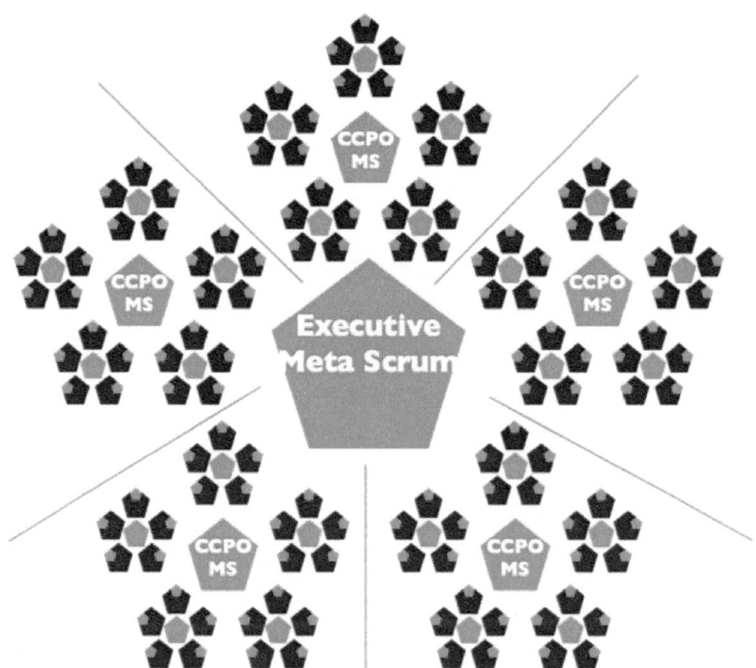

Outputs/Outcomes of the Product Owner Organization

The PO organization (various MetaScrums, the CPO's, and the Executive MetaScrum) work as a whole to satisfy the components of the Product Owner Cycle: **Strategic Vision, Backlog Prioritization, Backlog Decomposition & Refinement, and Release Planning**.

The goals of setting a Strategic Vision are to:

- clearly align the entire organization along a shared path forward.
- compellingly articulate why the organization exists.
- describe what the organization will do to leverage key assets in support of its mission.

- respond to rapidly changing market conditions.

The goals of Backlog Prioritization are to:

- identify a clear ordering for products, features, and services to be delivered.
- reflect value creation, risk mitigation and internal dependencies in ordering of the backlog.
- prioritize the high-level initiatives across the entire agile organization prior to Backlog Decomposition and Refinement.

The goals of Backlog Decomposition & Refinement are to:

- break complex products and projects into independent functional elements that can be completed by one team in one Sprint.
- capture and distill emerging requirements and customer feedback.
- ensure all backlog items are truly "Ready" so that they can be pulled by the individual teams.

The goals of Release Planning are to:

- forecast delivery of key features and capabilities.
- communicate delivery expectations to stakeholders.
- update prioritization, as needed.

Connecting the PO/SM Cycles

Understanding Feedback

The **Feedback** component is the second point where the PO & SM Cycles touch. Product feedback drives continuous improvement through adjusting the Product Backlog while Release feedback drives continuous improvement through adjusting the Deployment mechanisms. The goals of obtaining and analyzing Feedback are to:

- validate our assumptions.
- understand how customers use and interact with the product.
- capture ideas for new features and functionality.
- define improvements to existing functionality.
- update progress towards product/project completion to refine release planning and stakeholder alignment.
- identify improvements to deployment methods and mechanisms.

Metrics & Transparency

Radical transparency is essential for Scrum to function optimally, but it is only possible in an organization that has embraced the Scrum values. It gives the organization the ability to honestly assess its progress and to inspect and adapt its products and processes. This is the foundation of the empirical nature of Scrum as laid out in the Scrum Guide.

Both the SM & PO Cycles require metrics that will be decided upon by the separate SM and PO organizations. Metrics may be unique to both specific organizations as well as to specific functions within those organizations. Scrum@Scale does not require any specific set of metrics, but it does suggest that at a bare minimum, the organization should measure:

- Productivity - e.g. change in amount of Working Product delivered per Sprint
- Value Delivery - e.g. business value per unit of team effort
- Quality - e.g. defect rate or service downtime
- Sustainability - e.g. team happiness

The goals of having Metrics and Transparency are to:

- provide all decision makers, including team members, with appropriate context to make good decisions.
- shorten feedback cycles as much as possible to avoid over-correction.
- require minimal additional effort by teams, stakeholders or leadership.

Some notes on Organizational Design

The scale-free nature of Scrum@Scale allows the design of the organization to be component-based, just like the framework itself. This permits for rebalancing or refactoring of teams in response to the market. As an organization grows, capturing the benefits of distributed teams may be important. Some organizations reach talent otherwise unavailable and are able to expand and contract as needed through outsourced development. Scrum@Scale shows how to do this while avoiding long lag times, compromised communications, and inferior quality, enabling linear scalability both in size and global distribution.[296]

---

[296]Sutherland, Jeff and Schoonheim, Guido and Rustenburg, Eelco and Rijk, Maurits, "Fully distributed scrum: The secret sauce for hyperproductive offshored development teams", AG-ILE'08. Conference, IEEE: 339-344, 2008

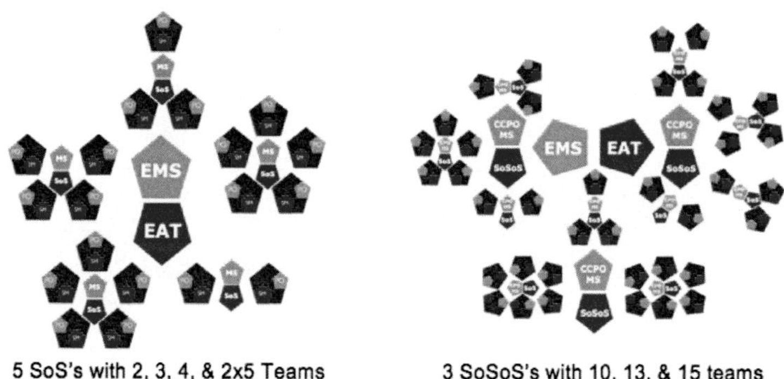

5 SoS's with 2, 3, 4, & 2x5 Teams

3 SoSoS's with 10, 13, & 15 teams

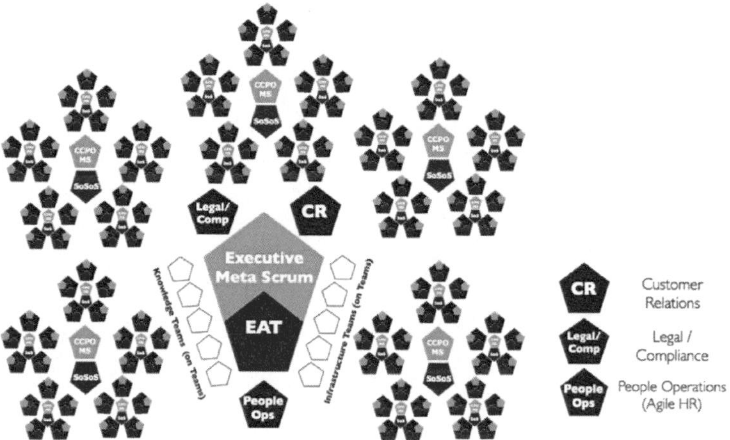

In this organizational diagram, the **Knowledge & Infrastructure Teams** represent virtual teams of specialists of which there are too few to staff each team. They coordinate with the Scrum teams as a group via service-level agreements where requests flow through a PO for each specialty who converts them into a transparent ordered backlog. An important note is that these teams are NOT silos of individuals who sit together (this is why they are represented as hollow pentagons); their team members sit on the actual Scrum teams, but they make up this virtual Scrum of their own for the purpose of backlog dissemination and process improvement.

Customer Relations, Legal / Compliance, and People Operations are included here since they are necessary parts of organizations and will exist as independent Scrum teams on their own, which all of the others may rely upon.

A final note on the representation of the EAT & EMS: in this diagram, they are shown as overlapping since some members sit on both of the teams. In very small organizations or implementations, the EAT & EMS may consist entirely of the same team members.

End Note

Scrum@Scale is designed to scale productivity, to get the entire organization doing twice the work in half the time with higher quality and in a significantly improved work environment. Large organizations that properly implement the framework can cut the cost of their products and services while improving quality and innovation.

Scrum@Scale is designed to saturate an organization with Scrum. All teams, including Leadership, Human Resources, Legal, Consulting & Training, and product & service teams, implement the same style of Scrum while streamlining and enhancing an organization.

Well implemented Scrum can run an entire organization.

Acknowledgements

We acknowledge IDX for the creation of the Scrum of Scrums which first allowed Scrum to scale to hundreds of teams,[297] PatientKeeper for the creation of the MetaScrum,[298] which enabled rapid deployment of innovative product, and OpenView Venture Partners for

[297]Sutherland, Jeff, "Inventing and Reinventing SCRUM in five Companies", Sur le site officiel de l'alliance agile, 2001

[298]Sutherland, Jeff, "Future of scrum: Parallel pipelining of sprints in complex projects", Proceedings of the Agile Development Conference, IEEE Computer Society 90-102, 2005.

scaling Scrum to the entire organization.[299] We value input from Intel with over 25,000 people doing Scrum who taught us "nothing scales" except a scale-free architecture, and SAP with the largest Scrum team product organization who taught us management involvement in the MetaScrum is essential to get 2,000 Scrum teams to work together.

The agile coaches and trainers implementing these concepts at Amazon, GE, 3M, Toyota, Spotify, Maersk, Comcast, AT&T and many other companies working with Jeff Sutherland have been helpful in testing these concepts across a wide range of companies in different domains.

And finally, Avi Schneier and Alex Sutherland have been invaluable in formulating and editing this document.

[299]Sutherland, Jeff and Altman, Igor, "Take no prisoners: How a venture capital group does scrum", Agile Conference, 2009. AGILE'09, IEEE 350-355. 2009

Cynefin

The complexity theory is a widely debated topic in various branches of science, and there is no generally defined definition of what **complexity** is. Cynefin[300] is a decision-making framework developed by Dave Snowden within IBM in the early 2000s that provides a simple and concise management strategy for each of the domains defined. In addition to being used in IBM, Cynefin is applied to product development, market analysis, supply chain management, branding and customer relationship management, emergency management and to several other critical areas by the government of many countries around the world. Now, let us examine the Cynefin Framework in greater detail.

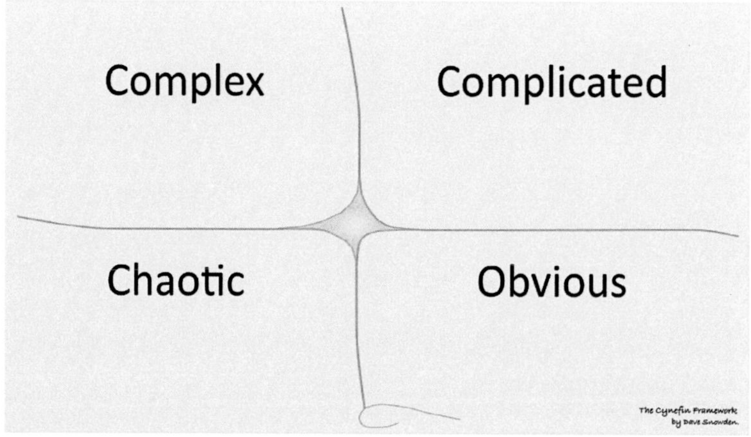

The Cynefin model has four domains (Obvious, Complicated, Complex, Chaotic), represented as four quadrants, for which it suggests a clear strategy; and a fifth domain, called Disorder, and represented

[300] https://en.wikipedia.org/wiki/Cynefin_framework

in the center, that is a situation where there is no clarity about which of the other domains apply.

Obvious Domain

In the Obvious domain, components are strongly coupled. This is a predictable and understandable domain; knowledge is enough to deal with the issues involved in this spectrum.

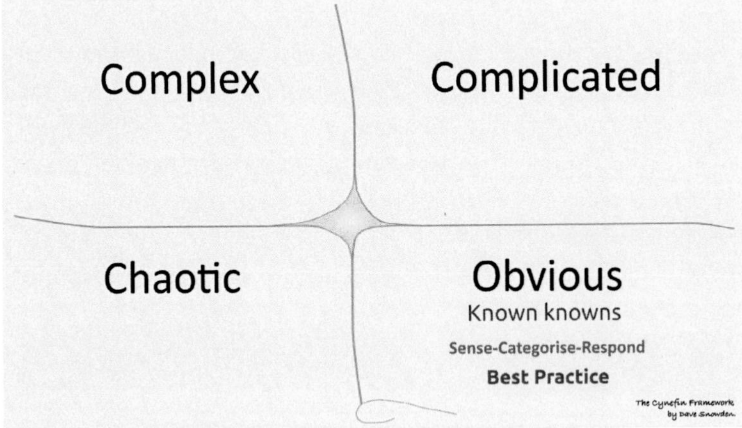

In an Obvious domain, the associated management strategy is **Sense - Categorise - Respond**: considering the type of problem (Sense), we use our knowledge to recognize its reference category (Categorise), and respond with the best solution (Respond). An Obvious domain is characterized by the Best Practices, where there is only one optimal way to solve the problem.

Complicated Domain

In the Complicated domain, components are coupled by a cause-effect relationship but this is not easily understandable. Our expertise is thus not sufficient to address immediately the problem as in Obvious domains.

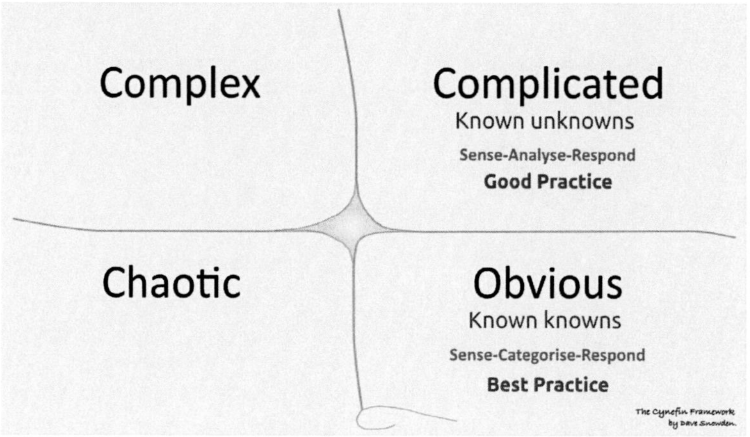

In a Complicated domain, the associated management strategy is **Sense – Analyse - Respond**; in other words, realizing the type of issue (Sense) we study it in detail (Analyse) and find the most appropriate response (Respond). A Complicated domain does not have a single optimal solution, but several Good Practices, different equally worth methods that allow solving the problem effectively.

Complex Domain

In a Complex domain, interactions between different components are not clearly perceptible a priori.

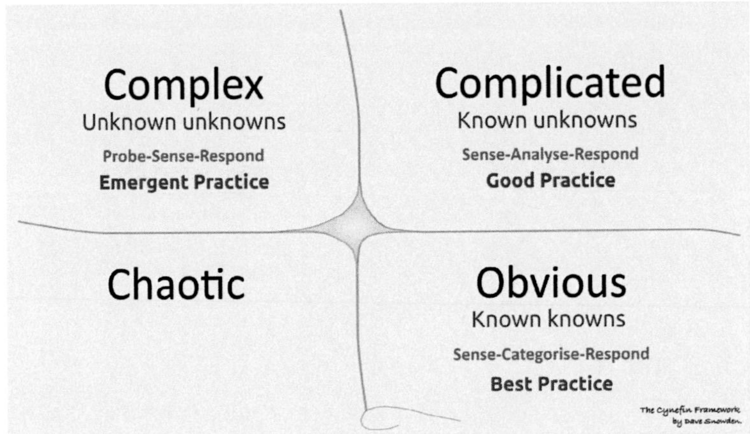

In a Complex domain, we do not know what we do not know (Unknown Unknowns). The management strategy associated with this domain is **Probe - Sense - Respond**, which involves performing an experiment (Probe), observing the results (Sense) and responding accordingly (Respond) probably with a new experiment capable to expand our knowledge. In this context, the approach is iterative and incremental and practices are called Emergent Practices precisely because they emerge during the discovery process.

Chaotic Domain

In the Chaotic domain, it is impossible to know what we do not know (Unknowable Unknowns). An experiment repeated infinitely in a Chaotic domain always produces different results, so it is useless. Studying a Chaotic domain is even more useless.

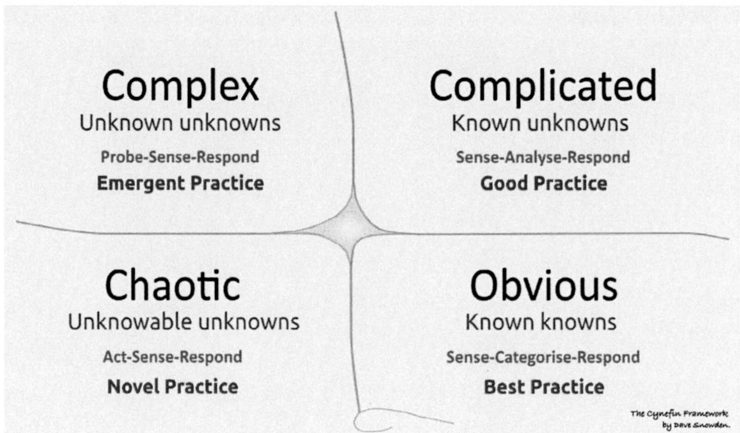

The management strategy in a Chaotic domain is **Act - Sense - Respond**. In practice, we need to act (Act), understand what happens while we act (Sense) and try to respond quickly (Respond). Fortunately, a Chaotic domain in nature is extremely short, and tends to stabilize towards a Complex domain.

Disorder

When we do not know the domain we are in, the Cynefin model calls it Disorder. It is represented by the dark area in the center of the diagram. In this area, the belonging domain is by definition very difficult to understand. According to Snowden, the way out of this domain is to break down the situation into constituent parts and assign each to one of the other four domains previously mentioned.

Conclusions

Cynefin provides a contextual approach extremely useful to managers to orient themselves in the growing complexity of today's challenges. This is a significant change from a cultural perspective, as it indicates that management, instead of obsessively trying to predict the future by understanding it, must have iterative and incremental processes that allow safe-to-fail experiments that can incorporate learning gained in successive strategic choices.

Popcorn Flow

In this chapter, you find the interview with Claudio Perrone[301], author of Popcorn Flow[302], where he explains his method.

Hi Claudio, thanks for your time. Let's start with the most obvious question: What is PopcornFlow?

PopcornFlow is a method to introduce, sustain, and accelerate continuous innovation & change. It promotes ultra-rapid experimentation to make better decisions under uncertainty.

It consists of two parts: a decision cycle and a set of principles.

Most people come across PopcornFlow through its 7-step decision cycle. No surprises there, as the word *Popcorn* stands for the initials of each step:

- Problems and observations
- Options
- Possible experiments
- Committed
- Ongoing
- Review
- Next

Teams and individuals reason about the problems they face, options to neutralize or reduce the impact of those problems, and possible experiments to explore one or more of those options. Either just-in-time or on a fast cadence, they capture the details on sticky

[301] https://www.linkedin.com/in/claudioperrone/

[302] https://popcornflow.com/

notes and place them on a PopcornFlow board - a visual board that represents each step as a column. They then *flow* experiments through the board, bringing to the surface (what I call) a *learning stream.* I often work with small teams where we co-design several experiments per week.

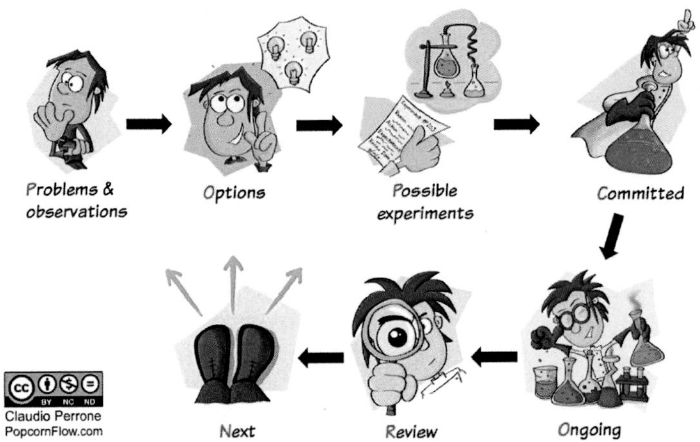

The decision cycle reveals only part of the story - the machinery. The secret to unleash PopcornFlow lies on its guiding principles:

1. If change is hard, make it continuous (The Virus Principle).
2. It's not only what you do but also what you learn by doing it that matters (The Ladder Principle).
3. Everybody is entitled to their own opinion, but a shared opinion is a fact (The Freedom Principle).
4. It's not "fail fast, fail often", it's "learn fast, learn often" (The Skateboarder Principle).
5. Small bets, big win. (Note: The wording of this last principle is still a work in progress, but it's based on Nassim Taleb's concept of "option asymmetry". In a nutshell, it's not about how frequently we meet or exceed our expectations, but rather about how to limit the cost of each experiment and how much we gain when we are - even if occasionally - right.)

How was PopcornFlow born?

I love origin stories!

I was still struggling to come to terms with the debacle of my latest entrepreneurial adventure when Eric Ries took the startup world by storm. He observed that startups operate under conditions of extreme uncertainty and promoted a sort-of scientific approach to validate assumptions and converge to a viable business model. The Lean Startup movement was born. Right away, I fiddled with those ideas, both for my own projects and for my clients - many of which were, in fact, fast-growing startups. As I needed to track experiments systematically, I created many Kanban board designs, which admittedly ranged from borderline simplistic to overly complex.

At a conference in Boston, however, something magical happened: Jeff Anderson[303] took the stage to show how he applied Lean Startup concepts to organizational change - something he called Lean Change[304] (an approach that was later forked and popularized by Jason Little[305]). Jeff argued that people react to change in highly contextual and unpredictable ways. As a result, a team of change agents involved in any large organizational transformation inevitably faces conditions of extreme uncertainty - a situation analogous to a startup. Wow, that was a smashing realization! It was early days, and the session was hotly debated. I chatted with Jeff right afterwards. Frankly, neither the scenario Jeff had described at the time - an appointed team of change agents experimenting *on* change recipients - nor most of the implementation details felt quite right. But it didn't matter: I realized I could devote my efforts and tools to co-design experiments and negotiate change *with* people in organizations.

I wasted no time. Back in Europe, a startup urged me to help

[303] https://www.linkedin.com/in/thomasjeffreyandersontwin/

[304] https://leanpub.com/leanchangemethod

[305] https://leanchange.org/

them address a situation that was critical to their survival. Their (anything-but) Scrum development team had been unable to release software for months due to quality and integration problems. People were distributed across several countries. The most troubling aspect was that the company had outsourced core parts of the platform to a third-party company whose management had since gone rogue: their lack of transparency and shady tactics had created an unsustainable situation.

With the motto "soft on people, hard on systems", we agreed to go back to basics and resume Scrum. My aim was to put a solid process in place, establish radical transparency, and treat with respect everyone involved in the production line - including the external partners.

I explained that Agile is not about ceremonies, it's about humility: we don't pretend to know and impose The One True Way to develop software. So, we start with we what we know so far, and then continuously inspect and adapt our approach. During our weekly retrospectives, we negotiated small change experiments to improve how we worked together - our communication, the tools we used, how we reviewed our code, and much more. We visually tracked problems and observations - facts, but also very personal opinions. We acted on the ones we could agree with (or, at least, not violently disagree with). It was all there for people to see. And so, with little fanfare, PopcornFlow became a natural way to facilitate our Scrum retrospectives.

Every week, I asked these questions:

- What experiments did we agree to do?
- Which one did we actually do?
- What did we expect to happen?
- What did we learn?
- Based on what we learned, what are we going to do next?

Some experiments met our expectations, others didn't. But as the co-designed experiments entered the cycle, the team's climate improved steadily. Little by little, people's confidence grew. They experimented several times throughout each Sprint. Even one improvement experiment each week would have been enough. Instead, they launched 5 or 6 of those every week - sometimes even 10! It didn't take long for the results to arrive and the company went from being unable to release the product for months to releasing it several times a day. My job was done.

I saw their PopcornFlow board once again, almost a year later. It had captured hundreds of experiments. Unsurprisingly, as the company grew, other boards had appeared in other parts of the organization, well outside the original development team. PopcornFlow had impacted marketing, sales, and strategy.

Then a friend of mine - an Agile coach who had introduced PopcornFlow in his organization - suggested: "Claudio, drop everything else and focus on PopcornFlow. This thing is freaking amazing."

So I did.

What makes PopcornFlow different?

Some practitioners have originally likened the PopcornFlow steps to PDCA/PDSA[306], the well-known Shewhart[307]/Deming[308] cycle. The similarity is only superficial, however. They operate in very different domains of complexity and, like two faces of a same coin, they are opposite and complementary.

With PDSA, we deliberately "go slow to go fast". With PopcornFlow, we "go fast to learn faster". The former is about *continuous improvement*, the latter is about *continuous change*. But above all, PDSA's approach is based on root-cause analysis and the scientific method, PopcornFlow is not! Consider the Freedom Principle I

[306]https://en.wikipedia.org/wiki/PDCA
[307]https://en.wikipedia.org/wiki/Walter_A._Shewhart
[308]https://en.wikipedia.org/wiki/W._Edwards_Deming

mentioned before, for example. (Don't worry: it has *metaphorical* rather than *literal* meaning.) Subjectivity plays a primary role and we can exploit it. It doesn't sound very *scientific*, does it?

Over time, I developed a finer sense of the forces at work and realized that PopcornFlow best operates in complex rather than complicated domains (see Dave Snowden's Cynefin[309] framework). In this context, PopcornFlow problems are, essentially, system *probes*. To a great extent, we use uncontrolled parallel experiments to *explore options* and change the system dynamics. In fact, I even came to question Lean Startup's scientific claims, particularly around the idea of *validated learning*. Is possible that maybe we are doing the right things for the wrong reasons?

And so, despite its origins, PopcornFlow has changed and evolved into something different. Its decision cycle is, perhaps, a very pragmatic expression of John Boyd's OODA loop[310]; its philosophy echoes Nassim Taleb's Antifragile[311] approach.

In which areas have you seen people using PopcornFlow?

My observation is that organizations want to innovate, but they don't know how.

PopcornFlow is relatively young and still evolving. Yet, it already found its way in startups, large financial institutions, well-known technology companies, and more. Last year, a group in the Canadian public sector, for example, won two prestigious national innovation awards; the secret - they revealed - was *a magic trick up their sleeve.*

I often use PopcornFlow to coach Agile teams and facilitate highly effective retrospectives. Teams trade options outside their immediate circle too - a crucial mechanism to reduce the inevitable

[309]https://en.wikipedia.org/wiki/Cynefin_framework
[310]https://en.wikipedia.org/wiki/OODA_loop
[311]https://en.wikipedia.org/wiki/Antifragile

bias. Combined with jobs-to-be-done theory, it also works well for product and service innovation. I'm occasionally called to help sales and marketing teams too.

Basically, if you need to introduce change, PopcornFlow may be a good fit. There is nothing intrinsically technological or "corporate" about it. I even use it to negotiate change with my kid (who is at the high-functioning end of the autism spectrum[312]). It's been used by families, job seekers, school teachers, life coaches, psychologists, and more. You see? It's about decisions. And life is full of those.

What can we expect from PopcornFlow in the future?

Workshops, coaching, and speaking gigs aside, these days I'm developing a digital platform and writing a book. I am trying hard to keep the technical jargon to a minimum and, hopefully, reach a wider audience. I designed PopcornFlow to be *so simple that even a five-year-old child could understand it.* "This way," I thought, "grown-ups will understand it too." My son became quite proficient at that age, but the jury's still out on some adults. Ah ah.

[312]https://www.autismspeaks.org/what-autism/asperger-syndrome

Additional material

In the electronic version, new stories and practical examples will be added over time. To obtain an electronic copy of this book **for free**, visit the following address:

https://leanpub.com/Scrum-for-Hardware/c/apaper

The code is valid until 31 December 2020.

Made in the USA
San Bernardino, CA
15 September 2018